# More praise for

## *In the*

## SANCTUARY *of* WOMEN

Desert ammas, medieval mystics, women quiltmakers and creative artists, biblical women from Eve to the beloved in the Song of Songs, as well as women working for justice: all these provide Jan Richardson with fodder for the fresh and sometimes unexpected reflections she has gathered into *In the Sanctuary of Women*. Through prayers and poetry, theological reflection and storytelling, Richardson opens up the rich possibilities of each day. Not your common prayer companion, Richardson will provoke thought and provide insight for any adventurous spiritual seeker.

—Wendy M. Wright, PhD
Professor of Theology, Creighton University

Here is a feast of spirit in which each word is born from hunger and satiated with delight. Jan yet again has provided a delicious reflection to lead men as well as women to our "secret room" and beyond.

—Alexander J. Shaia, PhD
Author of
*The Hidden Power of the Gospels: Four Questions, Four Paths, One Journey*

D0188115

# *In the*
# SANCTUARY
## *of*
# WOMEN

A COMPANION FOR *Reflection & Prayer*

## JAN L. RICHARDSON

UPPER
ROOM BOOKS®
NASHVILLE

IN THE SANCTUARY OF WOMEN
*A Companion for Reflection & Prayer*
Copyright © 2010 by Jan L. Richardson
All rights reserved.

No part of this book may be reproduced in any manner whatsoever without written permission of the publisher except in brief quotations embodied in critical articles or reviews. For information, write Upper Room Books, 1908 Grand Avenue, Nashville, TN 37212.

The Upper Room® Web site: http://www.upperroom.org

UPPER ROOM®, UPPER ROOM BOOKS®, and design logos are trademarks owned by The Upper Room®, a ministry of GBOD®, Nashville, Tennessee. All rights reserved.

Unless otherwise indicated, scripture quotations are from New Revised Standard Version Bible, copyright © 1989 National Council of the Churches of Christ in the United States of America. Used by permission. All rights reserved.

Scripture quotations marked NEB are from The New English Bible © 1989 by Oxford University Press and Cambridge University Press. Reprinted by permission.

At the time of publication, all Web sites referenced in this book were valid. However, due to the fluid nature of the Internet, some addresses may have changed or the content may no longer be relevant.

*Page 319 constitutes an extension of this copyright page.*

Cover design: Bruce Gore / www.gorestudio.com
Cover art: *In the Sanctuary of Women* © Jan L. Richardson

LIBRARY OF CONGRESS CATALOGING-IN-PUBLICATION DATA
Richardson, Jan L.
    In the sanctuary of women: a companion for reflection and prayer / Jan L. Richardson
        p. cm.
    ISBN 978-0-8358-1030-2
1. Christian women—Prayers and devotions.    2. Christian literature.
3. Devotional literature.  I. Title.
    BV4844.R56 2010
    242'.643—dc22                          2010001997

Printed in the United States of America

*For my sisters and brothers*
*in the community of*
*Saint Brigid of Kildare Monastery*

# Contents

## *Acknowledgments*

I AM GRATEFUL to those who helped: those who prayed, read, and offered sanctuary near and far. I carry their names with me like a litany. Among the many are Mary Stamps and Saint Brigid of Kildare Monastery, the artful community at the Grünewald Guild, Judy and Joe Richardson, and Maru Ladrón de Guevara.

At Upper Room Books, I am thankful to my editor, Rita Collett, and to Robin Pippin.

My longtime sweetheart, Garrison Doles, will be my husband by the time these words make their way into the world. He saw them all first and tended them well.

And to you, gratitude and blessing.

# INTO THE SANCTUARY

## *An Introduction*

THIS IS WHAT I KNOW:

There are prayers inscribed on our bones, prayers we carry in our marrow, prayers that run through our blood.

There are prayers we carry with ancestral memory, prayers passed down from generation to generation, prayers that spiral in us like DNA.

There are prayers that we carry in the most hidden parts of ourselves, prayers we have never breathed aloud, prayers we can barely acknowledge.

There are prayers that have taken form in this world, prayers that have made their way into letters and diaries and books, prayers that have taken the shape of stitches and poetry and paintings, prayers that have bodied forth as compassion, as justice, as mercy, as grace.

There are prayers of blessing and of lament, prayers we pour out for others, prayers we offer for our own selves. There are prayers whispered, wailed, shouted, groaned; prayers sung and laughed and wept and dreamed. There are prayers of stillness and of silence, prayers in the breath and in the belly, prayers in the beating heart and in the space between the beats.

There are prayers.

### HUNGRY

I have been searching for these prayers, hungry to find the ways they have taken shape in the lives of women across time. I have been looking for traces of them, seeking their imprint, following their wandering trail through the centuries. I have been peering into the gaps, wondering about the silences, piecing together the scraps of history, imagining the ways that women have sought the presence of God, attending to how they have articulated their longing for the sacred from generation to generation.

It has been a long looking.

Nearly two decades ago, I began to search for a resource for my personal prayer and reflection. I was eager to find a book that engaged my experience

11

as a woman in the church, a book that stretched and challenged that experience, a book where I didn't have to keep altering the language and changing the imagery. Failing to find it, I finally decided to write it. In the pages of *Sacred Journeys: A Woman's Book of Daily Prayer*, I gathered up the words of women from around the world and across the centuries and stitched them together with words born of my own hungering and praying and seeking.

*In the Sanctuary of Women* arises from a similar desire. I still hunger, still listen to the lives of women across time who have something to tell me about God, still look for a language to describe how the sacred shows up in this world. In offering these pages that you hold in your hands, I don't presume that women have always sought the Divine in the same way or that there is such a thing as a universal women's experience, a way of being that all women share. I do believe that in our desire for God and for the healing of the world, it is crucial that women listen to one another; that we acknowledge both the similarities and differences in the details of our lives; that we bring the fullness of our lives, with all the wonders and messiness, into our life of prayer; and that we hear our lives and pray with them in the context of the larger systems of which we are a part. Our practices of prayer, reflection, and contemplation call us not to stand in isolation from the world but rather to live in profound relationship with it: to acknowledge how we are, as one writer has put, inexplicably inextricable.[1]

## BENEATH THE FLOORBOARDS

Here is a story.

On a day in the middle of the twentieth century, in a sanctuary that had once belonged to a Cistercian convent in Lower Saxony, Germany, a team engaged in restoration work made a remarkable discovery. Pulling up the floorboards in the nuns' choir, where for generations the sisters had gathered to pray, the team found hundreds of objects that had belonged to the community. The objects spoke volumes about the daily and devotional lives of the nuns: the unearthed treasure included thimbles, spindles, looms, pilgrim badges, wax boards for writing, and the earliest known eyeglasses. Among these everyday objects was a collection of prayer books that the nuns had created about five hundred years earlier.

The prayer books had much in common, yet each one was distinctive to the woman who had used it. Created by the nuns for personal prayer and contemplation outside the more formal Liturgy of the Hours that the community shared together, these small books reveal and reflect the spiritual concerns of individual sisters as they sought Christ amidst the religious turmoil taking place in the wake of the Reformation. In a time when monastic reforms were being forced upon the sisters, fashioning their books of prayer offered a means for them to take an active role in choosing and expressing their spiritual path.

Half a millennium later, the prayer books that once lay buried beneath the floorboards offer an intimate link to a particular community of women who designed and used these books as a portal into prayer. Although they possess their own distinctive history, these books stand as part of a larger legacy that women of prayer across the ages have given to us. Despite the losses and erasures that have taken place in the history of women in the Judeo-Christian tradition, we yet have traces of these women in the trail of prayerful pages they left behind.[2]

## THE BOOK AS A THIN PLACE

Like the Cistercian sisters, women for generations have used books as thresholds into prayer. From the Middle Ages, hundreds of books survive that give us a glimpse of how women prayed, including Books of Hours, psalters, and breviaries. These books range from more humble ones, such as those belonging to the Cistercian women, to lavishly illuminated volumes that would have taken artists and scribes months or years to fashion. Simple or extravagant, each book offered an intimate space where the reader could encounter God. Opening the pages of a sacred book, a woman could enter into what Celtic folk have long called a *thin place:* a realm where heaven and earth meet.

Such books of prayer were not merely personal; they did not exist just for the benefit of one's own soul. In picking up a Book of Hours, a psalter, a breviary, a woman became part of a community, wherever she was: the very act of reading joined a woman to others who devoted themselves to contemplation and devotion. Although they might never meet in person, these reading women were linked by scriptures, by prayers and psalms that had been on the lips of their ancestors, and by a shared desire for the presence of God in the midst of their daily lives.[3]

Although women in the Middle Ages had much more limited access to education and literacy than did men, books became a way for many women to participate in the Word and also to share in passing the Word along. It is often in the very pages of these books that we glimpse the ways that women were intimately intertwined with books: we see women creating books, women acting as scribes, women serving as patrons for others who created books. We see women teaching their children to read from these books and women passing them along to others as gifts.

And time and again, in these pages that come to us across the centuries, we see the image of a woman with a book of prayer in her hand. The ubiquitous image of the reading woman is epitomized in medieval depictions of the Annunciation to Mary. In narrating the moment when the angel Gabriel seeks out Mary to become the mother of God, artists of the Middle Ages most often chose to portray her contemplating a book: the Hebrew scriptures, oftentimes, or—in an intriguing bit of anachronism—a medieval Book of Hours. Mary, these images tell us, was a woman immersed in the Word, long before the Word immersed itself in her.

## OFF THE PAGE

A kind of conversation took place among women who used these books of prayer. Their books tell us a little about what these women held to be important, how they sought God, how prayer was intertwined with their daily life and with significant events such as giving birth and entering into death.

Yet this prayerful conversation spills off the pages. Across the centuries, women have carried prayers in our bones and in our blood. We have passed down the sacred stories from body to body. We have struggled to know our lives as sacred texts, to perceive the ways that God has written God's own story within us, to understand how the Word still seeks to take flesh in and through us. And we have hungered for places of safety and of community in which to do this, to gather in the company of others whose stories and prayers both echo and challenge our own.

## INTO THE SANCTUARY

This book is an invitation into this conversation. Here amongst these pages, in the presence of women past and present, is a place to enter into the mysteries that lie at the heart of who we are. We do well to remember that the practice of prayer must do more than reinforce what we already know and believe. Instead, the act of praying prompts us to question, to move beyond familiar habits and patterns and routines, and to imagine possibilities beyond what we can see. Prayer draws us onto a threshold that lies between what we have known and what God may yet be calling us toward. In this calling, God challenges us to look into the layers of our lives, to offer up prayers of radical honesty, and to remember that since we are women created in God's own image, nothing in us is foreign to God or lies outside the circle of God's love and grace.

As we cross into the sanctuary within this book, I am here to ask you: what prayers are buried beneath the floorboards of your life? Are there pages of your story, your sacred text, that you have hidden from view, even from yourself?

In this place, may you find a space of hospitality for all of who you are. Here among these women, may there be comfort and challenge, mystery and grace to provide sustenance for your every step. For everything that lies within you, may there be a welcome. May this be for you a refuge, a place of meeting, a shelter. May it be a sanctuary.

## NOTES

1. "Cold Calling," from the blog SouthQuest, http://southquest.blogspot.com/2006_04_01_archive.html.

2. The story of the unearthed prayer books appears in June Mecham's article "Reading between the Lines: Compilation, Variation, and the Recovery of an Authentic Female Voice in the Dornenkron Prayer Books from Wienhausen," *Journal of Medieval History* 29 (2003):109–128.

3. I am grateful to Jessica Brantley for her ideas about how, in the medieval period, books fostered what she calls *devotional communities* and *textual communities* among people who had little or no face-to-face contact. See her book *Reading in the Wilderness: Private Devotion and Public Performance in Late Medieval England* (Chicago: University of Chicago Press, 2007), especially chapter 2, "'Silence Visible': Carthusian Devotional Reading and Meditative Practice," where she writes, "Devotional reading fundamentally allows for both an eremitic experience and a communal one" (54).

# THE LAY OF THE LAND

## *Using This Book*

THINK OF EACH CHAPTER as a book in itself: excavated from its hiding place, waiting for you to make it your own. Or think of it like this: a room, a place where a conversation has been unfolding for years, for generations. Or, still, like this: each chapter a chapel, where silence alternates with the murmuring of prayers that have been raised for centuries, seeping into the very stones of the place. Whatever they are, these gatherings of pages that fill this book, they open themselves to you.

At the outset of each chapter, a woman meets us. She invites us across the threshold. Offering hospitality and inspiration, this woman serves as companion as we explore the landscape that her life offers. As you travel through the chapter, you will find several features that will help you navigate and contemplate its terrain.

*Readings:* The readings in this book have emerged from my pondering of the lives and words of women who have offered sanctuary in my own journey. Beginning with glimpses of the story of the woman featured in the chapter, the readings invite you to reflect on the themes that surface in her life and how these unfold in your own life. Where do you find points of connection? What challenges do you encounter? What questions stir and stretch you, drawing you into a different landscape? How does entering this woman's story beckon you to enter your own? You may engage the readings on a daily basis or simply dip into them whenever you wish. If you reflect on one reading a day, this book will carry you through six months.

*The Secret Room:* Midway through each chapter, you will find a reading called "The Secret Room." These "secret rooms" were inspired by Phil Cousineau, who, in his book *The Art of Pilgrimage*, urges us to notice the often hidden places along the path that help us make sense of the journey.

> Everywhere you go there is a secret room. To discover it, you must knock on walls, as the detective does in mystery houses, and listen for the echo

that portends the secret passage. You must pull books off shelves to see if the library shelf swings open to reveal the hidden room.

I'll say this again: Everywhere has a secret room. You must find your own, in a small chapel, a tiny café, a quiet park, the home of a new friend, the pew where the morning light strikes the rose window just so.

As a pilgrim you must find it or you will never understand the hidden reasons why you really left home.[1]

These midpoint readings offer a glimpse into some of the secret rooms I have found along the way: places that called me to stop and look and be open to what I had not anticipated. I share these rooms by way of inviting you to discover a few of your own. As you travel through this book, what unexpected images open themselves to you? How do they help you to see in a different and deeper way? What do you find there?

*Blessings:* In their book *Earth Prayers*, Elizabeth Roberts and Elias Amidon write, "Invoking the powers of the universe or bestowing our blessing on the Earth or other beings is neither a simple benevolent wish nor an act of hubris. Rather it is an act of creative confidence."[2] A blessing reminds us that God has not designed us to live by our own devices: we are bound together with one another and with all of creation, and we are called to work for the well-being of those with whom we share this life—and those who will follow. Offering a blessing is an act of profound hope. In blessing one another, we recognize and ally ourselves with the presence of God who ever works to bring about the healing of the world. In that spirit, each reading in this book closes with a blessing to send you on your way. These blessings are born of a desire that the words will offer a moment of grace amid whatever is taking place within the landscape of your life. May these blessings sustain you for the path ahead, that you may offer—and be—a blessing in turn, that you will move from the sanctuary within these pages to become, in your own self, a sanctuary in this world.

*Digging deeper:* Each chapter closes with a brief listing of some books for further exploration of the woman and the themes featured in that chapter. You will find additional resources among the notes at the end of each chapter.

*Sharing the sanctuary:* As you enter the conversation taking place *within* these pages, I invite you to think about how you might take the conversation *beyond* these pages. Designed for personal prayer and contemplation, this book is meant also to foster shared reflection and discussion. What conversations might the women in this book inspire you to have with the women in your life? With a girlfriend, a sister, a daughter or mother, a book group, a Bible study, or in some other configuration: how might this book help you find and offer sanctuary to others in your circle—men as well as women?

Resources for sharing the conversation, including a Reading Guide for Groups and an interactive blog, are available at sanctuaryofwomen.com.

## NOTES

1. Phil Cousineau, *The Art of Pilgrimage: The Seeker's Guide to Making Travel Sacred* (Berkeley: CA, Conari Press, 1998), 126. Cousineau drew inspiration from the poet Donald Hall, who, in his essay "Poetry: The Unsayable Said" (Port Townsend, WA: Copper Canyon Press, 1993), tells of friends who found a secret room in the old house they had bought. Hall writes, "The unsayable builds a secret room, in the best poems. . . . This room is not a Hidden Meaning, to be paraphrased by the intellect; it conceals itself from reasonable explanation. The secret room is something to acknowledge, accept, and honor in a silence of assent; the secret room is where the unsayable gathers" (4).
2. Elizabeth Roberts and Elias Amidon, eds., *Earth Prayers: From Around the World: 365 Prayers, Poems, and Invocations for Honoring the Earth* (New York: HarperCollins, 1991), 170.

# THE BEGINNING
# OF ALL THINGS

*The Book of Eve*

## INTRODUCTION

In the beginning. With the opening words of the book of Genesis, our story is set in motion. Passed down from generation to generation, its lines etched into our history, this sacred text seeks to tell us who we are and where we have come from. This is the book of our beginnings.

As if one story could not contain the origins of Creation, those who laid down the lines of Genesis gave us two tellings. In the first Creation story, God makes the world with words. Syllable by syllable, God speaks into the formless chaos and, from it, speaks the world into being. Light. Darkness. Sky. Earth. Plants bearing seeds. Seasons and seas and all manner of creatures.

In the second Creation story, God makes the earth and the heavens, then scoops up dust, dirt, the stuff of the ground. *'Adamah*, in Hebrew. Breathes into it. Sets us on our way.

Words and dust: this is what we are made of.

Eve, first woman, chooses more than the words that have been inscribed on her, more than the story given to her. She reaches out her hand and, with that gesture, begins to create a vocabulary of her own. Takes and tastes and steps into her own story.

Eve chooses a complicated way. Her reaching, her taking, her tasting will stir her from the safety of Eden. Her act propels her into a future in which choices will not be laid out for her but where she will have to make decisions each step of the way.

We may find it difficult to engage this story without reading it through the lens of interpretation that has defined this as the story of the Fall, an explanation of how sin entered the world. The doctrine of original sin, however, didn't emerge until several centuries into Christian history, though it would be the one that would come to hold sway. Yet reading the text solely through this lens can occlude the intent of the scripture, keeping us from a fuller, richer reading of the text. Rather than accept the interpretations that have been handed down to us, how might it be for us to take the story of Eve into our own hands, to take and taste and chew on this sacred text, and so find for ourselves what her story has to tell us?

Sin and brokenness inhabit this tale, but they are not the whole story. The book of our beginnings holds mysteries that go deeper than doctrine. Eve challenges us to look at where we have come from and to look again. She beckons us to consider how we tell our stories, how we participate in the making of them and the telling of them. Her story prompts us to reconsider our own stories, to question what we think we know about their contours and their meanings.

This is a story of original hunger. It invites us to trace the lines of our longings and where they have led us. It calls us to reckon with the ways we have hidden ourselves from the Holy and from one another. And in beckoning us to look back, it offers us the sustenance that will help us create the path ahead.

As you travel with Eve, may her story draw you more deeply into your own.

# PRAYER FOR THE MORNING

Blessed are you, O God,
who created the world with a word
and who fashioned your people
from dust and from delight.
In our waking, may we know you
breathing in us,
breathing through us,
creating us anew
with your longing and love.

# PRAYER FOR THE EVENING

Blessed are you, O God,
who dwells even in darkness
and who restores your creation
with the gift of rest.
Deliver your people
from the troubles of the night,
and let your peacefulness and grace
be upon each place.

# 1
## THE PRAYERS BENEATH

Whenever my artist friends Peg and Chuck begin a new painting, they take a few quiet moments with the canvas. Before reaching for a paintbrush, they first pick up a pencil. They write a prayer onto the canvas. No one else will ever see the penciled words. With every stroke of the paintbrush, the prayer disappears. Yet the words infuse the work. Beneath the layers of paint, the prayer persists. Blessing and invocation, it calls to the viewer, both concealing and revealing its presence.

Here at the beginning of this book, I am writing prayers. Within these lines, between these lines, tucked between the words, scribbled onto the backs of the pages, I am writing. Line by line, the prayers will disappear, swallowed by the layers of words that will yet be inscribed on top of them, around them, across them. But the prayers will persist.

Perhaps, along the way, a word will show itself. *Enfold*, your eye will spot one day. *Encompass. Delight.* Or perhaps you'll be reading along and suddenly you think you've caught a glimpse of *courage*. Or *wisdom*. Or *grace*. Or *vision*. I cannot tell you the prayers—I just barely know them myself—but if you find in these pages a word that you most need, a phrase that you hardly knew you were hungry for, then perhaps you've stumbled across one of them that left itself exposed.

On this day of beginnings, know that you are an answered prayer. I have been waiting for you.

### BLESSING

On each threshold, wisdom;
at every doorway, love;
through every entry, grace;
with each beginning, peace.

# 2

## CLOSER

The story of Eve comes to us something like one of Peg and Chuck's paintings. She, along with her husband, Adam, is a wondrous creation, formed and fashioned by God, breathing with God's own breath. There are prayers inscribed within her story, blessings buried beneath the layers by her Creator, nearly impossible to discern. All the more difficult because of the layers that others have added over the centuries, a patina of interpretation and the crackling of conflict, lines laid down by those who have sought to inscribe their meaning across the canvas, have looked into the layers and said that they mean "original sin" and "seductress" and "devil's gateway."

But other words, different words, linger beneath the layers. Ancient words that we will never fully know but that shimmer under the surface, blessing us, bidding us to look more closely, and closer still.

What do you see within this story? What words hover between and beneath the lines of the text? What have you been told or taught about this story? What do you find with your own eyes?

### BLESSING

Throughout this day,
may you know the breath of God
breathing in you.

# 3

## TAKING THE FRUIT

A few years ago, the city of Orlando sponsored a juried art show with the theme "Still Life." I hadn't done a still life since childhood, but the theme set my imagination in motion. I began to think about fruit and Eden and Eve. *How about a still life that wasn't still?*

I found a rough ceramic bowl and painted a snake around the inside lip. Inside the bowl I placed a group of apples—artificial—that I had cut in half and connected with hinges. The apples became books: when opened, each one contained a text, a brief reflection on Eve and the garden. *Taking the Fruit*, I called it. The library of Eden.

### The First Apple

Each desire in my life leads
to another desire that lives
behind it or beneath it
or within it. In the midst of
paying attention to them all
I sometimes wonder if I'm
addicted to longing.

### The Second Apple

The Sufi poet Rumi
says that our longing is the
answer to our longing—that
our capacity for desire is the
reply to our desire. Some
days I find this comforting,
but on other days it doesn't
give much satisfaction.

### The Third Apple

Desire finds its way into a
lot of my writing so I've had
to stock up on my synonyms.
*Longing, yearning*, and
*hunger* are useful; and
*hankering* is fun. *Ache*
comes in handy if it's a hard
desire, as some of mine are.

*The Fourth Apple*

Maybe Eve left Eden
with a seed tucked under her
tongue and rolled it around
in her mouth and in her memory
when she was in danger of
forgetting the wisdom
she had nearly left untaken.

*The Fifth Apple*

Every now and again I try
to remember to stop and ask,
"Are there any lines
I should be crossing?"

*The Sixth Apple*

Cooper Edens writes,
"Longing, far more than it
haunts you, reminds you
of your true name."[1]
What's yours?

BLESSING

Desire, longing, and yearning;
hunger, hankering, and ache:
may you know the presence of the God
who makes a home in each of these.

4

THE FIRST QUEST

In my mind's eye I keep seeing Eve's gesture of reaching for the tree, fingers
not yet grasping the fruit but poised. I find myself wondering, *What hunger*

*gave rise to this?* What told her that Eden wasn't enough, that the landscape and the life she knew would not suffice? What hunger lay beneath her hunger?

> So when the woman saw that the tree was good for food, and that it was a delight to the eyes, and that the tree was to be desired to make one wise, she took of its fruit and ate (Gen. 3:6).

In her commentary on this story, Susan Niditch writes that "to be the curious one, the seeker of knowledge, the tester of limits is to be quintessentially human—to evidence traits of many of the culture-bringing heroes and heroines of Genesis."[2] We are built to stretch beyond what we know, to search for what lies beyond our known borders. Eve's reaching for the fruit is the first quest. Within her gesture lies the impulse that would animate the restless searching of all the following generations.

In her desire, Eve commits herself also to the requirement of every quest: the experience of exile. We cannot stretch beyond ourselves and yet cling to what we have known. Reaching means abandoning the familiar landscape in which we live our days; if not physically departing, then shifting the patterns and habits that have defined our terrain. Once undertaken, it is a leaving that we cannot undo or unlearn. The road by which we set out is never quite the same one by which we will return.

This is, perhaps, the curse of each quest but also its gift: with every departure, a new world. And each time we cross a threshold or make a choice for something new, every time we reach for some piece of knowing to make it our own—there is the presence of Eve, in shadow. Reaching. Tasting. Beyond.

## BLESSING

May your longings lead you far
and farther still
toward the place where what you desire
can be met only by God.
May your hungering bring you home
by another way.

# 5

## THE GEOGRAPHY OF DESIRE

Each summer I fly across the country to the Grünewald Guild, a remarkable retreat center in Washington State that focuses on faith and the arts. I go there to teach a course called "The Soul of the Book." In the class we spend time exploring some of the sacred books that have come to us across the ages, particularly medieval illuminated manuscripts such as the Book of Kells, the Lindisfarne Gospels, Books of Hours, Psalters, and Apocalypses. In their pages we see how, for centuries, artists and scribes have used the book as an art form, intertwining images and text as a way to make a home for the sacred. We look to those books as inspiration for creating books of our own. With art and with words, we make pages that convey something of the sacred text of our own lives.

I always invite the students to bring a book that has been a soulful companion on their journey. One year, a woman brought a book that had belonged to her grandmother. The book began its life as a geography textbook. Her grandmother had turned it into a cookbook, pasting in recipes that she gathered across the years.

The grandmother's literary alchemy spoke powerfully to me. As I turned the pages of the textbook-turned-cookbook, I found myself enchanted by the hints it offered that somewhere beneath our hungers are maps; that there is a geography to our desires; that our yearnings possess longitude and latitude; that if we follow their lines, they can help us find our way.

BLESSING

On this and all days,
may you go in the company
of the God who makes
a way for you.

# 6

# A WANTING WOMAN

The notion of looking at our hungers as a map, as clues to the path ahead, may seem a foreign one. The story of Eve, after all, has been used in large part as a cautionary tale against pursuing our desires, particularly as women. It's not a long trip, some would have it, from being a wanting woman to being a wanton woman.

At the very least, there tends to be a perception, both for women and for men, that God's desires often run counter to our own and that God calls us to pursue the path that is the least appealing to us. It's true that God seems to have a penchant for working in bizarre ways and that our resistance toward a possibility may indeed signal that God is drawing us in that direction. I say this as someone who actively did not want to become an ordained minister; who, as a twelve year old girl hearing her pastor preach about his call to ministry, was horrified by the thought that God might call me to such a path. I had my plan, and it did not involve preaching and whatever else pastors did.

Yet perhaps far more often than we think, God works within our desires. My twelve-year-old self found her way into ministry by pursuing the plan that I had, the passion that captured my heart and my imagination. That passion led me to the next one and to the next. Not different calls, I finally realized, but rather a deepening of one that had long been there.

It is often difficult, to be sure, to discern which of our desires belong to God and which are merely our own. To a great extent, the Christian tradition is right to teach us to be suspicious of our wanting, given how frequently our desires can deceive us. Yet this same tradition also gives us practices that help us examine what it is that we long for. Spiritual direction, *lectio divina*, fasting, prayer: these are among the practices that help us recognize and listen to our hungers as messengers that have something to tell us. Oftentimes a yearning lies buried beneath or within the initial desire, which makes this wanting thing so tricky: desire has a fondness for disguising itself, for not showing its true face right away. It can take sorting through many layers of yearnings before the real one reveals itself.

BLESSING

As you move from passion to passion,
may God draw you deeper
into the desires that God has for you.

# 7

## A HUNGER SHARED

One of the signs that we've found our way to a core desire, something that
God desires for us, is that in following it, we feed not only our own hunger
but that of others as well. When we pursue God's longing for our life, it
never serves only ourselves.

*Vocation* is a word that gets at this idea. With ancient roots in the Latin
word *vocare*—to call—vocation isn't merely about what job we have but
about who God has created us to be in this world. *Vocation* conveys the
notion that God has designs on us and has placed us within this world to
work for its flourishing in concert with our own. In writing about vocation,
Frederick Buechner says, "The place God calls you to is the place where
your deep gladness and the world's deep hunger meet."[3]

So what are you hungry for? What do you desire, and what desire lies
beneath that desire—or within it? What does your wanting teach you about
yourself; about what you love, what you fear, what is possible? How does
your longing meet the world's longing? How do you pray with your desires?

BLESSING

Where the hunger of the world beyond you
meets the hunger of the world within you:
may you find yourself in this place.

# 8

## BEYOND OUR WANTS

At a funeral Mass for a friend, I found myself deeply moved by the musical setting chosen for the Twenty-third Psalm. What especially struck me was the response that the congregation joined in singing: "Shepherd me, O God, beyond my wants, beyond my fears, from death into life."[4]

As someone who spends a lot of time trying to know and follow my desires, I was surprised to find myself drawn to this prayer that asked for guidance to lead us beyond our wants. Perhaps its attraction lay in how it spoke to me of the paradox of longing: that following our true longings leads us deep within ourselves but ultimately beyond ourselves; that pursuing the desires of our hearts and souls leads us beyond superficial impulses, beyond grasping, beyond fear of what will happen if we follow our yearnings.

Perhaps if we live out our longings in ways that are whole-making and enable others to live out the desires of their hearts as well, we will indeed move from death into new life. It will never be possible to reenter Eden, but there are new trees to be planted that bear the fruits of knowledge and wisdom and life. Like Eve, we may journey with bodies and souls whose desires have left us snakebitten; but, like Eve, we may journey also with a wholeness of vision that will bring forth new worlds.

### BLESSING

Peace in the longing,
peace in the leaving,
peace in the letting go.
In every step, peace.

# 9

## EXPOSED

When pondering the Garden—when wondering what broke there, what crack opened up, where things really started to go awry—my gaze goes not toward the taking but toward the hiding. Eve tasted and Adam tasted and with the tasting came knowing. "Then the eyes of both were opened," Genesis tells us. They were exposed. When they heard the voice of God on the evening breeze, Eve and Adam hid themselves. From the One who had formed them, from the One who had given them life, they fled.

And perhaps this is where the sin truly lay: that they hid their faces, that they refused to look upon the One who had created them, that they distanced themselves from the living God.

As well they might.

As well might we.

We condemn Eve and Adam, ourselves forgetting what it means to stand in the presence of God. Or, remembering, our courage fails us. What we have called "The Fall" we might better describe not as a plummet occasioned by Eve and Adam's taking and eating but rather, as Avivah Gottlieb Zornberg puts it in her reflection on Genesis, *The Beginning of Desire*, "a failure to stand upright in the presence of God, to take responsibility for what they have done."[5]

I know this impulse, the desire to hide, in my own self. I am well acquainted with the part of myself that yearns for God even at the same time that I put up resistance. Amid my searching for the holy, I periodically stop to wonder, *What am I doing anyway, asking for the living God to become known to me and to know me?* I think of Annie Dillard's questions in her book *Teaching a Stone to Talk*, where, in reflecting on the ways we speak to God in worship services, she asks,

> Does anyone have the foggiest idea what sort of power we so blithely invoke? Or, as I suspect, does no one believe a word of it? The churches are children playing on the floor with their chemistry sets, mixing up a batch of TNT to kill a Sunday morning. It is madness to wear ladies' straw hats and velvet hats to church; we should all be wearing crash helmets. Ushers should issue life preservers and signal flares; they should lash us to our pews. For the sleeping god may wake someday and take offense, or the waking god may draw us out to where we can never return.[6]

That's the crux of it, that latter possibility that Dillard offers: at the heart of my resistant longing for God is the knowledge that to call upon God, to cry out, as did the prophet Isaiah, "O that you would tear open the heavens and come down!" means giving myself to the prospect, the surety, that God will draw me out to places from which I can never return.[7]

BLESSING

That you may unhide yourself,
that you may turn and turn again
toward the Holy One,
that you may see the face of God
and live.

# 10

## WAKING

As Dillard hints, the real risk that we run in calling upon the living God is not that we might wake God up. Rather, the danger is that God might awaken us. Might open our eyes to the ways that God is ever present with us. Has been right under our noses, waiting for us to notice. Has been loitering in the places where we hang out. Has been calling to us in the cool of the evening and in the glare of the day.

We know that waking changes us, that perceiving God's presence asks something of us. This constitutes the terror and the wonder of waking: that it compels us to let go of the part of ourselves that has been content to pass through the world in a half-slumber, seeing only so far or only so much. Seeing invites responsibility, and this is where Eve and Adam falter: they take the fruit but do not want to take the responsibility that comes with it. They follow their desire but allow it to draw them away from God rather than deeper in.

The story of Eve invites us to ask, Where do we place our courage? Taking the fruit was a daring act. It changed everything. But what if Eve had been equally daring in refusing to hide herself? What if, when she and her mate heard the voice of God calling to them in the cool of the evening, she had stepped up and said, "Here am I"?

BLESSING

Know that the God who calls you
will stir up courage within you,
will accompany you in your waking,
will sustain you in your seeing.

## 11
## A PRAYER TO BE SAID UPON RISING
## AND AGAIN UPON GOING TO SLEEP

*for Daniel*

It's hard to keep the eyes clear
when they live
so close to the brain,
where circuits spark with information
piled up for processing
and thought-lines clog with questions
that play hockey between one's ears
in the dark hours.

I know of no substitute
for the work of cleaning out the crap;
no alternative
to the struggle for focus;
no tools other than
shovel and pickax,
backhoe and plow.

When I am lulled by the urge to settle,
dubious of my own desires,
it helps to breathe
until I find my point of resistance,
to listen beneath the fears
to the questions below the questions,

those messengers that run
barefoot till bloody,
leaving their scarlet map
painted in the dust.

It can also be told this way:

Wisdom and Courage are lovers.
Their secret is that
their dwelling has no lamps.
At sunset they say a prayer
that in the night
their ears hands noses tongues
will tell them what they need to know.

At sunrise they say another prayer:
that their vision will not depend
merely on what the daylight reveals.

The neighbors find them odd,
but their children—
Compassion, Integrity, and Hope—
have learned the wonder of
a heart unhiding itself,
coming as gift
to our deepest eye.

### BLESSING

Wisdom. And courage.
And more wisdom still.

# 12

## SHINING LIKE THE SUN

For a while I've had a sneaking suspicion that on those occasions when we're
tempted to hide ourselves, to turn our eyes from the world around us, it's

not because it's so terrible but because it's so stunning. I once commented to someone that I thought it was a wonder that anyone makes it through life sober. Even with its pain, its brokenness, and its terrors, the world that God wrought is astounding. It should come as no surprise that so many of us look for ways to turn down the volume, to insulate ourselves from the impact. It's too much to take in.

Genesis tells us that after Eve and Adam ate the fruit, "Then the eyes of both were opened, and they knew that they were naked; and they sewed fig leaves together and made loincloths for themselves" (Gen. 3:7). Many have read this and assumed Eve and Adam did this because they felt shame. What if it wasn't their shame that drove them to garb themselves but rather their beauty? What if seeing each other with eyes wide open was too overwhelming to bear? To fully see and be seen is dazzling. And fearsome. Adam tells God, after all, "I heard the sound of you in the garden, and I was afraid, because I was naked; and I hid myself" (Gen. 3:10). To see as Eve and Adam did after their eyes were opened is difficult to sustain.

Thomas Merton once wrote, "There is no way of telling people that they are all walking around shining like the sun."[8] Yet, as he knew, to make the attempt is part of our wondrous and terrible vocation. We are called, in this broken world, to open ourselves to the beauty that persists. To allow ourselves to see and to be stunned.

BLESSING

May you move through this day
with eyes open to the God
who shines like the sun
within and around you.

# 13

## A COMMUNION OF MORE THAN OUR BODIES

Of the beauty and pleasures that the world affords, food is among the most basic. So deeply is it bound to our personal and collective history, it's no wonder that food should figure with such prominence in the tale of our beginnings. Aside from whatever disobedience and rebellion may have lurked in the heart of Eve, Genesis tells us that Eve "saw that the tree was good for food, and that it was a delight to the eyes" (Gen. 3:6).

M. F. K. Fisher was a twentieth-century writer famed for the ways that she wrote about the pleasures of food—the preparing of it, the eating of it, the sharing of it. In the foreword to her book *The Gastronomical Me*, she offered these insights into the mysterious ways that our hungers and our histories intertwine:

> People ask me: Why do you write about food, and eating and drinking? Why don't you write about the struggle for power and security, and about love, the way others do? . . .
>
> The easiest answer is to say that, like most other humans, I am hungry. But there is more than that. It seems to me that our three basic needs, for food and security and love, are so mixed and mingled and entwined that we cannot straightly think of one without the others. So it happens that when I write of hunger, I am really writing about love and the hunger for it, and warmth and the love of it and the hunger for it . . . and then the warmth and richness and fine reality of hunger satisfied . . . and it is all one.
>
> I tell about myself, and how I ate bread on a lasting hillside, or drank red wine in a room now blown to bits, and it happens without my willing it that I am telling too about the people with me then, and their other deeper needs for love and happiness.
>
> There is food in the bowl, and more often than not, because of what honesty I have, there is nourishment in the heart, to feed the wilder, more insistent hungers. We must eat. If, in the face of that dread fact, we can find other nourishment, and tolerance and compassion for it, we'll be no less full of human dignity.
>
> There is a communion of more than our bodies when bread is broken and wine drunk. And that is my answer, when people ask me: Why do you write about hunger, and not wars or love?[9]

BLESSING

May you have food in the bowl, to feed what is basic,
and nourishment in the heart, to feed hungers more wild.

May the God of the feast draw you to a welcome table
where you know communion and delight and rest.


# 14

## APPETITES

In illuminating the entwining of food and security and love and how these
relationships are part of our histories, M. F. K. Fisher offers lovely and compelling images. Yet our hungers also have a deeply shadowed side. At a basic
level, the story of Eden helps to explain why we sometimes experience such
a tangle when it comes to desire and food. Anything involving these is certain to grow complicated at some point along the way. Eden speaks to how
these things—hunger, eating, pleasure, peril—are bound up together in our
personal as well as collective history.

Our patterns of eating, or not eating, manifest these complications.
Anorexia, bulimia, obesity, and other conditions related to diet and habits
of consumption: our bodies bear witness to the complexities of food and
desire, made all the more convoluted by the wildly conflicting messages
that some cultures convey. It can be extraordinarily difficult to find good
answers to the basic question: What do we eat? And, beneath that, What are
we hungry for?

In her book *Appetites: Why Women Want*, Caroline Knapp offers a
powerful reflection on the hungers of body and soul. Writing in particular of women's relationships with food with wisdom born of Knapp's own
struggle with anorexia, she traces the threads that link appetite, identity,
body image, pleasure, and love in contemporary culture. Near the close of
the book, she writes, "Appetite—naming it, satisfying it—*is* a monumental
struggle for many women, a long-distance swim against a current of painful
feeling." She goes on to state that she treasures the signs of hope given to her
by women "who have swum against that current of pain and finally made it
to another shore, new altars of desire built on the banks."[10]

How do you relate to food? What history lies within your hungers?
What did you eat as a child, or what did you do without? How does what
you eat tell you about who you are?

BLESSING

That you may know what it is
that you truly hunger for.
That eating may offer pleasure,
harmony, and deep delight.
That you may find God there.

# 15

*The Secret Room*

## IN THE GARDEN OF THE TEXT

It is a small book. A chapbook of sorts. Apple-red cover, two staples in its folded spine. The drawing on the front depicts an old, twisted tree whose branches are laden with books. In the corner, a woman. She reaches toward an open book.

The apple-red book came my way in college, a text for one of my classes. Published by the Woman's Institute for Continuing Jewish Education in San Diego, *Taking the Fruit: Modern Women's Tales of the Bible* is a contemporary introduction to the ancient practice of midrash (pl. midrashim), one of the treasures of the Jewish tradition. Midrashim are stories that first emerged orally, long centuries ago, as the rabbis pondered the Hebrew Bible. Where gaps, curiosities, and seeming contradictions existed in the text, the rabbis brought the gift of their imaginations. Spinning stories out of the spaces between the lines and reconciling the points of tension, they created tales of wisdom and wonder that were passed down from generation to generation, eventually taking written form.

The practice of midrash was born of the recognition that although the form of the scriptures remains essentially the same, the Bible is a living book that continues to ask us to engage it anew. While the boundaries of the written text of the Bible came to be fixed in a codified form, the practice of midrash pulls at and plays with those boundaries, finding abundant room to add its storied wisdom to the gaps and margins of the text.

The practice of creating midrash continues to this day. In the past several decades, Jewish women in particular have turned to midrash as a way to claim a voice of their own within a text that often relegates women to the margins. The creators of *Taking the Fruit* describe it this way:

> One way for women to relieve the tension that is created in a relationship which involves the static, codified Torah and the modern ever-changing world, is for each generation to create anew. Women's roles in the Torah were circumscribed and limited while women's roles in the modern world are expanding in vision and in practice. Therefore it is incumbent upon contemporary women to write modern stories which maintain their relationship with the text, and which incorporate their experience and consciousness into Judaism. This process allows Judaism to grow and develop a healthy relationship with all of its people.[11]

The midrashim in *Taking the Fruit* are new ones—or, at least, were new at the time that the book was published nearly thirty years ago—written by members of a class that the Woman's Institute offered. The writers drew inspiration from earlier midrashim, ancient as well as contemporary ones, and from their own lives. Within their pages we find imaginative stories of biblical women such as Eve, Sarah, Rachel and Leah, Dinah, the midwives Shiphrah and Puah, and Miriam. Also present among the pages is Lilith, an intriguing and complex character who emerged from a mix of folklore and rabbinic midrash. In the midrashic tales, Lilith appears prior to Eve: she is the *first* first woman, the woman of Genesis 1 who was created at the same time as the man, not the woman of Genesis 2 who was made from the rib of Adam.

*Taking the Fruit* initiated me into an ancient tradition of storytelling entirely new to me. The notion that between and within the words of the Bible lay worlds yet to explore enchanted me. With its invitation to bring the sacred gift of imagination to the holy ground of the scriptures, midrash beckons us to these sacred texts as to a garden where we are meant to tend and take and eat.

## BLESSING

So may you tend and take
and eat the gifts in the garden of the text.
In the gaps, in the margins,
in the secret spaces among the words,
may you find places to create stories anew.

# 16

## WHY I EAT PEARS

Their subtlety was lost on me
when I was a child,
when my tongue sought
the stronger taste of strawberry,
the crisper flesh of apple,
the darker sweetness of chocolate.

Pears had no place in the days
when I sucked sour lollipops,
stole chunks of fresh pineapple before dinner,
consumed ten pieces of garlic bread
in one sitting.

And if today I eat pears,
don't think that my taste has mellowed,
that my tongue has grown tired.
Though it's true I can't devour chocolate
quite the way I used to,
my mouth still finds its way
to lemon, to salsa,
to wine, and to salt.

Today I eat pears
because my mother eats them.
I eat pears

because they make me
pay attention.
I eat pears
because I have to wash my hands
after.
I eat pears
because of how they look
in ripe repose in my kitchen,
their golden and crimson curves
lounging in my cobalt colander.

I eat pears
because their flesh is so willing
and my knife
is so sharp.

BLESSING

This day and each day,
may you find something worth savoring.


# 17

## THE HUNGER TABLE

Eve and Adam found out that our eating exposes us. It says something about who we are and what we desire. This fact accounts for both the pleasure of eating and the challenge of it.

Jesus too knew the exposure involved in eating. That helps explain why he spent much of his ministry hanging out at tables—so much so that critics accused him of being "'a glutton and a drunkard, a friend of tax collectors and sinners'" (Matt. 11:19). Jesus understood the table as a place of revelation, as when he sits down with his companions on the road to Emmaus. Taking bread, he blesses it, breaks it, gives it to them. With words that offer a curious echo of Eden, Luke tells us, "Then their eyes were opened, and they recognized him" (Luke 24:31).

The kind of seeing to which eating invites us also helps account for why the central sacramental rite of the Christian tradition occurs at a table. It is a place that recognizes our sometimes conflicted hungers and offers the possibility of their redemption. The Communion table beckons us to unhide ourselves from one another and from the God who causes us to desire in the first place.

One day while I was in seminary, I stood in a line of people waiting to process into the chapel. I was carrying one of the Communion chalices, and I held it to a friend's ear. "Listen!" I said. "You can hear the Last Supper!"

It's not wholly a joke, though. That's part of what Communion does: it gathers us around the vessels that help us hear the story, that help us attend to the echoes of Jesus' blessing and offering, to listen to our history and enter into it. Gathering at the table of Communion, of Eucharist, invites us to listen also to the hollow places within us, to seek sustenance and nourishment, to be reminded we are not alone. The table invites us to meet Christ and one another at the point of our hunger. It confronts us with the knowledge that we can't get by on our own reserves. And it offers a place to hold those hungers.

In a culture that constantly tells us what we're hungry for and how to sate our desires, it is a marvel that the central sacramental space of the Christian tradition is a table that beckons us to acknowledge that we have deeper hungers and keener desires than the ones our televisions, magazines, and radios confront us with. To gather at the table of Christ is a countercultural act that challenges us to sort among our competing hungers, invites us to name the desire that lies beneath them, and beckons us to resist the urge to stuff ourselves not simply with food but with whatever keeps us from acknowledging the emptiness within us.

The table of Christ gives a glimpse of Paradise: not the innocent paradise of Eden but rather a redeemed creation in which our wounds have given way to wisdom and we perceive beauty in the scars we carry. Here we see with grown-up eyes that are yet capable of wonder. These glimpses sustain us as we go into the world to offer others the feeding that we have found.

BLESSING

O taste and see
the goodness of the God
who calls us to the table
and meets us in every feast.


# 18

## CURIOUS WOMEN

Across the ages, Eve has often found herself linked with myths and legends of women such as Pandora, the first woman in Greek mythology, who couldn't resist opening the jar that had been given her; Psyche, who turned a light on the lover who visited her only at night; and Bluebeard's wife, who could not let the forbidden door remain closed. In her book *Eve: A Biography*, Pamela Norris notes that the impulse to link these women is quite old; Pandora, for instance, appears alongside Eve in the writings of the early church father Tertullian. Both mythology and commentary have portrayed these as women whose curiosity wreaked havoc at best and, at worst, became a gateway for evil to enter the world. In the hands of their tellers and interpreters, these stories have often served as cautionary tales, warnings to women about the perils of inquisitiveness. Curiosity, they say, is a curse.

Yet *curiosity* is such a pale word to describe this desire to know, to discover, to push beyond the limits that defined these women. Within the very sphere of their intimate, domestic spaces, whether garden or house, these women found ways to cross the boundaries set for them. In doing so, they received something far deeper than a satisfaction of curiosity. Their crossings propelled them from the existence they had known into a life that would be, if more chaotic, then less constrained and confined. They would become actors in their own stories.

These women experience a form of initiation. As with all initiations, it comes not quite in the form that they anticipated but in one that they needed—one that their story required. In her book *Reinventing Eve*, Kim Chernin reminds us:

Initiation is not a predictable process. It moves forward fitfully, through moments of clear seeing, dramatic episodes of feeling, subtle intuitions, vague contemplative states. Dreams arrive, bringing guidance we frequently cannot accept. Years pass, during which we know that we are involved in something that cannot be easily named. We wake to a sense of confusion, know that we are in dangerous conflict, cannot define the nature of what troubles us. All change is like this. It circles around, snakes back on itself, finds detours, leads us a merry chase, starts us out it seems all over again from where we were in the first place. And then suddenly, when we least expect it, something opens a door, discovers a threshold, shoves us across.[12]

## BLESSING

May you have
the vision to recognize
the door that is yours,
courage to open it,
wisdom to walk through.

# 19

## CEREMONY

Sometimes the changes in our lives beg for recognition. Our initiations are occasions that give us the opportunity to take the pieces we accumulated in a season of living—pieces that may be beautiful or broken or some of both—and to gather them up in a fashion that seeks to make some sense of their presence, to incorporate them into the pattern of our lives.

I think of the years I spent as the artist-in-residence at San Pedro Center, a Catholic retreat center near Orlando. The first year, I lived on the property in a small cabin by the lake. There wasn't much ritual involved when I moved there (except for a pair of sandhill cranes standing welcome in the driveway when we pulled the moving truck into the entrance, which felt like some kind of blessing). Years later, though, when I left my position there and took up my new role with The Wellspring Studio, it felt like an occasion that needed some ceremonial action. The transition had been a lengthy and convoluted process, in part because it took a while to do the institutional sorting-through of the form that my new ministry would take. With all that past, it was time to celebrate—and to remember.

One afternoon I gathered at the retreat center with three friends who had been sustaining companions throughout the sometimes complicated and sometimes wondrous (and sometimes both) turnings of my path within and beyond that place. I shared some reflections with them about what I had found there and who I had become because of it. I talked about how I had imagined having a Big Ritual to mark what a huge transition had taken place for me in leaving and what a deep transformation had occurred within me over the course of my years there. But as the day of celebration approached, I realized that I didn't need a Big Ritual. Having already put copious amounts of energy into getting to this point in my life, I found that I needed a ritual that would be simple. Gathering together, telling some stories, and being in that landscape: this would be ceremony enough.

And, of course, we had cake.

It was an occasion of learning that rites of passage don't have to be lavish affairs. Each passage asks something different of us. They do, however, ask. Our passages invite us to consider how we move from one part of our life to another, how we can do so with mindfulness, how we will gather up the pieces and fashion from them a doorway, a path.

How do you mark the beginnings and endings of the lifetimes that unfold within your life? How would you describe the different selves you've been across the years? Did you know when you were passing from one phase of your life into another? Have you gone or are going through or are anticipating a change that could benefit from some ritual attention? How might you set aside a time, alone or with friends, in order to remember and to mark the passage; to name who you have been and who you are becoming?

BLESSING

In the beginning,
in the ending,
in the beginning again:

may the God of the threshold
encompass you in every turning.


# 20
## THE THRESHOLD RITES

Eve's taking of the fruit is, in some fashion, a ritual gesture, a rite of passage.
A rebellious one, to be sure, but a passage nonetheless. It marks the beginning of Eve's growing up, and of ours.

These days, many of us live in a culture that gives little attention to
recognizing and naming the thresholds that we cross in the spiral of a life.
"Where are the threshold rites," Joan Halifax asks, "that mark living and
dying, mourning and marriage, birth and childhood, vision and darkness?"[13]

In the absence of such rites, we sometimes manufacture our own initiations, not always recognizing this is what we're doing. Something in our
souls stirs up situations that propel us into a territory we might not have
gotten to otherwise. We pursue these initiations, these passages, not always
consciously, not always mindful of their consequences but needing the wisdom that they bear. As Eve discovered, our choices give us a past that may
appear flawed, broken, in pieces. These pieces give us, however, something
to work with, something from which a world can be made.

### BLESSING

When all about you lies in pieces,
may the Holy One make of them a passage.


# 21
## THE POSSIBILITY OF A PAST

There is this too: how else do we gain our deepest wisdom, save with our
grand mistakes? Wisdom comes mostly with experience; and on the day
the serpent approaches her, Eve has had precious little of that. She has no

earthly parents, no ancestral relationships or records, no cultural memory or traditions to help her know who she is, not even a group of girlfriends to warn her away from seductive strangers or to take her in when Eden expels her. Eve has developed no collection of consequences from previous choices she has made; she possesses no insights gained from occasions of having chosen well or poorly. She is a woman without history, floating in the perpetual nowness of Paradise.

Without chronology, Eve would have had little idea of what it meant to have a past. I wonder, then, if part of her desire to reach for that fruit lay in a hunger for something to happen that would alter the shape of her days— something that would give her a sense of days in the first place, would drive her from the formless timelessness that she had known, beyond which she could not imagine but about which she had some intuition, some suspicion, some inkling. By stepping across a threshold, by moving into choice, into consequence, into time, Eve gives herself—and us—not only the possibility of a future, but the possibility of a past as well.

BLESSING

May the Ancient of Days inhabit
not only your future but also your past.
May you know the grace, wisdom, and redemption
that yet dwell in what has gone before.


# 22

## PAGES AND WINGS

What does Eve's story invite us to see about our own past? What does this woman of beginnings beckon us to know about our own beginnings? What is the ground from which our lives have been made? What were our earliest hungers, and where did they lead us?

As a child, I loved birds. I don't remember the origins of this love, what prompted it or precisely when it showed itself. I was no more than ten when I decided I wanted to be an ornithologist. I read hungrily. I collected feathers, keeping my treasures in a small suitcase and, later, a large, clear plastic bag, the kind that bedspreads come in. The core of my collection came from the Jacksonville Zoo. When I wrote to the zoo asking for some feathers, the letter found its way to a kind bird curator. In response, he sent a manila envelope from which tumbled an exultation of feathers. I suppose he had merely gathered a day's worth of feathers the birds had left behind; but for a ten-year-old girl, it was a treasure. An enchantment. The feathers turned to dust long ago—the work of mites—and my avian absorption gave way to other interests that consumed me. Yet those birds have haunted every subsequent passion.

I have thought of those birds in recent years, as my passion has turned toward the medieval illuminated manuscripts that feed and fascinate my imagination. One day as we were walking, I talked with Gary about this. He asked what I thought the connection was—those birds, these books. I thought for a few paces, then replied that I thought it had something to do with pages and wings. The feathers that tumbled from the bird curator's envelope had the same hues that I see in the books I now pore over. The birds of my childhood hover among the leaves; opening a book, I see not the shadow of wings but rather their vivid colors bleeding into the pages, drenching them, their imprint indelible across the years, still offering the possibility of flight.

### BLESSING

In the pondering of your past,
in the contemplation of your present,
in the hungers that persist
and in those that fall away:
peace to you, deep peace.

# 23

## AT THE POINT OF OUR PASSIONS

About my bird days I remember not just reading but also making. I naturally responded to what I was taking in by creating. I rolled clay between my palms and made eggs. I drew pictures of birds. I wrote. I made posters. I have some memory of inflicting "talks" about birds upon my family and anyone else who would listen.

I remember too that birds occasioned my first experience of seeking connections around a shared interest, of reaching out to someone who could offer insight and guidance. I wrote to Oliver L. Austin, the author of a massive book titled *Birds of the World* that had offered me many happy hours. He served as curator emeritus of ornithology at the nearby Florida Museum of Natural History in Gainesville. Somewhere among my boxes in storage resides a scrapbook with correspondence from both Dr. Austin and his wife, who also wrote about birds. I remember them both as gracious and generous to my young self.

What do your passions call you to create, to offer, to leave behind? How do your interests draw you toward others? How do you participate in passing along the knowledge, wisdom, experiences, and questions that come to you in your searching?

### BLESSING

That the desires of your heart
may draw you toward creation
and connection.
That community and kindred
will attend your path.
That you will not go alone.

# 24

## VANISHED

Much of my fascination with birds was devoted to extinct and endangered birds. Where did this preoccupation come from? Early curiosity about loss? Desire to figure out how to prevent disappearance?

Browsing through the library recently, I came across a book by Christopher Cokinos. Borrowing a line from a poem by Emily Dickinson, its title is *Hope Is the Thing with Feathers: A Personal Chronicle of Vanished Birds*. Cokinos writes at the intersection of personal curiosity, natural history, and American history: telling the story of birds that have gone missing, he observes that he is telling too about such aspects of cultural history as logging, millinery, and urbanization.

Cokinos tells his own history as well. His interest in extinct birds was ignited when, walking in a forest with his wife, he saw a flash of green swoop past, then another. In his search to figure out what he rightly assumed to be a pair of escaped parrots, Cokinos came across references to the Carolina Parakeet, the only species of parrot that was native to the United States; it became extinct in the early twentieth century. Reading about the Carolina Parakeet led him to read and write about other vanished birds.

Tonight, thinking about the birds among my own beginnings, I pull out a roll of yellowed newsprint. I unfurl it and read my young printing. "A Few Extinct Birds," I had written across the top, more than three decades ago. The newsprint displays five pencil sketches. In one column appear the Dodo (which I always loved drawing, probably for its distinctive beak), the Seychelles Black Parrot, the Jamaican Wood Rail, and the Mauritius Blue Pigeon. A single bird hovers in the second column: a Carolina Parakeet, the bird that launched Cokinos's journey.

Cokinos writes that though we may not restore these birds to the physical landscape, "we can restore—we can *restory*—these vanished birds to our consciousness."[14] Perhaps this is what I was doing even then: telling their story with words and with drawings, reclaiming the lost birds, making them live as part of my personal story, my history.

And am doing still, now with women instead of wildlife: women whose stories have gone missing, whose stories were suppressed or simply slipped away; women whose lives exist in fragments, in scraps, their remnants left behind like feathers to be gathered up, evidence of flight and movement and migration. In telling their stories, we tell our own.

BLESSING

May we bear witness
to what we have lost in this world:
what has disappeared, what has gone missing.
May we see and safeguard what remains.

# 25

## WHERE I'M FROM

In her poem "Where I'm From," Appalachian poet George Ella Lyon offers a litany of the places and people, the artifacts and experiences that hold her roots. In the opening stanza, she writes,

I am from clothespins,
from Clorox and carbon-tetrachloride,
I am from the dirt under the back porch.
(Black, glistening,
it tasted like beets.)[15]

For years, the poem has served as a writing prompt that invites others to reflect on their roots. Commenting on how widely the poem has traveled, Lyon writes, "People have used it at their family reunions, teachers have used it with kids all over the United States, in Ecuador and China; they have taken it to girls in juvenile detention, to men in prison for life, and to refugees in a camp in the Sudan. Its life beyond my notebook is a testimony to the power of poetry, of roots, and of teachers."[16]

In our mobile society, it's often hard to say where we're from, hard to name the roots that hold us as more and more of us live at a distance from the places and people we grew up with. Yet Lyon's poem reminds us that roots occur in many ways, sometimes but not always tied to one particular place.

Here's where I'm from.

*Where I'm From*

I am from orange groves
and old Florida,
from a house my parents built
in a field my grandfather gave them.
Black-eyed Susans grew there in the spring,
so thick we played hide-and-seek
simply by kneeling among them.

I am from a town
with more cows than people,
from Judy and from Joe,
from generations that have grown up
in one place.

I am from peanut butter and
honey sandwiches every morning,
from my grandmothers' kitchens,
from Thanksgiving feasts in the
community park,
from Christmas Eves in the
white painted church
among the pine trees.

I am from the dictionary we kept
by the dinner table
where we ate words like food,
from hours and days in libraries,
from miles of books.
I am from the path they have made.

I am from solitude and silence,
from the monks and mystics who lived
between the choir and the cell,
from the scribes bent over their books,

from parchment and paint,
from ancient ink and from gold
that turned pages into lamps,
into light.

I am from women less quiet,
women of the shout and the stomp,
testifying wherever they could make
their voices heard.
I am from Miriam and Mary and Magdalena
and from women unknown and unnamed,
women who carried their prayers
not in books
but in their blood
and in their bones;
women who passed down the sacred stories
from body to body.

I am from them,
listening for their voices,
aching to hear,
to tell, to cry out,
to make a way for those
yet to come.

So where are you from? What are the places, the people, the experiences that carved your path? What holds your roots? How does where you're from help you understand who you are? How does your past help you find the path ahead? What might your own "Where I'm From" poem sound like?

BLESSING

Blessed be the people we carry in our blood.
Blessed be the places we carry in our bones.
May our living make a way for those who come after:
a path of blessing, a path of beauty.

# 26
## UNFOLD YOUR OWN MYTH

"Unfold your own myth," the medieval Persian poet Rumi exhorted his hearers.[17] Pondering Eve, I think of how she does this, how in the midst of the script that has been given her, she chooses not to accept it. She steps into her own story.

Choosing not to follow a prescribed script, a template, brings its own consequences. Among them: questions from people trying to figure us out. These questions are an attempt to locate us within our shared human story, to get a fix on us, especially when we don't fit the usual patterns. "Are you on sabbatical?" colleagues repeatedly asked me when I became artist-in-residence at San Pedro Center. "Are you married, honey?" a woman asked me a few days ago.

And this question: "Where's your baby?" It comes from Kyla. She is a neighbor, perhaps two years old. I love to cross paths with her when I'm out for a walk. She greets me like I am the greatest person in the world, and she can hardly believe her luck that I have turned up. I've seen her greet other people the same way, so I know she doesn't reserve her enthusiasm just for me. I don't mind.

"I don't have a baby, Kyla."

"Why?"

"Oh, Kyla, let me tell you about the complexities of life choices . . ."

Her father flashes a knowing smile. Kyla seems flabbergasted but lets it go.

I used to assume that my life would follow a certain template, at least with respect to family: fall in love, marry, have children. Blessed with a wonderful family, both immediate and extended, I had a growing up that was graced. I expected to pass the gift along.

I don't know just where it happened, but at some point I began to realize that parenthood was a calling, and I hadn't discerned that calling in my life. The knowledge has become a sure but bittersweet clarity. Yet the clarity has stirred questions of my own. Without children, how do I pass along what I have received? If I am not bringing up a new generation, how do I offer beginnings?

BLESSING

That you may have
the wisdom to know the story
to which God calls you,
the power to pursue it,
the courage to abide its mysteries,
and love in every step.


# 27

## HERE

There are days when the question suddenly surfaces: How did I get *here*? Here, as an artist and writer and minister living in this place in this town, sharing my life with these particular people? Why this and not some other path? Why here and not another place?

I don't mean to say that these questions stir up deep doubts, uncertainties, or qualms about where I am and the path I have found (most days). I recognize how fortunate I am in the life that I have. Yet the question still surfaces: how did I get here? Is this what I intended? Did I come here by insightful choosing, or have I allowed myself to be swept along?

When the question surfaces, when I find myself asking how I got here, it provides a good opportunity to ponder whether I am living more by intention or by reaction. How much do I allow myself to be carried along by choices I have already made or by the choices of others or by circumstances over which I think I have no control? Is there something in my life that I need to view from a different perspective—to ask, Does this still fit for me? Do my present commitments enable me to live into what God has called me to do and to be in this world?

BLESSING

Blessed the place where you are,
blessed where you are going.

# 28

## MESSENGERS

Recently it struck me that I have lived long enough to have some sense of the consequences of the choices I have made. I can look back and see the grace of the good choices. I can recognize the grief that has come in the choices that were less wise. I am not a woman of many regrets, and so it came as a surprise when I found myself visited by grief over decisions that were wise at the time but yet held sorrow. Closed doors cracked themselves open, beckoning me to see what I didn't have the eyes to notice at the time.

I have learned to understand regrets as invitations, as messengers. Rather than being thugs from the past, come to beat me up for decisions I cannot possibly retrieve, they come instead with a word to offer. The word often speaks of something missing in my life, some connection I need to make. With time and with giving attention to the regrets, they have become not so much about loss as about what is yet possible. What path can I still make from the choices gone before?

### BLESSING

That you may welcome your regrets
not as sorrows
but as messengers, as invitations,
as doorways to what yet lies ahead.

# 29

## WILDNESS AND TIME

My books always begin on index cards—stray thoughts, a few sentences, sometimes just a few words that might otherwise slip away. I save them, let them simmer and stew and accumulate, then return to them, often much later, to ponder which of them I'll flesh out.

I have one index card on which, years ago, I wrote just three words:

*wildness and time*

Are these words my shortest poem? A prayer? I don't recall what was on my mind when I jotted them down—perhaps nothing, else I would have added to them. Pondering Eve, I've been thinking of these words again. Perhaps they are a blessing for Eve, a hope, a promise for a woman cast out from Paradise, that perhaps the wildness will be precisely what she needs as she learns to live within chronological time. Perhaps the words are Eve's blessing and prayer for us: that we will not be domesticated. That we will not be tamed.

## BLESSING

May you resist
all that would confine you
and constrain you.
May you have time enough
and wildness enough.
May you have the words
that will help light your way.

# 30

## TRACES

"Yet the beginning is not the beginning," writes Alicia Ostriker. "Inside the oldest stories are older stories, not destroyed but hidden. Swallowed. Mouth songs. Wafers of parchment, layer underneath layer. Nobody knows how many. The texts retain traces, leakages, lacunae, curious figures of speech, jagged irruptions. What if I say these traces too are mine?"[18]

## BLESSING

May you know the hidden stories
of your life, your lineage, your tradition.
May you look into the layers
with courage and imagination.
Among the gaps, the absences,

the traces and fragments,
may you find stories to create anew.


# 31

## AFTER EDEN

The ancient texts tell
that my husband accumulated
nine hundred and thirty years
before he died.

They do not tell
that I survived him,
nothing but sinew
and muscle and bone
shed of everything.

Mother of All Living,
my mate had named me,
but what of my sons
dead or gone?
Abel in the ground
long ages now
and Cain forever wandering.

After we buried Adam
(dust to dust)
I returned to the borders of Eden.

The cherubim at the gate
looked tired
and the sword, once flaming,
now gave a dull glow.

A snakeskin
twisted in the breeze

rasping and hollow
an empty thing.

A hundred years from now
if they unearth my bones
they will see
the imprint of leaves
along every one,
testimony to the secret
that even Adam
(bone of my bone,
flesh of my flesh)
did not know:

I took the tree with me
the day I left Eden,
the day I decided not to die,
the day I chose instead
to sink my roots in the soil
of this terrible, stunning world.

## BLESSING

May the Holy One,
who created you from words and dust
and called you good,
inhabit your every hunger,
dwell in each desire,
and encompass you
in all the choosing that lies ahead.

## FURTHER READING

*Appetites: Why Women Want* by Caroline Knapp. New York: Counterpoint, 2003.

*The Beginning of Desire: Reflections on Genesis* by Avivah Gottlieb Zornberg. New York: Three Leaves Press/Doubleday, 1995.

*Eve: A Biography* by Pamela Norris. New York: New York University Press, 2001.

*Four Centuries of Jewish Women's Spirituality: A Sourcebook* ed. Ellen M. Umansky and Dianne Ashton. Lebanon, NH: University Press of New England, 2008.

*Reinventing Eve: Modern Woman in Search of Herself* by Kim Chernin. New York: Times Books/Random House, 1987.

## NOTES

1. Cooper Edens, *Nineteen Hats, Ten Teacups, an Empty Birdcage & the Art of Longing* (New York: Green Tiger Press/Simon & Schuster, 1981).

2. Susan Niditch, "Genesis," in Carol A. Newsom and Sharon H. Ringe, eds., *The Women's Bible Commentary* (Louisville, KY: Westminster/John Knox Press, 1992), 13.

3. Frederick Buechner, *Wishful Thinking: A Seeker's ABC*, revised (SanFrancisco: HarperSanFrancisco, 1993), 119.

4. Marty Haugen, "Shepherd Me, O God" (Copyright © GIA Publications, Inc., 1986).

5. Avivah Gottlieb Zornberg, *The Beginning of Desire: Reflections on Genesis* (New York: Three Leaves Press/Doubleday, 1995), 23–24.

6. Annie Dillard, *Teaching a Stone to Talk: Expeditions and Encounters* (New York: Perennial Library/Harper & Row Publishers, 1988), 40–41.

7. Isaiah 64:1.

8. Thomas Merton, *Conjectures of a Guilty Bystander* (New York: Image Books/Doubleday, 1989), 157.

9. M. F. K. Fisher, *The Gastronomical Me,* in *The Art of Eating: The Collected Gastronomical Works of M. F. K. Fisher* (Cleveland, OH: World Publishing Company, 1954), 353.

10. Caroline Knapp, *Appetites: Why Women Want* (New York: Counterpoint, 2003), 179.

11. Jane Sprague Zones, ed., *Taking the Fruit: Modern Women's Tales of the Bible* (San Diego, CA: Woman's Institute for Continuing Jewish Education, 1981), 9–10.

12. Kim Chernin, *Reinventing Eve: Modern Woman in Search of Herself* (New York: Times Books/Random House, 1987), 16.

13. Joan Halifax, *The Fruitful Darkness: Reconnecting with the Body of the Earth* (San Francisco: HarperSanFrancisco, 1994), xx.

14. Christopher Cokinos, *Hope Is the Thing with Feathers: A Personal Chronicle of Vanished Birds* (New York: Jeremy P. Tarcher/Putnam, 2000), 3.

15. George Ella Lyon, "Where I'm From," in *Where I'm From: Where Poems Come From* (Spring, TX: Absey & Co., 1999), 3.

16. George Ella Lyon, http://www.georgeellalyon.com/where.html.

17. Rumi, "Unfold Your Own Myth," in *The Essential Rumi*, trans. Coleman Barks (Edison, NJ: Castle Books, 1997), 40–41.

18. Alicia Suskin Ostriker, *The Nakedness of the Fathers: Biblical Visions and Revisions* (New Brunswick, NJ: Rutgers University Press, 1997), 15–16.

# A HABIT OF THE
# WILDEST BOUNTY

*The Book of Brigid*

## INTRODUCTION

Ireland, *Isle of the Saints.* Nearly a thousand years ago, the Irish chronicler Maelbrigte used the term to describe the island whose landscape seemed to abound with women and men who had given themselves to God. Of the Irish saints, one of the most beloved has been Brigid of Kildare. Born in 452 CE as the new faith of Christianity began to take root in her homeland, Brigid became a woman whose life would engage people's imaginations for centuries to come.

The facts we know about Brigid (whose name also appears in such spellings as Brigit, Brighid, and Bride) are so few that some scholars have concluded she never actually existed. The historical information that has survived is like a handful of threads spun from the mists and mysteries of early Christianity on the island. The first written evidence of Brigid's life didn't emerge until about a hundred and fifty years after her death. The writer of the earliest *Life* of Brigid, which is also the earliest extant *Life* of an Irish saint, was a monk named Cogitosus, who lived at one of the monasteries that Brigid established. (A *Life* is a written account of a saint.) Cogitosus tells us that Brigid was born of Christian parents named Broicsech and Dubthach (other accounts refer to Dubthach as being pagan), that she possessed miraculous abilities from an early age, and that she grew into a powerful and revered preacher and monastic leader whose concern "was to provide for the orderly direction of souls in all things and to care for the churches of many provinces which were associated with her."[1] The literature suggests that Brigid founded a number of monasteries, the most influential one being the double monastery—comprised of both women and men—that she established at Cill Dara (the "Church of the Oak"), now known as Kildare.

Other writers who followed Cogitosus expanded on Brigid's story. The other two oldest *Lives* of Brigid—the *Bethu Brigte* (*Irish Life of Brigit*) and the *Vita Prima* (so called because it was long thought to have been the first written *Life* of Brigid)—expand on Brigid's saintly qualities. While the details of each of these *Lives* sometimes conflict, owing in part to certain political aims of their authors, they accord in presenting Brigid as a groundbreaking woman whose gifts and powers helped shape the landscape of early Christian Ireland.

Many of the tales of Brigid's life read much like those of other female saints: her saintly qualities were evident from an early age; she forsook marriage in order to follow Christ in a monastic way of life (she even caused her eye to burst in order to avoid being married off); she was a wonder-worker who brought healing and justice; she exercised miraculous influence over the weather, animals, and the landscape. "She stilled the rain and wind," the final line of *The Irish Life* tells us.[2]

The *Lives* particularly emphasize the hospitality that brought Brigid renown. In her charming book *St. Brigid of Ireland*, Alice Curtayne describes Brigid as someone who "found the poor irresistible"[3] and ministered to them with "a habit of the wildest bounty."[4] Her lavish generosity tended to put her at odds with her family and, as she became a monastic leader, with her community. In one account of Brigid's life, her father became so exasperated with the benevolence she displayed with his possessions ("holy thieving," as one writer has put it) that he carted her off to the king, intending to sell her to him. While Brigid waited for her father to talk with the king, a man with leprosy came along; she immediately gave him her father's precious sword. When her father returned and inquired about the sword, Brigid responded, "Christ has taken it." In a fury, her father left her with the king, but she mysteriously reappeared at home. "Truly, Dubthach," the king tells her father, "this girl can neither be sold nor bought."[5]

A strong domestic quality pervades Brigid's wonderwork, a homeliness to the miraculous that runs throughout her tales. A sense of gracefulness shimmers in the utterly mundane quality of the material of Brigid's miracles, underscoring the dignity of the daily tasks to which the women of her day—and women across centuries—devoted so much of their lives. Esther de Waal's phrase, by which she describes an imagined Celtic woman, is apt for Brigid: "She has made the mundane the edge of glory."[6]

Those who wrote Brigid's *Lives*, however, were keen to portray her as much more than a wonder-working dairymaid. Within the workaday landscape of her stories, signs of the mystery and power of God flicker and flash with a brilliance that illuminates the saint and sparks the imagination. As we will see, the symbol of fire appears throughout her stories, highlighting and underscoring Brigid's role as not only a worker of domestic miracles but also a woman of transcendent power. As a charismatic leader, she wields influence in monastic, civic, and natural realms; she is ever at ease among kings and bishops; she brings healing to body and soul; she displays gifts of exhortation; she has prophetic dreams and sees far into the hidden reaches of the heart. Brigid possesses a sense of justice that prompts her to secure the freedom of prisoners and slaves, to reveal the truth when a bishop has been wrongly accused of fathering a child, and even to move a river in the cause of fairness.

Brigid died sometime around 525. According to Cogitosus, she was buried in the abbey church she established at Kildare, and she continued to work miracles after her death. Tradition tells that she was moved from Kildare and laid to rest in Dunpatrick alongside two other great saints of Ireland, Patrick and Columba. Her physical grave remains a mystery, but the landscape of Ireland continues to testify to her presence, with forms of the name *Brigid* appearing in the names of towns, holy wells, and churches. Legends, prayers, rituals, and celebrations continue to expand and sometimes complicate her story, adding their threads to the mysterious tapestry of Brigid's legacy.

Throughout the coming days, this fiery saint will prompt us to ponder where we notice and enact habits of wild bounty. Brigid's story will invite us to observe our own patterns of hospitality, to reflect on our rhythms of abundance and lack, and to explore the riches as well as the challenges that come to us from Celtic spiritual traditions. In Brigid's company, may the deep generosity of God attend your days.

# PRAYER FOR THE MORNING

Christ our Light,
with every morning
you welcome us into the world
and with your lavish care
you meet our hunger and our thirst.
Give us eyes to see the feast
you have placed within these hours:
hallowed, holy,
blessed day.

# PRAYER FOR THE EVENING

Into your hands, O God,
we give this day.
We enter this dark with you.
With peace and with plenitude,
inhabit these hours.
In shadow, in silence,
let your face shine.

# 1
## THE FRAGMENTS OF THE FEAST

For generations, the deep reverence for Saint Brigid has manifested in a rich pattern of folklore, prayers, and rituals in Ireland and beyond. Legends and litanies reveal how people have called upon her help in daily life, invoking her assistance and protection in childbirth, in travel, in daily labor, and at the coming of night and rest.

The depth of devotion to Brigid is particularly apparent in the festivities associated with her feast day. Falling on February 1, Brigid's day coincides with the celebration of Imbolc. One of the four major festivals of the ancient Celtic calendar, Imbolc, whose name refers to the pregnancy or lactation of ewes, heralds the arrival of spring. The ceremonies of the day are marked by joy at the turning of seasons and by reverence for the saint known as a provider of bounty.

As with other saints' days, Brigid's feast day has traditionally offered an opportunity not only to celebrate her life but also, in a sense, to continue it through remembering and reenacting the stories and qualities associated with her. Across the centuries, this has taken a variety of forms.

Lisa Bitel remarks that the writers of Brigid's early *Lives* "were writing not prose, but liturgical drama." She observes,

> During the early Middle Ages the reading of a saint's vita was a public event on the saint's feast-day, part of a ritual cycle or pilgrimage, accompanied by various celebrations. . . . No doubt the abbess-saint's successors distributed charitable gifts on her feast-day, since generosity towards the poor and ill was one of the saint's major characteristics.[7]

Indeed, Alexander Carmichael relates stories of such generosity and celebration on Brigid's feast in the *Carmina Gadelica*, a collection of hymns, prayers, poetry, and tales that he gathered in Scotland in the nineteenth century. Carmichael observes that "Bride [Brigid] with her white wand is said to breathe life into the mouth of the dead Winter and to bring him to open his eyes to the tears and the smiles, the sighs and the laughter of Spring. The venom of the cold," he continues, "is said to tremble for its safety on Bride's Day."[8] He tells of practices of celebration that flow both from the people's reverence for Brigid as a bearer of bounty, and their relief as winter begins to pass.

Carmichael tells of how, on the eve of Brigid's feast, girls would take sheaves of corn or a butter churn and fashion a doll, called a *Brideag* (Little Bride), in the shape of Brigid. The girls would walk in procession with the *Brideag*, singing the song *Bride bhoidheach oigh nam mile beus* (Beauteous Bride, virgin of a thousand charms) and stopping at the homes of townspeople who would decorate the doll with small offerings or provide food that would become part of the feast.[9]

As Carmichael recounts it, the celebration began on the eve of the feast, as Celtic festivals have always done, and lasted far into the night. "As the grey dawn of the Day of Bride breaks," he writes, "[the young women and men] form a circle and sing the hymn of *Bride bhoidheach muime chorr Chriosda* (Beauteous Bride, choice foster-mother of Christ). They then distribute *fuidheal na feisde* (the fragments of the feast)—practically the whole, for they have partaken very sparingly, in order to have the more to give—among the poor women of the place."[10]

Nearly fifteen centuries since her death, the habit of celebration still persists on Brigid's feast day. Among the diverse festivities, it is Carmichael's image of the fragments of the feast—fragments that the revelers place in the hands of hungry women—that haunts my imagination. As I ponder the scraps of Brigid's life, as I attend to the pieces of my own life, what fragments will serve as nourishment, not only for me but also for others who long for a feast? What miracles lie in wait among the mundane; what holiness will fill those who hunger?

## BLESSING

May the spirit of Saint Brigid,
woman of lavish hospitality,
inspire you this day.
Amid the fragments, may you find wild bounty
and in every moment, a feast.

# 2
## BRIGID OF THE CANDLES

In the rhythm of the Christian liturgical year, the Feast of Saint Brigid is followed by the Feast of the Presentation of Jesus on February 2. Also called the Feast of the Purification of Mary, the day bids us remember Mary and Joseph's visit to the Temple to present their child Jesus on the fortieth day following his birth, as Jewish law required, and for Mary to undergo the postpartum rites of cleansing. Luke's Gospel tells us that a resident prophet named Anna and a man named Simeon immediately recognize and welcome Jesus. Taking the child into his arms, Simeon turns his voice toward God and offers praise for the "light for revelation" that has come into the world (2:32).

Taking a cue from Simeon, some churches began, in time, to mark the day with a celebration of light: the Candle Mass, during which priests would bless the candles to be used in the year to come. Coinciding with the turn toward spring and lengthening of light in the Northern Hemisphere, Candlemas offers a liturgical celebration of the renewing of light and life that comes to us both in the story of Jesus and in the natural world. As we emerge from the deep of winter, the feast reminds us of the perpetual presence of Christ our Light in every season.

With her feast day just next door, it's no surprise that Brigid makes an appearance among the Candlemas legends. In the *Carmina Gadelica*, Alexander Carmichael conveys this story of Brigid as an anachronistic acolyte:

> It is said in Ireland that Bride walked before Mary with a lighted candle in each hand when she went up to the Temple for purification. The winds were strong on the Temple heights, and the tapers were unprotected, yet they did not flicker nor fail. From this incident Bride is called *Bride boillsge* (Bride of brightness). This day is occasionally called *La Fheill Bride nan Coinnle* (the Feast Day of Bride of the Candles), but more generally *La Fheill Moire nan Coinnle* (the Feast Day of Mary of the Candles)— Candlemas Day.[11]

Where do you find yourself in this story? Are you Mary, graced by the light that another sheds on your path? Or are you Brigid this day, carrying the light for another in need?

Before you, beside you, behind you,
may Christ our Light
attend your way.

# 3

## GOLDEN, RADIANT FLAME

The image of fire pervades Brigid's story. From before her birth until long after her death, the presence of flame persists, invoking the Judeo-Christian memory of fire as a sign of the presence and power of the Divine. In one of the earliest prayers to Brigid, known as "Ultán's Hymn," the writer calls upon the protection of Brigid, whom he addresses as a "golden, radiant flame."[12] In the *Vita Prima*, a druid offers assurance to Brigid's mother, telling Broicsech that she will "give birth to an illustrious daughter who will shine in the world like the sun in the vault of heaven."[13] Cogitosus describes how, in prayer, Brigid burned "with the flame of an inextinguishable faith."[14] the *Vita Prima* and *The Irish Life* relate occasions during Brigid's childhood when her family's house appeared to be on fire but was not consumed.[15] *The Irish Life* also describes how, during Brigid's consecration as a nun (at which the bishop inadvertently ordained her as a bishop), a flame stretched from her head to the heavens.[16] The twelfth-century writer Gerald of Wales, after visiting the abbey that Brigid established at Kildare, recounts a tale of a perpetual flame tended by nineteen nuns of Kildare, adding that Brigid, now long dead, took a turn on the twentieth night.[17]

In one of my favorite legends, Brigid, who has leapt across chronology to become present at the nativity of Christ, spots Herod's soldiers entering Bethlehem. Weaving a wreath of candles for her head, the intrepid saint dances in front of the soldiers to distract them, enabling the Holy Family to flee to safety.

BLESSING

Fire of wisdom to bless you,
fire of insight to enlighten you,
fire of mercy to protect you,
fire of God to encircle you
and grant you peace.

# 4

# THE LIVES OF THE SAINTS

Immersing myself in the *Lives* and legends of Brigid, I find myself contemplating what I'm looking for in these lines. How do we read the life of a saint? Those who told the stories of saints wrote, of course, with the sensibilities of a much different time, and they approached their narratives with purposes that often diverge markedly from those that contemporary readers and scholars bring to the texts. Although we can usually cull at least a few historical facts from the saints' *Lives*, these writings do not present us with the kind of biographies we are accustomed to.

*Hagiography* is the word we attach to the rough art of writing about saints. Hagiography constitutes a unique sort of literature, with elements borrowed from sagas, mythology, romance, history, and, of course, scripture, particularly the Gospels. In seeking to convey the truth of a saint's life—a process that often didn't depend too heavily upon the facts—hagiographers turned to motifs found in the *Lives* of other saints, as well as to other forms of storytelling.

It was important to the hagiographers to depict their saints as persons imbued with sacred power that they exercised in physical and spiritual realms. The stories of the saints are replete with displays of influence over the elements, animals, and other people; they could also alter the course of illness, injury, and even death. Most important, the miraculous signs and wonders that weave through the saints' *Lives* confirmed that they shared in the power of Christ. The hagiographers intended to convey that such power did not originate with the saints themselves but instead flowed from their kinship with Christ and their intense desire to model their lives on his own.

While these authors grounded their reflections in the historical lives and ministries of their subjects, their writings reflect a broader array of theological, spiritual, and political purposes. This reality, combined with the variety of literary influences from which they drew, means that reading and interpreting the stories of the saints can be a complicated undertaking. Commenting on this complexity, Esther de Waal observes in her book *The Celtic Way of Prayer* that "we have to handle the *Lives* at many different levels: historical, mythical, psychological, and, not least, spiritual."[18]

Though the textual landscape that the hagiographers have left us can be demanding to navigate, their ultimate purpose lay in drawing us into the life of the saint and thereby into the life of Christ. The *Lives* of the saints remind us that the miraculous power that infused Jesus, the apostles, and the saints still remains available to those who seek God.

The *Lives* may intrigue the intellect, but they aim to feed the imagination and quicken the soul. They inhabit the realm of poetry, drama, liturgy, dreams—those landscapes where God draws us toward a knowing that doesn't rest on facts alone. In addressing our imagination, the *Lives* seek not simply to inform but to inspire; they invite us to engage the saints' lives by enacting them. We do this in celebration and ritual and storytelling, yes, but, far beyond that, by embracing the God-hunger that inhabited them. The lives of the saints present us with mystery in order to summon us toward ministry.

BLESSING

May the lovers of God
who went before you,
whose devotion to Christ
helped make a path for you,
grace the way ahead of you
with their company
and good cheer.

# 5

## THE WORK OF ANGELS

It is said that Brigid founded a scriptorium and school for artists at Kildare, administered by Conlaedh, whom she also chose as bishop of Kildare. We know little about the school or the scriptorium, but one medieval writer offers an intriguing insight into a work that the scriptorium may have produced, and into Kildare itself.

In the twelfth century, the traveler and writer Gerald of Wales paid a visit to the abbey at Kildare. His lively (if not always factual) recounting of his impressions, which he records in *The History and Topography of Ireland*, indicates that although Brigid and her original companions were centuries gone by the time Gerald arrived, her powerful presence lingered throughout the abbey that she had established. In a section that he titled "A book miraculously written," Gerald observes, "Among all the miracles of Kildare nothing seems to me more miraculous than that wonderful book which they say was written at the dictation of an angel during the lifetime of the virgin." He goes on to write,

> This book contains the concordance of the four gospels according to Saint Jerome, with almost as many drawings as pages, and all of them in marvellous colours. Here you can look upon the face of the divine majesty drawn in a miraculous way; here too upon the mystical representations of the Evangelists, now having six, now four, and now two, wings. Here you will see the eagle; there the calf. Here the face of a man; there that of a lion. And there are almost innumerable other drawings. If you look at them carelessly and casually and not too closely, you may judge them to be mere daubs rather than careful compositions. You will see nothing subtle where everything is subtle. But if you take the trouble to look very closely, and penetrate with your eyes to the secrets of the artistry, you will notice such intricacies, so delicate and subtle, so close together and well-knitted, so involved and bound together, and so fresh still in their colourings that you will not hesitate to declare that all these things must have been the result of the work, not of men, but of angels.[19]

In Gerald's telling, Brigid is closely involved in the making of this Book of Kildare, her prayers supporting, enabling, and entwining with the work of the artist-scribe as he works on this book whose design, as Gerald tells it, he received from an angel in a dream.[20]

The Book of Kildare disappeared long ago, Gerald's words the only trace of it. Surviving manuscripts such as the exquisite Book of Kells, created in the British Isles around 800 CE, offer a glimpse of what the Book of Kildare might have looked like. Across the vellum pages of the Book of Kells, scribes and artists set forth the text of the Gospels, intertwining words and images so intimately that the boundary between text and art became a blur. Among and around the words, the artists tucked in layers of symbols that hint at deeper and more complex meanings. Chalices, vines, eucharistic hosts, books, peacocks, doves, lions, fish, snakes, human heads, wrestling men, and an array of other images that the artists borrowed from the symbolic and natural worlds: the artists entwined and surrounded these all with the intricate knotwork so characteristic of their art. The pages appear not decorated but drenched; vivid and haunting, the book testifies to the mysteries of the Word made visible and incarnate on the page.

What corner of the world did Brigid's fantastical book find its way to? Borne away on the waters or carried off in the spoils of war or engulfed by earth, does its radiance still show forth somewhere? Or, abandoned to the currents of history, did its luminous pages simply loosen from their bindings, one by one; did the brilliant drawings slip from their pages, did the words loosen their hold, letter by letter; did every last illuminated stroke dissolve in the waters, in the earth, in the wind, until nothing remained, save for the prayers that Brigid had breathed into its beginning?

BLESSING

In the fire of revelation,
in the clarity of illumination,
in the shadows of mystery,
in the silence of prayer,
may the Word of God
inscribe itself on your soul
and illumine your way.

# 6

## THE GOSPEL OF A WOMAN'S LIFE

The tale of the lost Book of Kildare, along with the other artful Gospelbooks that did survive the centuries, offers some clues to how we might look at the legends of Brigid. Fashioning the *Life* of a saint, after all, was an art akin to that of fashioning the Gospelbooks: each involved a complex mix of fact and legend. When I find myself stymied in trying to sort through the mysteries of Brigid's life, it helps to spend some time contemplating a few pages from the intricate, ancient gospel pages. Wandering their mysterious landscapes compels me to look beneath the surface.

Those who created such books went far beyond simply penning the words onto the page; rather, in their devotion to the Word in Christ, they summoned the greatest gifts of their artistry to produce pages that shimmer with layers of meaning and complexity. In a book where little is straightforward or plain, where it is difficult at times even to make out the words in all their artful convolutions, much is left to the viewer to interpret, decipher, and discern.

Reflecting on the Book of Kells, Bernard Meehan writes of how "certain pages and motifs are capable of carrying different layers of meaning, or at least of interpretation" and that "the images on the page should be read in a number of different ways simultaneously."[21]

Like the scribes and artists who poured themselves into the Gospelbooks, Brigid's devotion to the Word in Christ spilled forth with a holy extravagance. This kind of extravagance is difficult to capture in historical fact. The impulse of her hagiographers, like the impulse of the manuscript artists, was to draw on the landscape of story and symbol to engage the reader's and viewer's imagination. As with the manuscript pages, the meaning of Brigid's life is not tidy, cannot be fully contained in the facts, grows ever larger in the telling. Mystery and history swirl together in Brigid's life like the spirals and knotwork that pervade the pages of the Book of Kells. Given the near impossibility of separating fact from invention, perhaps the invitation is to give in to the mystery, allowing ourselves to move more deeply into its labyrinthine path.

Perhaps, as Meehan describes the Book of Kells, the life of Brigid is simply "an enigma, a work to be wondered at rather than understood."[22] As with the pages of Kells, whose intertwined letters nearly defy deciphering, Brigid both reveals and conceals the gospel of a woman's life.

BLESSING

That you will let yourself be lost
from time to time
in the labyrinth of the Word.
That you may, for a while,
empty yourself of all the words you know.
That Christ the living Word
will find you
and fill you
with his wisdom.
That he will write himself anew
across the pages of your life.

# 7

## SACRED COMPLICATIONS

The pages of the illuminated Gospelbooks such as the Book of Kells and the vanished Book of Kildare remind us that complexity is a quality the soul needs in its journey. At first glance, such pages can nearly overwhelm with the intricacy of their turning, twisting, spiraling patterns. Seeking to follow the lines, one risks becoming lost among the paths where symbols and stories entwine and ensnare. It is in this very quality, however, that the books display their genius and extend their invitation to us. They remind us that a place for mystery exists within the landscape of our faith, that we never really know a terrain until we allow ourselves to get lost in it, and that the complexities and complications of our lives can offer beauty.

The pages of these Gospelbooks both challenge me and comfort me because I am a creature drawn to complication. Given the choice between making the way easy and making the way difficult, I sometimes tilt toward difficulty. I've learned that my soul often needs to have something to push against, something to forge and form it. I feel rather like Jacob sometimes: occasionally I need a heated wrestling match with the Divine, a struggle that will help me find a new name.

There's a difference, though, between the complications and complexities that forge the soul and those that drain it. I can wax poetic about the holy disruptions that have deepened me, but I recognize too my capacity for choosing complications that stem from some other, less sacred impulse. Sometimes I make the way difficult for myself by taking on too much or by avoiding an issue that needs attention. I recognize that I'm capable of manufacturing my own complications rather than waiting for the ones that come around naturally in traveling with Christ.

The artists and scribes who created the lavish Gospelbooks did so to glorify God, not merely to create wondrous books. As they turned their gaze toward Christ, the intricate patterns and paths followed, not the other way around. With the pages they left behind, these lovers of God beckon me to look to the One who leads me and let the path unfold from there.

BLESSING

When the path is simple, peace.
When the way is complicated, peace.
May Christ not only show you the way
but also be the way you travel:
way of blessing, way of peace.

8

CROSSING THE LINE

As one absorbs the prayers and legends in which Brigid appears, it becomes clear that their crafters weren't dealing with history as a hard science. As Brigid's fame grew, so did the fantastical elements of her story. For those who told her tales, fidelity to chronology was not always a priority.

I'm intrigued by the anachronism that attends Brigid, how the few facts we know about her life don't always fit the stories that surround her.

A number of legends and prayers, for instance, place Brigid in the story of Jesus' nativity. The fifth-century abbess slips backward across centuries; at an overcrowded inn, she provides food for a traveling couple in desperate need; she becomes the midwife to Mary; she assumes the role of foster-mother to Jesus. In these tales, the woman born on the threshold crosses back and forth over the boundaries of chronology, her prodigious wonder-work seemingly extending to time itself.

I've grown fond of this sort of playing with time that pops up in the lives of the saints, this impulse toward anachronism that inhabits not just Brigid's story but others as well. Something about this juxtaposition of time, the placing of characters in a calendar not their own, jars us and inspires us toward a different kind of seeing. As we encounter persons in a landscape where we think they don't belong, they invite us to notice something about them that we might otherwise miss, some truth that dwells beneath the often sparse facts of history.

In the Middle Ages, when most of the writings and legends about Brigid took shape, this kind of time-play with sacred stories was widespread. Often it took visual form; for instance, as the artists adorned canvases and wood and walls and manuscript pages with images of biblical characters as well as saints, they garbed them in the clothing of the artist's own day.

Such artwork beckons us to see that the biblical characters aren't stuck among the pages of the scriptures, aren't confined to that ancient moment of history. Abraham and Sarah, Moses and Miriam, Jesus and Mary and Joseph, and all the biblical figures walking across the paintings in the fashion of the day: they come alive under our gaze, they walk off the page and out of the painting into our world.

But maybe there are not two landscapes, two separate realms separated by a line drawn in the historical sand. Perhaps this is what the phrase means, *I believe . . . in the communion of saints*: that we inhabit not two worlds, but one.

BLESSING

> May the God who dwells behind time
> and the God who dwells within time
> bless you with the gift of time.
> May it be for you an open door,

a spacious place,
a realm of meeting,
a world of grace.


# 9

# THE SOUL OF TIME

I've never been a big fan of linear time. So with their occasionally relaxed attitude toward historical facts, the legends that surround Brigid's life hold a certain appeal for me. Spilling across the confines of chronology, the tales acknowledge the fluidity of time and invite us into a different kind of remembering.

What is it that I think about time?

Many have written about how the proper relationship with time involves inhabiting the present moment. Giving attention to the moment is among the practices I try to cultivate around time, but I've come to suspect that mindfulness of what is unfolding right now is not always the most important thing.

Thomas Moore addresses this in his book *Original Self*. "Being present to the life that presses upon us," he writes, "does not mean simply being alert and full of consciousness." He continues,

> Surrendering to a daydream or a memory may be a way of being engaged with the present. Drifting into reverie might bring us to the full immediacy of the moment, which may be properly focused on invisible things. Turned inward, we might be completely present, and conversely, being wide awake to life might be a distraction and, to the soul, a kind of sleep.
>
> The principle of being present to life is also complicated by the soul's odd sense of time, so different from the literal measurements of the clock and calendar. The soul exists in cycles of time, full of repetition, and it has equal portions of flowing temporality and static eternity. Responsive to the soul, we may easily drift out of literal life several times a day to revisit people and places of the past or to imagine the future.[23]

What time zone does your imagination most often live in? What do you find in visiting the past or envisioning the future? What place do daydreaming, remembering, musing, and imagining have in your life?

BLESSING

That your soul may live
in the cycles it needs.
That time may work
its wisdom in you.
Repetition, return,
reverie, and rest:
may the heart
of each moment
open to you.

# 10

## INTERTWINED

We learn something—one hopes—with the accumulation of years, not because the years always proceed in an orderly fashion but because they spiral us back around the same questions, lead us past familiar landscapes from other angles, encourage us to think again about what has gone before, confront us with patterns of repetition and return.

The curious way that past, present, and future intertwine—much like the intricate designs of Celtic art—doesn't always make sense to me; in fact, thinking about the mysteries of time tends to give me a headache. Yet it does lend a certain grace when I'm feeling burdened by thinking it moves only in a linear, orderly fashion. Like when I find myself dogged by regret about the times I didn't accomplish what I thought I should have accomplished or have given my energy to something that didn't pan out as hoped, or when I'm not as far along as I would like to be at this point in my life.

Sometimes, when vexed by the weight of time that seems wasted, I have found myself the fortunate recipient of the generosity of folks who ask me to think otherwise. These people help me remember there are seeds in these times. And I find the kernels, sometimes so tiny. I gather them up and fling them—is it ahead or behind? Wherever they go, it is an act of prayer, of redemption, of grace.

BLESSING

May time spiral well for you,
leading you around
and around yet again
to the landscapes where remembering
offers redemption and grace.

## 11

## THIN PLACES

In Celtic spiritual traditions, the fluidity of time extends far beyond the stories of the saints. We encounter it, for instance, in the notion of thin places: spaces where the veil between worlds becomes transparent, and heaven and earth meet. In Ireland and elsewhere, the physical landscape offers such places in the form of holy wells, sacred ruins, stone circles, and in the architecture of nature: in forests, fields, seacoasts, hills—places where the lay of the land evokes an awareness of the sacred. These spaces are haunted by the holy. Time runs differently here, and the presence and prayers of generations of visitors have made the veil ever more thin.

The presence of thin places prompts one to wonder whether the Spirit has a particular fondness for some favorite hangouts. Yet our tradition tells us that God stubbornly insists on dwelling *everywhere*, that God pervades the entire creation; and I think God cannot be more *there* in some places than in others, no matter how godforsaken some corners of the earth may seem. Perhaps the mystery of thin places is that when we find ourselves in them, when we recognize them, we become more present to the God who is always present to us. Something in the landscape meets us, inhabits us. The veil that falls away is not external to us; it is within.

BLESSING

That the holy
will haunt you.
That the terrain of your days
will give way to God.
Each moment. Each step.
Each circling and turning.
Every breath an opening
tearing the veil.

# 12

## THIN PLACES IN TIME

This thinning between worlds happens not only in the physical terrain but also in the landscape of time, in the turning of the wheel of the year. The ancient Celts believed that at certain festival times, the gates to the otherworld opened. The living developed practices designed either to entice the spirits or—depending on the spirit—to keep them at bay. This awareness of those who have gone before us persists in the Christian tradition—as, for example, in the Feast of All Saints, which we celebrate on November 1, the traditional new year of the Celtic calendar, when the veil was at its thinnest.

The rhythm of the Christian year offers its own thresholds, inviting us to enter into a deeper awareness of the God who dwells both within and beyond chronological time. As we spiral again and again through the liturgical seasons and holy days, we are called to move more deeply into the story of God, to notice how this story has unfolded in the lives of those who have gone before us, and in our own lives. As we move deeper into the story, it moves deeper into us.

Thin places remind us that we travel in the presence of the communion of saints and in the company of the God who, in the person of Jesus, intersected and inhabited time. In taking flesh, God opened wide to time, to the effects of its passing, to the weight of chronology. Yet this God dwells also beyond time. It is a mystery, this simultaneous entering and shedding that God does with time. In the thin places, we are given a glimpse.

May your journey through this day
offer a thin, thin place
where heaven and earth meet
and time falls away.

# 13

## THIN PLACES WITHIN

There are also thin places that we carry within ourselves, our own stories, our own internal terrain. I know the places in my soul where the past makes its presence known, the occasions when memories surface, inviting my attention, encouraging me to see within them what I had not seen before. They come bearing comfort, or they come to offer questions.

In these thin places I sometimes have a keen sense of the shadows of other lives—fleeting impressions of what might have happened if I had made a different choice or if another path had opened to me at a crucial juncture or a seemingly ordinary one. I am not meant to inhabit or linger too long amid these glimpses of other lives, yet they visit nonetheless. They come as reminders of how it matters what we choose. They come too as a reminder of grace: that God can work within every choice, even the ones we made long ago.

What is time like for you these days? How do you experience the meetings and crossings of past, present, and future?

BLESSING

In the choices of your past,
in the choices of your present,
in the choices yet to come:
the God of wisdom inhabit you
and inspire the way you go.

# 14

## PROVISION

Most of Brigid's recorded miracles are feats of provisioning by which she secures an abundance of fare for daily sustenance as well as for festive occasions. In Brigid's presence, butter is replenished; the bacon she slips to a dog miraculously reappears in the pot; a stone turns to salt; water becomes milk or beer or, in one instance, an aphrodisiac. Her plenitude consciously echoes Christ's miracles of provisioning—water into wine, a few loaves and fish into a feast—and embodies God's abundant generosity. In a poem attributed to Brigid, she wishes she had a "lake of ale" to offer to the King of Kings.

The *Vita Prima* relates this story:

> Some clerics came to Brigit and preached the word of God. Afterwards Brigit said to her cook, "Get a meal ready for our distinguished guests." The cook said in reply, "What shall I give them for dinner?" And Brigit said, "Give them bread and butter and onions and lots of courses." The cook replied, "Yes, I will, but do you go to the church first because the cook hasn't any of the things you mention!" And Brigit said to the cook, "Sweep the floor of the kitchen and shut it and go home and pray there and I shall go to the church." Now at the sixth hour Brigit called the cook by clapping her hands and said to her, "It's time to give food to the guests. Go to the kitchen and give them a generous helping of whatever you find there." Then on opening the kitchen she found all the provisions that Brigit had mentioned and the provisions did not run short for seven days but were ample for both the guests and all of Brigit's community, and nobody except Brigit and her holy cook knew where these provisions had come from or who had brought them.[24]

As someone whose ministry involves raising my entire income, I find myself thinking a lot about provision. *How do I keep food on my table and a roof over my head by my own power?* Part of the answer lies in remembering that I don't, in fact, do this alone. Over time I've learned to be more intentional about praying for provision. "Ask, seek, knock," Jesus said. It stretches me sometimes, opening myself to pray about matters that seem so basic. Yet what we find in Brigid's life—not to mention in the Gospels—is a persistent reminder that the mundane and the miraculous are inextricable.

In the very stuff of our daily lives—food, shelter, work, community—God makes a home, looking for ways to offer us what we most need.

I've also learned to give thought to what I *really* need. For more than a decade I've lived in a studio apartment, a small space that affords continual opportunities for spiritual practice regarding possessions. I have to be vigilant about what crosses the threshold, discerning about what I bring in and what I need to let go of. Part of what I've discovered in this space is that often it takes only the tiniest thing to blow me away with its loveliness, its power, its provision.

*Plenitude*

At lunch today
it was the purple
of the olive pits
against my cobalt plate
that stunned me.

At tea,
the gold of peach
bloodstained by its stone.

I do not know
where the greater part
of the miracle lies:
that I should pause
to notice this,

or that I,
a woman of
such great hungers,
should be so well satisfied
by such small things.

BLESSING

May the God of small things
delight you this day.

# 15

## *The Secret Room*

## SAINT BRIGID OF KILDARE MONASTERY

According to the *Vita Prima*, Brigid was born as her mother crossed the threshold into her home.[25] The story provides an evocative image of the woman Brigid would become: a bridge between traditions as Christianity emerged in Ireland, a threshold figure in her own being.

This threshold image helped inspire Mary Stamps as she began to form an innovative new monastery, itself a bridge between traditions. Mary established Saint Brigid of Kildare Monastery more than a decade ago on the grounds of Saint John's Abbey in Collegeville, Minnesota. Saint Brigid's is a new expression of monasticism in that it draws from both Methodist and Benedictine traditions. It is distinctive also in that except for Mary, who has taken full monastic vows, the community is comprised primarily of *oblates*, a word that describes people who are drawn to associate with a monastery without making the same commitment as a vowed monastic.

Mary and I became friends while I was in seminary at Emory University, where she was working on a PhD in her pre-Saint Brigid's days. One of the great gifts of my life has come in knowing Mary as she has navigated her journey as a Methodist woman called to a monastic way of life—a call that has been marked by great challenges and wondrous synchronicities. ("If you ever begin to doubt God's grace," Mary once wrote, "call me and I will talk you through it!")[26]

The community, which I joined in its early years, is a colorful bunch of contemplatives who feel extraordinarily blessed both to be the recipients of what Mary has found on her long journey to become a Methodist monastic and also to participate with her in discerning how this threshold community will continue to grow. Saint Brigid's is comprised of women and men, both lay and clergy; we are mostly Methodist but include people of other denominations as well. We extend across the United States and into the Dominican Republic, which requires us to be creative in tending our connections: phone conversations, e-mails, and an annual retreat are among the ways we engage one another.

In the spirit of the famed generosity of Saint Brigid, her namesake community offers good hospitality despite being dispersed. As someone who understood myself as a contemplative long before I had the word for it and who has often had to venture far afield in search of wellsprings to sustain my spirit, this community has offered a kind of homecoming. I feel less alone on a path that has sometimes seemed solitary and strange. Within this community that we are creating across the distance, the gifts of the monastic tradition that speak with such power to my soul come to life. In this space, with these people, we work to live out the values that mark both the Benedictine and the Methodist way of life, including practices of hospitality, prayer, simplicity, and community. Doing this comes with challenge, struggle, joy, and delight. Most of all, it comes *together* in God's wild abundance and grace.[27]

BLESSING

That you will have sisters,
that you will have brothers,
that you will have the company
of the kindred of your soul.

# 16

## GODDESS AND SAINT

Part of Brigid's appeal in contemporary times owes to the fact that her name is said to belong also to a pre-Christian goddess named Brigit, who was the goddess of healing, poetry, and smithcraft. The stories and depictions of the goddess and the saint share some common ground in their motifs, such as the symbol of fire. Because of this, it was long assumed that Brigid the saint was an evolutionary figure—a goddess who put on a Christian cloak after the faith came to Ireland.

More recent scholarship, however, has suggested that the reverse is true: that to emphasize certain powers and qualities of Brigid the saint, her hagiographers drew upon the familiar symbols and stories of pre-Christian goddesses. In her book *Landscape with Two Saints*, Lisa Bitel writes that with shifts in the religious structures and the curtailing of women's authority, "the writers of Brigit's cult developed new tactics for describing her authority. . . . By 900," she continues, "the nexus of symbols produced the goddess Brigit known in early medieval literature."[28] It was long after the life of the saint, then, that references to a goddess named Brigit or Brig began to emerge. The first mention appears in the tenth-century work of Cormac mac Cuilennáin; he describes a goddess named Brigit, who is actually three sisters, all named Brigit. One is a poet, one is a healer, and one practices smithcraft.[29]

However the evolution happened, in whatever direction the symbols and stories of Brigid the goddess and Brigid the saint began to intertwine, what emerges is a compelling woman of power and grace who continues to engage our imaginations. Each age has told the story of Brigid in a way that reflected its needs. The authors of her early *Lives* did this, and this practice has continued across the centuries.

The diverse tellings do not diminish Brigid. Rather, they testify to her power as a multivalent figure who continues to inspire devotion in each age. Brigid the goddess and Brigid the saint both draw from a well of story, symbol, and myth that has nourished spirits across the centuries. How does Saint Brigid speak to you in this day, in this time? What intrigues or compels you about her story?

## BLESSING

May the power of Brigid inspire you,
the grace of Brigid attend you,
the flame of Brigid enliven you,
the story of Brigid engage you.
May the God who provided her
all these gifts
provide them also to us,
that we may go into the world
with her lavish generosity
and her creative fire.

# 17

## THE TREASURES OF THE TRADITION

Brigid's present popularity owes much to the contemporary fascination with what is sometimes labeled as "Celtic spirituality" and, within the Christian faith, the "Celtic church." The term *Celtic* itself is hard to define: generally, what we today call Celtic Christianity refers to the varied ways that the Christian faith took form in the lands of Ireland, Scotland, Wales, Brittany, Cornwall, and the Isle of Man.

In seeking to draw from the rich sources that lie within Celtic expressions of the faith, much of the literature has distorted the religious traditions of those called Celtic. It often generalizes about Celtic religious expressions as a whole, overemphasizes the distinctions between Celtic and Roman Christianity, and depicts a seamless evolution from pre-Christian spiritual traditions to a Christian landscape with little real distinction between the two. Because the Celtic lands were not part of the far-flung Roman Empire, Christianity did evolve somewhat differently there than in countries under Roman rule. Yet Christians of the Celtic lands were members of the wider Catholic faith, and the Celtic church—which was never a cohesive institution as such—had more in common with Rome than it had different, though it certainly had its points of conflict. Some of these distinctions, such as the dating of Easter and what style of tonsure the monks would wear, found their resolution at the Synod of Whitby in 664. Hosting the synod was Hilda, the abbess who founded the double monastery where the synod took place and a woman famed for her wisdom and counsel.

Rome prevailed at the Synod of Whitby. As the already present common ground between the Celtic churches and Rome grew, the Celts continued to put their distinctive stamp on the faith. Among their many gifts, they are known for the depth of imagination and devotion by which they offered contributions such as:

- a vibrant monastic tradition in which monks and nuns—many of whom lived as hermits in the wilderness—formed the backbone of the church for centuries

- lively stories of saints known for their wisdom, miracles, and utter devotion to God

- a passionate engagement with and reverence for the Word, which included the creation of remarkable manuscripts such as the Book of Kells and the Lindisfarne Gospels
- distinctive visual art that borrowed from other cultures yet which the Celts made uniquely their own
- appreciation of creation as a place of encounter with God
- prayers that bear witness to the ways they sought the holy in the daily rhythm of their lives

BLESSING

May the Spirit who has enlivened
the Celtic people for generations
now enliven and inspire us,
that we too may place
our distinctive mark
on this Christian tradition
that has been entrusted to us.

# 18

## A QUEST FOR CLARITY

The Celtic saints, known for their wisdom and no-nonsense clearheadedness, might themselves caution us against seeing the Celtic legacy with a romantic eye. Attempting to view Celtic religious traditions with fewer distortions, however, takes away none of their distinctiveness or their ability to capture our imaginations. It is true that the Celtic church shared much in common with Christianity on the European continent and elsewhere: Ireland and its neighbors didn't hold a monopoly on love of the Word, emphasis on community, service to those in need, lively saints, love of creation, and the like. Yet the Christians of Celtic lands imprinted, influenced, and configured the faith in ways that continue to speak powerfully to us across time.

Oliver Davies points out in his book *Celtic Spirituality* that "the issue is a particular patterning of emphases, which cohere theologically into what we might describe as a distinctive spirituality."[30] In this age, when people experience such a hunger for community, for a sense of wholeness, for a life of prayer and ritual that engages us in our daily lives, and for words and images that intrigue and nourish us, it's no wonder so many of us find such appeal in this tradition that offers us such riches.

The Christian church has never existed in an idyllic state—not even in its earliest days, as we can see in Paul's letters. So perhaps the invitation the Celtic Christians offer is to see the past as clearly as we can and to draw from it with integrity, not replicating it but rather letting its treasures inspire us as we create new patterns of prayer and worship for our own day and time.

BLESSING

May the God of the ages
clear our vision
to see the past,
deepen our wisdom
to find its wellsprings,
quicken our thirst
to drink with integrity.

# 19

## THE WAY OF THE GREEN MARTYR

One of the distinctions in the way that the faith took shape in Ireland and its neighbors is that the arrival of Christianity produced relatively few martyrs in these lands. In contrast to many other countries where the coming of Christianity was attended by deadly resistance, the Celtic people welcomed the new faith with comparative ease, though not without difficulty. In the absence of opportunities to suffer death as a sign of their faith, Celtic Christians developed other forms of martyrdom by which they sought to declare and deepen their devotion to God.

Esther de Waal, who writes, "Unless we appreciate the deeply ascetic strand that runs throughout Celtic Christianity we cannot do justice to the fullness of the Celtic tradition," describes Celtic martyrdom this way:

Much is said of martyrdom, in three kinds, the red, the white, and the blue or green. The first is the generally accepted martyrdom of being killed for the faith. The second is renunciation of the world, the way of exile, or *peregrinatio*, which can by definition be the vocation of only a chosen few. But the third, the blue or the green, devotion to austerities, can be pursued by anyone; it is the life of denial, of daily repentance, hidden, secret, which can be experienced without leaving home, and which is essentially about the disposition of the heart, bringing body and mind under control so that men and women can serve God more fully and freely.[31]

Though preserving the life of the body, these practices served as ways for a soul to die to all that would hinder it from God.

How is it with your heart? What practices help you do what de Waal describes, habits that draw you into this third way? How do you divest your heart of what hinders you from seeing God fully and with freedom?

BLESSING

That all that confines you
will fall away.
That you will loose yourself
into the love of God
with devotion and desire.
That you may know the way
that makes for peace
in your soul and in this world.
That you will give your life
to its path.

20

THE FRIEND OF THE SOUL

A young cleric, a member of a community led by a foster-son of Brigid's, was eating with her after Communion one day. "Well, young cleric there," says Brigid, "hast thou a soulfriend?" The cleric replies, "I have." "Let us sing his requiem," Brigid tells him, "for he has died. I saw when half thy portion had gone, that thy quota was put into thy trunk, and thou without any head on thee, for thy soulfriend died, and anyone without a soulfriend is a body without a head; and eat no more till thou gettest a soulfriend."[32]

The tale may be rather gruesome by our sensibilities, yet it demonstrates Brigid's understanding of the importance of a practice that was widespread in Celtic Christianity: having an *anam ċara*, a soul friend. In his book *Anam Ċara*, John O'Donohue writes,

> In the early Celtic church, a person who acted as a teacher, companion, or spiritual guide was called an *anam ċara*. It originally referred to someone to whom you confessed, revealing the hidden intimacies of your life. With the *anam ċara* you could share your innermost self, your mind and your heart. This friendship was an act of recognition and belonging. When you had an *anam ċara*, your friendship cut across all convention, morality, and category. You were joined in an ancient and eternal way with the "friend of your soul." The Celtic understanding did not set limitations of space or time on the soul. There is no cage for the soul.[33]

Such a friendship between souls is a form of hospitality. In this kind of friendship, we welcome and make room for another in our lives. Soul friendship recognizes and honors the place within us that can only truly know itself in the company of another. In its space, we both give and receive sanctuary.

"It is the soul-friend who helps above all," writes Esther de Waal in *The Celtic Way of Prayer*, "who brings medicine for the soul, who supports and who challenges throughout one's life."[34]

### BLESSING

May there be no cage
for your soul.
May you have a friend
by whom you know this.
In the space between you,
may there be
medicine, hospitality, sanctuary.

# 21

## A SPIRAL-SHAPED GOD

Some years ago, at a retreat center in Ontario, I led a retreat in which we explored some of the riches that come to us from Celtic Christian traditions. When I saw that our meeting room had a smooth linoleum floor, an idea stirred. After tracking down several rolls of masking tape, I returned to the gathering space and got to work. When I finished a couple hours later, the center of the room held a circle with a triple spiral inside, large enough to use for walking prayer and meditation.

The symbol of the triple spiral is particularly prevalent in Celtic lands, where, in Christian times, it came to signify the Trinity. Evoking the energy, interconnection, and mystery of the triune God, the triple spiral graces such works as the remarkable insular Gospelbooks of the early medieval period, including the aforementioned Book of Kells as well as the Book of Durrow. We see it in metalwork and in stonework, as in the high crosses that still mark the landscape. The spiral evokes the God who both exists in a dynamic wholeness within itself yet also reaches out (or is it in?) to embrace us.

Historically, Celtic Christians offered no systematic theology by which they sought to define the nature and work of the Trinity, but evidence of their experience of the triune God abounds. Beyond their artistic and symbolic depictions of the Trinity, they left a remarkable body of prayers and poetry that offer us an incarnate experience of the Trinity. In their poems and prayers, Celtic Christians moved from the abstract to the actual; for them, the triune deity was not a theological concept but rather was God deeply embedded in daily life. In the Celtic imagination, God, Christ, and Spirit intertwine with one another and with all of creation.

In the Celtic triple spiral, there is a central space where the three spirals touch: it is a place of meeting and of sheer mystery. Its vast, vibrant emptiness reminds me that, in this life, we will never know all the names of God. Even as the Trinity evokes, it conceals. We will never exhaust the images we use to describe the One who holds us and sends us, who enfolds us and impels us in our eternal turning.

I continue to carry that image of the triple spiral and the community in whose company I walked its path: inward, outward, journeying ever around the mystery at its center. Those walking companions remind me of how we are to be a living sign of the Trinity who dwells in eternal relationship within itself and with all creation. As individuals and as communities, we are called to times of spiraling inward, to attend to our own souls. We are propelled, in turn, into times of spiraling outward, to attend to the world beyond us. In all our turnings, the presence of God persists.

How do you experience the God who exists as a community and invites us to a life with others? How does this God become incarnate in the rhythm of your days?

BLESSING

God of the Twisting Path,
God of the Turning Spiral,
God of Revelation,
God of Infinite Mystery:
may this God enfold
and entwine you
in every step.

# 22

## A MIND GIVEN TO GOD

Throughout her life, Brigid's deep grounding in God fosters a keen clarity about what is most important. Given our human tendency to lose sight of what is essential, such wisdom appears miraculous in itself. Brigid's insight shows forth in such tales as the one recounted in the fifteenth-century *Leabhar Breac* (*Speckled Book*), in which Brigid receives a visit from Brendan, the famed navigator-monk. As they enter her house, Brigid hangs her wet cloak on a sunbeam. Brendan's attendant endeavors to do the same, failing twice in the effort; taking the cloak, Brendan achieves success, but "with anger and wrath." Brendan tells Brigid, "Not usual is it for me to go over seven ridges without [giving] my mind to God." Brigid replies, "Since I first gave my mind to God, I never took it from Him at all."[35]

To what are you giving your mind today?

BLESSING

Let it be
that you will ever
turn yourself Godward.
In clarity
and in confusion,
in distress
and in delight,
may your mind
find its home and its rest
in the One whose thoughts
are ever stayed on you.

# 23

## TAKE A BLESSING

Brigid's hospitality displayed the same quality of wisdom and purpose as did her consuming devotion to God. Profligate in her generosity, she nonetheless brought to it a spirit of discernment. *The Irish Life* tells the story of a man with leprosy who approaches the saint one day, saying, "For God's sake, Brigit, give me a cow." With the air of someone who has perhaps been approached by the man a number of times before, Brigid tells him to leave her alone. He persists. Brigid asks him how it would be if they prayed to God for the removal of the man's leprosy. "No," he replies, "I get more this way than if I were clean." Brigid disagrees with his priorities and insists that he "take a blessing and be cleansed." The man acquiesces, acknowledging that he is in much pain. Upon receiving his cure, the man vows his devotion to Brigid, pledging to be her servant and woodman.[36]

What do you need for this day? Does another need underlie this, one that would be more difficult to ask for help with but would bring a deeper blessing?

BLESSING

May you take a blessing
and be cleansed
of all that would turn
your mind and heart from God.
May insight and discernment
be your ever-present companions.

# 24

## CHRIST OUR GUEST

Those who wrote Brigid's *Lives* emphasized her wonderwork in order to call to mind Jesus' miracles. They wanted readers to understand how Brigid's utter devotion to Christ enabled her to share in his powers of healing and provision. Her miracles, however, echo not only the actions of Christ; they exemplify the lavish generosity of women whose stories intersected with the story of Jesus.

Think of the impoverished widow who gives two coins to the Temple treasury, how Jesus points her out to his companions and praises the way that she gives all she has in the midst of her poverty (Mark 12:41-44). Or Mary Magdalene and the other women who traveled with Jesus and provided for him out of their own resources (Luke 8:1-3).

In every Gospel we read of a woman who anoints Jesus as he sits at table. In Matthew, for instance, an unnamed woman pours costly oil over Jesus' head. Although her graceful action toward Jesus incurs the ridicule of his companions, he recognizes the prophetic, priestly qualities of the woman's actions and honors the hospitality with which she has drenched him (Matt. 26:6-13).

Hospitality is an action that goes against logic, against what makes sense. It goes beyond what may be convenient or conventional. In extending hospitality, we acknowledge our resources are not our own: that everything belongs to God. Hospitality is an act by which we return these gifts to God, even if, like the widow, our lives are marked by material lack; or, like Mary Magdalene, our words are not believed; or, like the woman who anointed Jesus, we become an object of ridicule.

Such hospitality also provides a way of ministering to Christ, as Jesus makes quite clear to his hearers just a few verses before Matthew's story of the woman who anoints Jesus. "'Truly I tell you,'" he says, "'just as you did it to one of the least of these who are members of my family, you did it to me'" (Matt. 25:40).

"Every guest is Christ," Brigid said.[37]

BLESSING

With your deepest grace,
amid your keenest lack,
by your most lavish devotion,
from your truest self,
may you minister to the Christ
who goes hungering and thirsting
in this world.

# 25

## THE DOMESTIC GOD

On the Feast of Saint Brigid this year, I invited my sweetheart, Gary, and our friend Linda over for afternoon tea. Like me, Linda belongs to Saint Brigid of Kildare Monastery. We three had time for a cup of jasmine tea, a slice of cappuccino cheesecake (Brigid would have loved cheesecake if she'd known of it), and a few strawberries before the next phase of our celebration: a conference call with a bunch of other folks from the Saint Brigid's community. Scattered across the physical distance, we joined together for a feast day liturgy that brought us close across the miles.

Then Linda, Gary, and I had more cheesecake.

I don't do a huge amount of entertaining. This owes to many factors, including my need for copious amounts of solitude and the fact of my wee living space, which tends to discourage the gathering of more than, say, a half dozen folks at once. My cozy studio apartment has an efficiency kitchen that Gary calls my yoga kitchen, because getting items out of the tiny refrigerator that sits under the sink sometimes involves doing contortions. Since I'm not wildly domestic, my two burners, microwave, and toaster oven arrangement suits me okay most days.

Still, when I get my act together to invite even a friend or two over for a cup of tea or a meal, I love sharing my home and receiving the gift of a loved one's presence in my quiet space. At times such an occasion feels like a miracle. In the cup, in the conversation: sustenance and grace.

I sometimes tend to overlook the ordinary miracles that unfold in the domestic realm. I often take for granted that on a daily basis, several times a day, I will have food to fill my hunger and I will be able to reach for it. Sharing the festive Saint Brigid's tea, however, and recalling her domestic wonderwork caused me to turn my attention to what happens within the everyday sphere of home, looking to see where the mundane gives way to the miraculous.

What ordinary miracles hide out in the rhythm of your days, waiting for you to see them or help enact them? What's going on in your home, and how might Christ be wanting to show up within it?

BLESSING

The blessing of Brigid
rest upon your home,
wherever or whatever it may be.
May a spirit of welcome
meet all whom you invite
within your walls.

# 26
## A STRANGE ECONOMY

The practice of hospitality as a holy act, of course, goes back long before the beginnings of Christianity. We learned many of our hospitable habits from our Jewish forebears, and the Hebrew scriptures are filled with examples of the sacred art of welcoming another.

One of my favorites among these stories is that of a woman who welcomed a prophet. Her name, like that of so many women, went unrecorded; history recalls her simply as the Shunammite woman. Having befriended the prophet Elisha, she recognizes him as a holy man and convinces her husband that they should provide a space for him. I love the homely, hospitable details that the story in 2 Kings 4:8-37 provides. "Let us make a small roof chamber with walls," says the woman of Shunem, "and put there for him a bed, a table, a chair, and a lamp, so that he can stay there whenever he comes to us."

Elisha recognizes the gift and, after a time, wants to know how he can repay the woman for her hospitality. "What may be done for you?" the prophet asks. And thus begins a tale of birth, death, and the raising of the dead: a story that echoes in Jesus' sending of the disciples to do the same kind of work. It echoes too in the tales of Brigid.

Jesus warns his followers about how those who welcome a prophet in the name of a prophet will receive a prophet's reward. At first, this doesn't hold much appeal, given the usual "rewards" bestowed upon prophets: imprisonment. Beheading. Crucifixion. Slaughter by various methods.

But in the land of Shunem, a woman welcomed a prophet with a room, a bed, a table, a chair, a lamp. Looking for no reward, the woman provided a sacred space for a holy man. And within the space of her very self, an unexpected child began to grow.

It's a strange economy, this kind of hospitality. We can't know what we will set in motion when we offer some space to the ones whom Jesus tells us to welcome. We give a cup of cold water or a place to rest or an extra room or a corner of our heart; we cede some precious territory to one who comes with a word from God; we open ourselves to remembering who God put us here to be and suddenly we're carrying something we never expected to carry. Maybe it's not a literal child, as it was for the Shunammite woman. But this kind of hospitality always makes room for new life to take root and come through us in ways that we can't predict. That's part of the curious ecosystem of hospitality: open a space to the holy stranger, and God creates a sacred space within us, an extra room in our souls. A place for God to grow.

What is hospitality like for you these days? How do you make room for those who bid you remember who God created you to be? What kind of holy space might God be wanting to create in your life? in you?

BLESSING
May you discern
where to extend a welcome,
and where to receive one.


# 27

## SISTERS IN THE LANDSCAPE

Although Brigid emerged as the most famous holy woman of the early church in Ireland, the writings about her are populated with other women who devoted their lives to God. In addition to the women in the communities she established, some of whom she often traveled with, she regularly crossed paths with other women in the course of her journeys. Cogitosus tells that while "journeying across the wide plain of Mag Breg," Brigid stayed the night at the home of a "certain faithful woman" who, in the midst of her poverty, extends extraordinary hospitality to Brigid, who works a miracle in her gratitude.[38] *The Irish Life* tells of "an old pious nun" who lives near the house of Brigid's father.[39] A pair of virgins named Tol and Etol greet Brigid and her companions on the day they go to be consecrated as nuns.[40] A "certain devout virgin" named Bríg asks Brigid to come visit her.[41] The virgins Induae and Indiu invite Brigid to "go with them to consecrate their foundation and house together with them."[42] A virgin named Lassar—called Saint Laisre in the *Vita Prima*—shares her hospitality not only with Brigid but also, while Brigid is there, with Saint Patrick.[43] Brigid visits also a holy woman named Fine who, with a group of virgins, lives at a place called Cell Fhine.[44]

The holy women who make their appearance in Brigid's *Lives* inhabit a wide spectrum of human behavior: they display both the wonders and demands of devoting oneself fully to God. They serve as examples of hospitality and remind us that even a saint known for her wild generosity sometimes needed someone to welcome her and minister to her. These women struggle too with the temptations that attend our human lives. Their stories attest to how pursuing the holy does not protect us from spiritual struggle; rather, it is often true that the more intently we pursue the holy, the more we find ourselves beset by forces that work against us. With both women and men, Brigid is fearless and creative as she confronts the presence of brokenness, injustice, and wrongdoing within and beyond her community. At the same time she embodies the quality of mercy.

If you created a map of your life, where would you mark the presence of holy women who are or have been part of your landscape? Who has carved out a place in your terrain with friendship, hospitality, and a needed gift?

BLESSING

Amid your labors,
along your road,
may there be sisters
to tend you
and welcome you in.

# 28

## HEAVEN FROM ANY PLACE

Celtic literature gives us *Lives* written about three women in addition to Brigid: Samthann, Ita, and Moninna, also known as Darerca. These women shared many of the qualities that we find in the stories of Brigid. Commonalities that arise in their stories include their establishment or expansion of monastic communities, miracles of healing and provisioning, the spirit of prophecy, winning the release of captives, ability to battle the demons, and working on behalf of the dead—either raising them from death or effecting their release from torment in the afterlife. Each *Life* patterned these qualities in different ways.

In the stories and sayings of these women, we can see how they were heirs to the desert tradition. Samthann, for instance, lived in the eighth century and served as the abbess of the community at Clonbroney. In the *Life of the Holy Virgin Samthann*, we read, "Once a monk consulted Samthann as to the proper manner in which to pray, whether one should be prone, seated, or standing. She replied to him that one ought to pray in every stance."[45]

Samthann's *Life* relates this story as well:

At one point Daircellach the teacher came to the virgin [Samthann], and told her, "I propose to defer study, and leave off prayer." She said to him, "What, then, can steady your mind lest it stray, if you shall have neglected spiritual cultivation?" The sage responded, "I wish to go abroad on pilgrimage." She retorted, "If God is not to be found on this side of the sea, certainly we may go abroad. For since God is near all who summon him, no need of voyaging besets us. One can reach heaven from any place on earth."[46]

BLESSING

May you be at prayer
in every stance,
and reach heaven
from the place where you are.

# 29

## THE FAMILIAR OF GOD

Born around 475, the holy woman Ita (or Ite) founded a monastic community in what became known as Killeedy ("Church of Ita") in County Limerick. She became foster-mother to Brendan the Navigator, famed for his amazing journey recorded in *The Voyage of Brendan*. The writer of Ita's *Life* calls her "a second Brigit"[47] and the "familiar of God."[48]

Ita's *Life* tells of a holy virgin who, talking with Ita of holy things one day, says to her,

Tell us in God's name, why you are held in higher esteem by God than the other virgins whom we know to be in the world. For to you sustenance from heaven is given by God; you cure all the feeble with your prayer; you speak of past and future events; everywhere you drive out the demonic, daily God's angels speak with you; you carry on in meditation and prayer to the holy Trinity without hindrance.

Ita responds, "You answered your own question by saying 'Without hindrance you carry on in prayer to and meditation on the holy Trinity.' For who ever shall have done so, will always have God with him, and if I was such a one from infancy, all these things, as you have said, properly pertain to me." Ita's *Life* goes on to recount that the "holy virgin, having heard this speech from the blessed Ita about prayer and meditation on God, departed rejoicing for her cell."[49]

The *Life* tells too that Brendan asks his foster-mother "about the three works which are fully pleasing to God, and the three which are fully displeasing." Ita replies, "True belief in God in a pure heart, the simple life with religion, generosity with charity; these three please God fully. However, a mouth vilifying people, and a tenacious love of evil in the heart, confidence in wealth; these three fully displease God."[50]

## BLESSING

May you be a familiar of God,
devoting yourself without hindrance
to all that the Holy One finds pleasing.

# 30

## A HOLY WELL

Daughter of a king, Moninna (or Moninne), also known as Darerca, was born around 435. Her *Life* tells that she was baptized by Saint Patrick, who, filled with the Holy Spirit, "observed her closely and understood her fervent desire to serve God." Patrick consecrated her as a nun.[51]

Moninna founded several communities for women and is particularly remembered for the one she established at Killeevy (Killeavy) in County Armagh. Her *Life* recounts that she visited Brigid on at least two occasions, serving as keeper of the guesthouse during her first stay. It also includes a blessing that Brigid offered to Moninna and her companions: "May God protect you on the road you follow; and may He guide you to the dwelling place you wish for." [52]

Celtic saints are often associated with holy wells, and Moninna has hers. Situated near a grave said to belong to Moninna, on the north side of the cemetery at Killeavy Old Church, Moninna's well continues to be a place of pilgrimage and prayer.

BLESSING

May you draw deep
from the wells of the holy
and have the protection
and guidance of God
on every path.

# 31
## A BLESSING OF BEADS

While working on this book, I received a package in the mail one afternoon. Inside I found a beautiful string of prayer beads, fashioned by my friend Mary, who founded Saint Brigid of Kildare Monastery. These prayer beads, infused with the prayers of a woman who herself is infused with the spirit of Saint Brigid and, more important, with the spirit of Christ, have stayed close to me as I have searched for the words to share with you.

A cross hangs from the beads. It is a Saint Brigid's cross, carved from the green marble of Connemara, Ireland. Legend has it that as Brigid sat by the bedside of a pagan chieftain—possibly her father—while he lay dying, she gathered up some of the rushes strewn across the floor and began to weave them into a cross as she told him about her faith.

Along with the beads, Mary sent a blessing. I pass it along to you, with prayers that in your life and work you will know the presence of the One who provides the wildest bounty.

BLESSING

Blessings on your work.
May your inspiration be Saint Brigid,

the generous, patron of artisans,
who once having set her mind
on Christ
never took it off.
May your strength
be your community
whose prayers are ever with you.
And may your love
be friends and family,
dearest kin of the heart.
Grace be with you, my sister.

FURTHER READING

*The Book of Kells: An Illustrated Introduction to the Manuscript in Trinity College Dublin* by Bernard Meehan. London: Thames and Hudson, 1994.

*Celtic Spirituality*, trans. Oliver Davies. New York: Paulist Press, 1999. (Includes *The Life of Saint Brigit the Virgin* by Cogitosus and *The Irish Life of Brigit*.)

*The Celtic Way of Prayer* by Esther de Waal. New York: Doubleday, 1997.

*Christianity and the Celts* by Ted Olsen. Downers Grove, IL: InterVarsity Press, 2003.

*Every Earthly Blessing: Rediscovering the Celtic Tradition* by Esther de Waal. Harrisburg, PA: Morehouse Publishing, 1999.

*Journeys on the Edges: The Celtic Tradition* by Thomas O'Loughlin. Maryknoll, NY: Orbis Books, 2000.

*Landscape with Two Saints: How Genovefa of Paris and Brigit of Kildare Built Christianity in Barbarian Europe* by Lisa M. Bitel. New York: Oxford University Press, 2009.

*Women in a Celtic Church: Ireland 450–1150* by Christina Harrington. New York: Oxford University Press, 2002.

NOTES

1. Cogitosus, *The Life of Saint Brigit the Virgin,* in *Celtic Spirituality*, trans. Oliver Davies (New York: Paulist Press, 1999), 122.

2. *The Irish Life of Brigit*, in Davies, *Celtic Spirituality*, 154.

3. Alice Curtayne, *St. Brigid of Ireland* (New York: Sheed & Ward, 1954), 29.

4. Ibid., 24.

5. Davies, *Celtic Spirituality*, 143.

6. Esther de Waal, "The Extraordinary in the Ordinary," in John S. Mogabgab, ed., *The Weavings Reader: Living with God in the World* (Nashville, TN: Upper Room Books, 1993), 128.

7. Lisa M. Bitel, "Body of a Saint, Story of a Goddess: Origins of the Brigidine Tradition," *Textual Practice* 16, no. 2 (2002): 213.

8. Alexander Carmichael, *Carmina Gadelica*, ed. C. J. Moore (Edinburgh: Floris Books, 1994), 585, n. 70.

9. Ibid., 582, n. 70.

10. Ibid.

11. Ibid., 583, n. 70.

12. Davies, *Celtic Spirituality*, 121.

13. Sean Connolly, "Vita Prima Sanctae Brigitae: Background and Historical Value," *The Journal of the Royal Society of Antiquaries of Ireland* 119 (1989): 14.

14. Davies, *Celtic Spirituality*, 124.

15. Connolly, "Vita Prima," 15; Davies, *Celtic Spirituality*, 140.

16. Davies, *Celtic Spirituality*, 145.

17. Gerald of Wales, *The History and Topography of Ireland*, trans. John O'Meara (New York: Penguin Books, 1982), 81–82.

18. Esther de Waal, *The Celtic Way of Prayer* (New York: Doubleday, 1997), 169–170.

19. Gerald of Wales, *History and Topography of Ireland*, 84.

20. Ibid., 84–85.

21. Bernard Meehan, *The Book of Kells: An Illustrated Introduction to the Manuscript in Trinity College Dublin* (London: Thames and Hudson, 1994), 16.

22. Ibid., 89.

23. Thomas Moore, *Original Self: Living with Paradox and Authenticity* (New York: HarperCollins Publishers, 2000), 7.

24. Connolly, "Vita Prima," 38.

25. Ibid., 15.

26. Mary Ewing Stamps, "Learning to Trust God Along the Way: My Vocation in Community," in *Conversations Along the Way: St. Brigid of Kildare Methodist-Benedictine Consultation, Occasional Papers #1* (Indianapolis: University of Indianapolis and Nashville, TN: The Upper Room, 2004), 9.

27. For more information about Saint Brigid of Kildare Monastery, visit janrichardson.com/saintbrigidmonastery.

28. Lisa M. Bitel, *Landscape with Two Saints: How Genovefa of Paris and Brigit of Kildare Built Christianity in Barbarian Europe* (New York: Oxford University Press, 2009), 192.

29. Ibid., 192–93.

30. Davies, *Celtic Spirituality*, 11–12.

31. De Waal, *The Celtic Way of Prayer*, 132.

32. Whitley Stokes, ed., *The Martyrology of Oengus the Culdee* (London: Henry Bradshaw Society, 1905), 65. Online at http://www.archive.org/details/martyrologyofoen29oenguoft.

33. John O'Donohue, *Anam Ċara: A Book of Celtic Wisdom* (New York: HarperCollins Publishers, 1998), 13–14.

34. De Waal, *The Celtic Way of Prayer*, 134.

35. Whitley Stokes, trans., *On the Life of St. Brigit (Leabhar Breac)*, CELT: Corpus of Electronic Texts: a project of University College, Cork, Ireland, http://www.ucc.ie/celt/online/T201010.

36. Davies, *Celtic Spirituality*, 146.

37. Connolly, "Vita Prima," 17.

38. Davies, *Celtic Spirituality*, 133.

39. Ibid., 142.

40. Ibid., 144.

41. Ibid., 149.

42. Ibid., 150.

43. Ibid., 153–54.

44. Ibid., 154.

45. *Life of the Holy Virgin Samthann*, trans. Dorothy Africa, in Thomas Head, ed., *Medieval Hagiography: An Anthology* (New York: Routledge, 2001), 107.

46. Ibid., 108.

47. *Vita sancta Ite (Life of Ita)*, trans. Dorothy Africa. (As edited by Charles Plummer in *Vitae Sanctorum Hiberniae*, vol. 2, 116–130. Originally published in 1910, reissued by Four Courts Press, Dublin, 1997), para. 36.

48. Ibid., para. 15.

49. Ibid., para. 11.

50. Ibid., para. 22.

51. "The Life of St. Darerca, or Moninna, the Abbess," Liam de Paor, trans., in *St Patrick's World: The Christian Culture of Ireland's Apostolic Age* (Notre Dame, IN: University of Notre Dame Press, 1993), 281.

52. Ibid., 285.

# A WAY IN THE WILDERNESS

## The Book of the Desert Mothers

### INTRODUCTION

In the early centuries of the church, as Christianity continued to find its form, women and men who sought to follow Christ began to move into the deserts of Egypt, Palestine, and Syria. Leaving behind the familiar landscapes they had known, they went into the wilderness to divest themselves of all that separated them from God.

These women and men, who became known as *ammas* (mothers) and *abbas* (fathers), undertook a way of life that we describe as ascetic—from the Greek *askein*, meaning "exercise" or "work," as an athlete does. The ammas and abbas sought the desert as a place to do this practicing, this exercising, this stretching of themselves toward God. They established a rhythm of life around practices that included prayer, reflection on the scriptures, silence, and fasting. For women in particular, life in the desert enabled them to leave behind their prescribed roles in the city.

In her book *The Forgotten Desert Mothers*, Laura Swan describes some of the changes within early Christianity that contributed to the movement into the desert. The church began as a faith that found its organizational center in the home, with communities gathering for worship in domestic settings in which women had roles that included leading worship, teaching, evangelizing, and ministry to those who were sick, poor, or in prison. As Christianity became an established religion, gaining official status in the Roman Empire in the fourth century and moving into a more public sphere, women's roles began to shift accordingly, with women receiving pressure to remain in the domestic realm. Swan observes that "women who had played significant roles in the ministry and leadership of Christianity found their participation dwindling as Christianity merged with the larger society and its male leaders grew increasingly uncomfortable with women in public roles. As leadership opportunities within mainstream Christianity decreased," Swam continues, "the desert and the monastery offered women a greater sense of physical and spiritual autonomy."[1]

The lives of the desert mothers took many forms. As with the men, some of the desert women lived as solitaries, others in community; many found a rhythm that incorporated the two. In time, as both the church and the monastic movement continued to evolve, the term *desert mother* came to refer not only to those who lived in the literal wilderness but also to those who undertook a monastic way of life in the city, either in community or as solitaries within a home or attached to a church. Some of these desert mothers were married and ministered alongside their husbands. Other women resisted marriage, sometimes at great risk to their lives, given the strong cultural expectation to marry. Many stories tell of women who took on the appearance of men in order to live a monastic way of life.

We know about these women because some of their teachings were preserved and included in the collection of sayings of the desert fathers. We have stories too, particularly of the later desert mothers, *Lives* that tell of their seeking after God. Probably the vast majority of the desert mothers accomplished their aim: to disappear entirely, known only to God.

In each setting, whether in the desert or the city, women grappled with core questions about what it meant to follow Christ and what rhythms of solitude and community would foster their discipleship. The desert mothers invite us to reflect on our practices—the means by which we seek after God and the attitudes of heart that dispose us to deeper relationship with God. In the coming days, as we reflect on these women of the desert, we will explore such practices as prayer, humility, *lectio divina*, and discernment, asking along the way, How do we practice? By what particular path will we follow Christ? What habits enable us to unhide ourselves from God?

In the company of these ammas, may we meet again the God who provides manna in the desert and wellsprings in every wilderness.

# PRAYER FOR THE MORNING

We are waking, God.
We are waking,
and we pray
that we may know you
as manna in the desert,
wellsprings in the wilderness,
honey from the rock,
O God our habitation
and our way.

# PRAYER FOR THE EVENING

God of the daylight,
you come also in darkness,
and even in shadows
you make a home.
Be rest to the weary
and solace to the brokenhearted;
be healing to the sick,
and to the troubled, be peace.
Be our comfort, our dreaming,
our sleep, our delight;
breathe through these hours,
O great God of night.

# 1
## INTO THE DESERT

Why the desert? Its harsh terrain held many hazards, especially for women. In her book *Praying with the Desert Mothers*, Mary Forman writes,

> The desert was not only sterile, but also "the region of the tombs, the domain of the dead, where the Egyptian never ventured without fear." It was the area of bands of nomads who were often hostile to strangers. Moreover, the desert was home to such dangerous animals as serpents, hyenas, snakes, and jackals that inhabited its abandoned temples and ruins. No better description of this desert exists than that of the *Life of Antony* (chapters 12, 50–52), as a wilderness of wild beasts, creeping things, and demons.[2]

It's not the kind of description that makes for a compelling travel brochure.

The qualities that made the desert perilous, however, provided just what the desert Christians sought. In the wilderness, they found the external landscape that their interior terrain needed. A desert exposes everything; it provides little room to hide from others, from God, or from oneself. Divested of the possessions, relationships, and rhythms of life that defined them in the city, the ammas found a freedom in the desert that would have been hard to come by otherwise.

### BLESSING

May the One who dwells
in every landscape
divest you of all that hinders
your path into God.

# 2
## IN THE WILDERNESS, WINGS

Brave as the desert mothers were, the notion of a woman finding God in the wilderness was hardly a new one. Many women had gone before the ammas into that terrain. Think of Miriam, a woman of the Exodus: a woman who, in helping to save her brother Moses, helped make the Exodus possible in the first place, and who shared in leading the children of Israel toward freedom.

And think of Hagar, mother of Ishmael the son of Abraham, driven into the wilderness not once but twice; first when she was pregnant and fleeing the harsh treatment of Sarah, then as the mother of a young son and cast out by Sarah and Abraham. Yet Hagar finds wellsprings in the wilderness and experiences God's presence so clearly that at one point she dares even to name God: "'You are El-roi'; for she said, 'Have I really seen God and remained alive after seeing him?'" (Gen. 16:13).

One of the most stunning images of a woman finding provision in the wilderness comes from John, author of the book of Revelation. In chapter 12, he relates his vision of a celestial woman who wears the sun for clothing, stars for a crown, and the moon for shoes. Crying out in the labor of delivering a child, the woman is beset by a dragon that waits to devour her son. Her son is saved and taken to God; the woman flees to the wilderness, where she finds nourishment in a place that God has prepared for her.

For this celestial woman, later interpreted as Mary the mother of Jesus, the wilderness becomes a place of refuge not once but twice: war breaks out, and the dragon, enraged by his defeat at the hands of the archangel Michael, goes after the woman once again. "But the woman," John tells us, "was given the two wings of the great eagle, so that she could fly from the serpent into the wilderness, to her place where she is nourished for a time, and times, and half a time" (Rev. 12:14).

Women such as Miriam and Hagar whose names were known, women of the wilderness whose names went unrecorded, and women who existed only in vision or dream: perhaps it was these women whose stories helped inspire and sustain those who followed after them in the desert. Perhaps the presence of these desert foremothers lingered in the landscape and assured the women who came after that even in the deepest desert there are wellsprings and in the wilderness, wings.

BLESSING

May you know the presence
of those who have passed

through the desert before you.
May they point the way
toward freedom
and sustain you
with their stories.
In the wilderness,
may there be wellsprings.
May there be wings.

# 3

## MEETING THE DEMONS OF THE DESERT

Many of the ammas and abbas went to the desert thinking they could escape the forces, which they sometimes described as demons, that plagued them in the city. Once in the wilderness, however, they discovered their demons waiting for them there.

Those who persisted learned that the desert does not offer a place of escape from who we are. Rather, it provides a landscape where what besets us becomes more apparent, more visible. The desert doesn't allow for leaving our internal landscape behind; instead, it confronts us with whatever distortions and brokenness we have allowed to creep into our terrain. Perhaps more than dealing with matters of physical survival, such confrontation was the most challenging work of the wilderness. "Entering the physical desert was never an easy prospect for the early spiritual fathers and mothers," notes Wendy Wright.

> Theirs was a harsh life, fraught with danger and marked by hardship. So, too, with the inner desert of the heart. Journeying through the treacherous maze of "worldly" temptations was not over when they left the world. In the desert they discovered that the image of the world was engraved deep in their own spirit. Thus the greater and more difficult journey was not from the cities of the Roman Empire to the solitudes of Egypt, Syria, or Palestine; it was through the crooked pathways of the heart. To make those paths straight for the advent of the Lord was the spiritual struggle in the wilderness.[3]

In such a terrain, it became crucial for the ammas to develop patterns of life that would sustain the spiritual work of the wilderness and help them navigate its challenges. Laura Swan writes, "Desert spirituality developed around all practices, passed on from amma to disciple, that dispossessed the ascetic of *all* that kept her or him from God."[4] These practices, however, held their own perils. In the midst of their earnest desire for God, wise ammas and abbas recognized how seemingly holy habits could sometimes distance them from God and one another. It was one thing to undertake a spiritual practice—fasting, prayer, vigils, and the like—for the purpose of drawing closer to God; quite another to allow these practices to become a point of pride, an occasion for competition, a source of division, or a cause for lack of hospitality to a guest. They learned that the forces they sometimes described as demons often loved to hide in the very practices that the desert folk pursued with such diligence. Recognizing this, Amma Syncletica observed,

> There is an asceticism which is determined by the enemy and his disciples practice it. So how are we to distinguish between the divine and royal asceticism and the demonic tyranny? Clearly through its quality of balance. Always use a single rule of fasting. Do not fast four or five days and break it the following day with any amount of food. In truth lack of proportion always corrupts. While you are young and healthy, fast, for old age with its weakness will come. As long as you can, lay up treasure, so that when you cannot, you will be at peace.[5]

BLESSING
May you find the practices
that offer you a doorway
into the heart of God.

4

## IN SEARCH OF STABILITY

Many of the ammas of the desert greatly valued stability, a spiritual practice that simply means to stay put. Stability is still one of the vows taken by those who become monastics. The vow recognizes that in committing ourselves to a particular place and staying rooted despite changes around and within us, we grow in a way that is different than if we are constantly on the move.

"There was a monk," Amma Theodora said, "who, because of the great number of his temptations said, 'I will go away from here.' As he was putting on his sandals, he saw another man who was also putting on his sandals and this other monk said to him, 'Is it on my account that you are going away? Because I go before you wherever you are going.'"[6]

Amma Syncletica put it this way: "If you find yourself in a monastery do not go to another place, for that will harm you a great deal. Just as the bird who abandons the eggs she was sitting on prevents them from hatching, so the monk or the nun grows cold and their faith dies, when they go from one place to another."[7] Reflecting on this saying, Laura Swan adds, "The desert journey is one inch long and many miles deep."[8]

This doesn't mean we should never go anywhere; the Christian tradition, and most other spiritual traditions, offers many stories of those who find God on the journey. Rather, Amma Theodora and Amma Syncletica challenge us to examine what prompts our perpetual motion. When we hit the road, literally or figuratively, is it because of distraction? Fear of what's before us? Boredom? Resistance? Restlessness?

Stability is not just about physically remaining in one place. The practice of stability impels us to find something worth giving ourselves to for a long, long time—a place, a community, a person, a path—and in that, to grow deeper in relationship with the God who dwells there. In navigating the changes, in wrestling with boredom, in confronting our restlessness, in learning to pay attention to what is before us rather than forever moving on to something or someplace that looks more appealing, we come to know regions of our souls that we could never enter otherwise.

Where do you find sources of stability? What do you learn in committing to something—a place, a person, a way of life—over the long haul?

"Go, sit in your cell," Abba Moses said, "and your cell will teach you everything."[9]

BLESSING

May your roots go deep
and deeper still
into the holy ground of God.

# 5

## SACRED READING

For the desert mothers and fathers, the center of their life lay in their relationship with the living word of scripture. "Desert ascetics were grounded in sacred scripture," writes Laura Swan.

> Knowing there were multiple senses of any text, they rejected a rigid approach to understanding scripture. Seeking to interiorize the word and make it a part of their very being, ascetics often began their desert journey in deep inner struggle to reflect upon, understand, and become one with the word. Reverenced as a source of life, the word was seen as having a capacity to awaken deep sensitivity and to transmit life energy. Meaning was found when word and life corresponded. Wrestling with God's word cultivated in the ascetic a way of understanding and reflecting on the world.[10]

This prayerful approach to reading scripture would come to be known in the Christian tradition as *lectio divina*, "sacred reading," a practice that the Benedictine monk Father Luke Dysinger describes as "a slow, contemplative praying of the Scriptures which enables the Bible, the Word of God, to become a means of union with God."[11] *Lectio* invites us to take a small bite of a text—a few verses or perhaps just a few words—and slowly chew on them, ponder them, and pray with them until they give up something that will provide sustenance for our soul and nourishment for our work in the world. The Dominican nun who first introduced me to this practice sometimes calls it *lectio bovina* for its ruminative, meditative, contemplative quality.

*Lectio* offers a terrain that in some ways resembles the landscape of a dream. Doing this kind of sacred reading with a text bears similarities to how we might reflect on a dream. In the contemplative space of *lectio* we ponder the variety of associations and connections between the text and our own story. If the text offers characters to us, we may look for how they reflect different parts of ourselves and what they might have to say to us. We imaginatively engage the symbols and metaphors that the written words present to us. And we look for the possibilities that our more rational minds might never have conjured—those soul-invitations that we sometimes have a hard time noticing otherwise. In the midst of even the most familiar texts, *lectio* opens new doors to us, telling us, *Look! Wake up! There are treasures here you have never seen.*

BLESSING

Among the most familiar words,
may God open you to new worlds.

6

THE SACRED TEXT OF YOUR LIFE

One of the most intriguing qualities of *lectio* for me is that we can bring this practice not only to the scriptures but to other sacred texts as well, for God inhabits words that we find not only within but also beyond the ones that we find in the Bible. We can also practice *lectio* with our own lives. Our experiences, our memories, our stories, all that we carry around within us: this is material for pondering, for reflection, for prayer. Inscribed with the word of God in our very being, we are ourselves sacred texts. In becoming prayerfully present to a layer of our lives, we may realize that God inhabited that layer in a way that we didn't perceive at the time. *Lectio* provides a way to recognize and to read God's unfolding story within us. "*Lectio* on life," Father Luke Dysinger calls this.[12] Such a practice helps us remember that as with a written text, our experiences rarely contain just one meaning; much more often, they contain multiple meanings or deepening meanings that only reveal themselves with time and attention.

BLESSING

That you may know your life
as a sacred text.
That God will lead you
to read your story anew.
That you may see how the holy
inhabits each line
and breathes across
every page.


7

A PILGRIM INTO THE WORD

Whether with a written text or with the sacred text of our own lives, *lectio* invites us to approach the text not as a map that will precisely show us our path but rather as a doorway into the presence of the living God who goes with us and prepares a way that we cannot always see. *Lectio* cultivates in us an ability to be surprised by the Word, to be open to it, to give up our assumptions about what it means or what shape it may take. This can be risky, because in order to truly encounter the God who dwells in the landscape of the text and of our own lives, we have to give up the belief that we know the lay of the land.

In his book *Sacred Reading: The Ancient Art of Lectio Divina*, Michael Casey observes that if we want to open ourselves to the working of the Holy Spirit in *lectio*, we must give up our attempts to control the process. This includes letting go of our tendency to gravitate only toward the familiar passages or to use a text merely to reinforce what we think we already know. "The Bible," Casey writes, "is an instrument of salvation only because it challenges our habitual beliefs, attitudes, and behavior. As soon as it begins only to confirm and reinforce our own views it is reduced to the status of a hand puppet. It no longer conveys an alternative; it simply parrots our own opinions."[13]

In the contemplative space of *lectio*, which complements serious study of a text but is distinct from it, we let go of the impulse to approach a text as something to be dissected, made to cough up its secrets or a singular meaning. *Lectio* acknowledges that even in the midst of our desire to understand a text, there is a place for sacred ambiguity, even for seeming chaos as we acknowledge that a text can have many layers of meaning and therefore many doors to the God for whom we search.

*Lectio* reminds us that living with the scriptures is a journey, a pilgrimage into holy terrain. As with any pilgrimage, *lectio* allows us to open to the gifts of the path, not just the goal. "As pilgrims," writes Michael Casey, "seeking may be more truthful for us than finding. In our practice of *lectio divina*, a patient receptivity may serve us better than a clamorous urgency to be enlightened."[14]

BLESSING

May you travel well
across the sacred words
that surround you.
May you be open of heart,
of mind, of spirit
to receive their surprises,
their treasures untold.

# 8
## THE INHABITED PSALTER

The desert mothers shaped their lives around the scriptures and in particular the psalms, which lay at the heart of their practice of *lectio* and prayer, whether private or communal. "Ascetics did not simply 'recite' the psalms," writes Laura Swan. "In their pondering of the word, they allowed it to permeate their inner being in order to pray from their gut."[15]

The ammas understood that the book of Psalms, perhaps more than any other book of the Bible, carries our collective memory as people who have sought the presence of God in every circumstance. The psalms give voice to the full range of human emotion. Desire, rage, hope, vindictiveness, love, despair: nearly everything we are capable of, both exalted and base, is at play in their pages. The psalmists incorporate it all, with no visible fear of judgment for bringing their emotions into God's presence. It reminds me of one of the desert fathers, Abba Poemen, who wisely counseled us, "Teach your mouth to say that which you have in your heart."[16] The psalmists did. A lot.

Because they did and because these words were gathered together in a book, we have inherited this remarkable body of poetry that has served as a central sacred text for the ages, both for Jews and for Christians. As prayers for both public worship and private contemplation, the psalms link us with all those, Jewish and Christian alike, who have prayed these words in solitude and in community across generations.

When I open a book that contains the psalms, it often stirs particular connections with others to whom I am linked by those words. I have a Bible that belonged to a beloved great-aunt. When I read the beautiful cadences of the psalms in the King James Version, I am mindful that she once prayed these same prayers. Her open Bible becomes a thin place where the veil between worlds is permeable.

During the graveside service for a family friend who influenced me greatly, the pastor invited us to pray Psalm 23 together (King James, of course, the version inextricably and beautifully bound with that psalm). The collective voice of the community gave me shivers; it tapped into a deep well of memory, and the voices lifted by the grave of that beloved mentor, friend, mother, and wife were not our voices alone.

The psalms are haunted. Generation upon generation, in dozens of languages, in every circumstance, the people of God have turned to them. The psalms are inhabited, filled with the presences of all who have prayed them, who have chanted or spoken or whispered or wailed these words in desert or sanctuary or home.

Whom do you hear when you turn to the psalms? Who inhabits their lines? Who prays them with you?

BLESSING

Among the pages of the psalms,
may you know the presence
of those who pray with you.

# 9

# LOITERING IN THE NEIGHBORHOOD OF THE WORD

Although many of the desert mothers and fathers went to the desert seeking solitude, there were times they sought out community. And there were also times that community came looking for them: word would get out about this wise amma or that wise abba dwelling in the desert, and women and men who had made a habit of aloneness found themselves surrounded by followers in search of teaching.

Desert communities took on various shapes—some became more formal, with shared space for life, prayer, and work; others remained informal, as with ammas or abbas who lived mostly alone but came together at certain times, sometimes joined by the guests who sought them out. Amid the various forms of community, the primary point of connection came in sharing their life of prayer. Monastic prayer became known as the Liturgy of the Hours, a rhythm of prayer throughout the day and night that called them to remember the God who dwells in every hour. The psalms form the core of the Liturgy of the Hours.

The ancient practices of the Liturgy of the Hours and of *lectio divina* enable us to be loiterers in the neighborhood of the Word, to hang out and dawdle with it, rather than moving through it with a briskness that assumes we know what it has to say. Kathleen Norris writes that "liturgical time is essentially poetic time, oriented toward process rather than productivity, willing to wait attentively in stillness rather than always pushing to 'get the job done.'"[17] The Liturgy of the Hours and *lectio* invite us to consider how we are allowing God to cultivate us, how we are tending our interior earth as a place where the Word can take root and grow—not just for ourselves but for the life of the world.

## BLESSING

So may you loiter,
so may you linger
in the places and practices
where the Word makes a home.

# 10

## DRY

And the well runs dry. It's one of the most common experiences in the spiritual life. A practice that we have cherished, a habit that has deepened us and drawn us closer to God, a discipline that we perhaps have engaged in for years no longer seems to work. Gradually over time or overnight with no warning, its familiar contours turn foreign, dull, perhaps even painful.

These times call us to some of our deepest discernment. They dare us to ask, Am I being called to go deeper in this practice, to persist, to keep digging toward the wellspring that surely must be here somewhere? Am I being invited to wait and to listen? Or is God leading me toward a different practice than the one I have known?

This kind of discernment, of course, is its own practice. Pondering the questions that lie at the bottom of a dry well offers a journey of its own. What I know is this: to find the answers, we have to pay attention to the dryness. This is a desert place. As uncomfortable as it may be, there is no substitute for these desert places in the spiritual life. They offer a wisdom that we cannot get any other way.

### BLESSING

When the well goes dry, listen.
Sit by it, your ear pressed to its rim.
Hear the empty and the hollow of it.
Let be. Let be.
When finally you hear your breath
echo back to you,
let this sound be your first prayer.
Where there is breath,
there is water somewhere.
Breathe.

# 11

## DRENCHED

Sometimes I grow attached to those dry, desert places in myself because on some level they're comfortable. I know them. Even though the grass really may be greener on the other side, it probably requires a really expensive lawn service. It costs.

When Jesus met a woman at the well on a dusty day, he told her that he could give her living water. Everyone who drinks of the water of the well, he told her, would become thirsty again, "'but those who drink of the water that I will give them will never be thirsty. The water that I will give will become in them a spring of water gushing up to eternal life.'"

"'Give me this water,'" the parched woman said to Jesus (John 4:14-15).

The kind of drinking that Jesus invites us to is not the polite, sipping from our teacups with pinkies extended kind of drinking. It's a drinking that drenches us, that causes rivers of living water to flow out of our hearts. The cost of this drinking—the cost of giving ourselves to the flow—is that we can't control where it goes.

Knowing this, it's sometimes easier to stay thirsty, to remain in the desert, to resist the responsibility that living into our thirst and living out God's dreams for us demands. I know folks who do this; I have felt this impulse in myself, to let the thirst burn me through to nothing but a pile of dry bones.

Ah, but God has a way even with dry bones, as the prophet Ezekiel found out in his vision of the desolate, skeletal valley. Even dry bones learn to dance.

What are you thirsty for, down to your bones?

### BLESSING

When you come
to the depth of your thirst—
its dryness, its dust;
when you arrive at the far reaches
of a desert within,
may the God of the wilderness
bring forth a well;

may you open wide to the drenching
of the water of life.

# 12

## HOLY ABSENCE

But there is this too. Respite. Rest. Letting the desert be the desert, without feeling compelled to bulldoze our way through it.

I think of a long stretch when I found myself in a soul struggle that had caught me entirely by surprise. Consumed by the wrestling and working and searching, I felt exhausted. After a time, my spiritual director, Maru, gave me this phrase: *holy absence.*

*There are times*, she said, *sometimes seasons, for removing ourselves from the struggle. Time for sabbath. Time for rest.*

### BLESSING

Even in the desert,
even in the wilderness,
sabbath comes.
May you keep it.
Light the candles,
say the prayers:

Welcome, sabbath.
Welcome, rest.
Enter in
and be our guest.

# 13

## GETTING SLEEPY

In pondering the practices that draw us deeper into God, I've found myself remembering an article that Thomas Moore, known for such books as *Care of the Soul* and *Soul Mates*, wrote in *Parabola* magazine. Reflecting on threshold spaces as crucial places for our soul's journey, Moore offers an intriguing take on our approach to awareness. He writes, "Religion is in the business of finding and constructing methods of getting sleepy, feeling lost, arriving and departing: pilgrimage, procession, fasting, incense, chanting, illuminated books." He goes on to observe, "Often we attain thresholds best through inadvertence. If we want their benefits, we might not always aim for consciousness and awareness, but rather a gap in our attention. In my view, the emphasis in some spiritual communities on continuing consciousness defeats the purpose."[18]

Moore is not arguing against awareness, of course; he is making a case that awareness, wisdom, and soulfulness do not arrive solely through perpetually vigilant consciousness. There is a different kind of waking that comes in giving ourselves to practices that cultivate a mindfulness of mystery. I love the litany of examples that Moore offers, and I add my own: walking, *lectio divina*, lingering at the dinner table with friends, creating or encountering artwork, poetry.

How do you let yourself get sleepy? What practices help you be present to the God who delights in meeting us not only in our focused awareness but also in the gaps in our attention, in dreams, in mystery?

BLESSING

May you grow sleepy enough
to find the gap where God lives.
May your soul find its waking there.

14

LISTENING IN THE DESERT

In reflecting on the lives of those who went into the desert, Wendy Wright notes, "The harsh ascetic impulse of these early Christians may be far from the spiritual needs of twentieth-century North America, but the quest for intentional listening is not." She writes,

We too urgently need to ferret out the still small whisper of divine prompting that so easily gets submerged in the rowdy chorus of voices that clamor for our attention in each day's busyness. We all need to be able to listen deeply; to listen with a tender, yielding heart; to listen adventurously enough to be utterly surprised at what we hear. We all need, in one way or another, at one time or another, to enter the desert and listen there mutely, intently for God.[19]

I experience this kind of listening in spiritual direction. With ancient roots, spiritual direction is a practice in which a person gifted (and usually trained) for this ministry accompanies others as they listen for God's presence in their life. Though called *spiritual* direction, this practice acknowledges that everything in our lives is of consequence to our spirits and our relationship with God; nothing is off limits in a spiritual direction conversation. And though called spiritual *direction*, it's not about having someone tell you what you should do.

One of the great gifts of the director I work with, Maru, is her ability to ask good questions, questions that arise from her long knowing of me, questions that come from her ability to listen well both to God and to me. Questions that offer not a map but a doorway that helps me find my way.

*What's the invitation?* she asked me in a conversation one day. I scribble down these things she says sometimes, not wanting to forget. I find them later; don't always remember what we were talking about but know it helped get me to a different place. A question that might need visiting again. *What do you have energy for? What can you do where you really are?*

And this more recent one on a day when I was looking back: *What would it take for you not to have any regrets now?*

Although Maru stops short of telling me what to do, I keep going back to her because she's willing to say what she sees. *There are no mistakes when it comes to the heart,* she told me once. *There is just the landscape of mystery. I sometimes wonder,* she told me another day, *if we're cowards when it comes to love.*

*We need ancient stones for this one,* she said to me in a time of much mystery. *A garden maze on the grounds of an old castle . . .*

In the labyrinth of your life, how do you do the listening that Wendy Wright describes? What helps you listen intently for God? What people or practices enable you to do this? In what ways do you long to listen but are resisting? What's in the resistance? As Maru might ask, *What's the invitation? What can you do where you really are?*

BLESSING

May God send you someone
to ask the sacred questions,
to listen you through the mysteries,
to go with you on the way.

# 15

*The Secret Room*

## INHABITING THE HOURS

On one of my early visits to Saint Brigid of Kildare Monastery, I had the opportunity to stay for a month. I arrived on the heels of a season that had been intensely draining. I was spent, and I was sad. I was in the desert.

I arrived at Saint Brigid's in time for Compline, the final prayer before sleep. After Compline I lingered in the oratory. In the quiet, amid shadows and candlelight, I found myself enveloped by the sense that I had come to a place that could provide a container for all I had brought with me. Not a container by which to preserve the weariness and sorrow, but instead one that could hold what I had brought, let it rest, and transform it.

Over the course of the month, I gave myself into the keeping of the Liturgy of the Hours. In a time when I hardly knew how to pray myself, the voices that surfaced in the Liturgy gave me what I couldn't manufacture on my own. They were medicine: the words of the psalmists, the ancient prayers of the church, and the actual voices of my friend Mary, the Methodist monk, and of other guests who visited during that month. In giving myself over to the rhythm of the Hours—even to the 7:00 morning prayer that was a great stretch for my inner night owl—I was able to release myself into the good care of those who had navigated centuries of bright and dark seasons and who had found the sacred in each time.

I sometimes think of my monastic month at Saint Brigid's when I pray the Liturgy of the Hours now. Where during that time I clung to the Liturgy as medicine, as solace in a weary season, the season has turned. Most times I bring to the Liturgy a centered contentment, hoping that my praying offers to others the kind of strength that the Hours offered me when I didn't have that strength on my own. That's one of the gifts of the Liturgy of the Hours: it is open to us whenever we are. Sometimes we can only curl up in the container it offers. Other times we can hold it as a container for others.

I experience the Hours best when praying it with others. When the Saint Brigid's community gathers for our summer retreat, our days together unfold around the Hours: morning prayer, noon prayer, evening prayer, and Compline. It is one of the great gifts of our time together, to hear the voices of my sisters and brothers sharing in this ancient rhythm. I miss having that kind of presence in my daily life and prayer. When I pray the Hours at home, in my abbreviated fashion, I am usually by myself. Yet when I open the prayer book that we use, a breviary especially for Benedictine oblates, I am mindful that I do not pray alone. Though I may be in solitude, I am praying in community. The Hours link me not only to my sisters and brothers of Saint Brigid's but also to Benedictines and other monastics around the world and across the ages.

BLESSING

In every season, in every hour,
may the love of God find you,
enfold you, gather you in.

# 16

## ONE WILD WORD

I'll tell you a secret. Though I am drawn to the Liturgy of the Hours and to its ancient beauty, it still stirs up a fight in me. I resist its regularity and orderliness. Some days, when faced with the Liturgy, I give up and pray for one wild word, one plea that is the most honest prayer I know in that moment, that sums up the deepest longing I am feeling.

One of my ongoing prayers is this: *God, teach me to pray.* On those days when I find the one wild word, when I offer it and know the place from which it has come and the God who dwells there: on those days, I think perhaps I have begun to learn what it is to pray.

BLESSING

That you will learn how to pray.
That you will forget how to pray
and so learn again and again.
That you will find one wild word.
That it will open your heart.

# 17

## A DIZZYING WAY

"Personal discernment," writes Wendy Wright, "is not a practice that can be easily systematized into any formula, especially not a simple one. . . . Spiritual listening is not listening to words, to arguments, to pros and cons, to positions and opinions. It involves listening to the delicate intersection of the human heart, with its desires and dreams, and the vast and silent mystery that is God."[20]

One day, taking a walk with Brother David, a friend who's a Franciscan friar, I asked him, "What's discernment like for you?" I was in the midst of making some decisions and found myself curious to know how he sorted through the choices in his own life. In good Franciscan fashion, David's response included a couple of stories about Saint Francis.

In the first story, Saint Francis and Brother Masseo are on a journey and come to a crossroads. Not knowing which path to take, Saint Francis tells Brother Masseo to stand at the center of the crossroads and spin himself around. When Masseo finally falls down, Francis and his dizzy brother set off in the direction in which Masseo had landed.[21]

In the second story, Francis is trying to discern whether he should spend all his time in prayer or whether he should also go out and do some preaching. He senses this decision is not his to make alone, so he enlists Brother Masseo's aid once again. He sends Masseo to two trusted souls, Saint Clare and Brother Silvester, to ask them to pray about this question. In prayer, each discerns the same response: Go and preach. When Brother Masseo takes this word back to Francis, he leaps up, saying, "Then, let us go, in the name of God!"[22]

As someone capable of making the act of discernment a long and involved process, I have found great companions in both of these tales that David shared. The first story may strike us as silly, but it reminds me that on those occasions when there's no one path that's obviously the right one to take, it's often better to set off in *some* direction if the alternative means staying stuck at the crossroads. God knows how to make use of any path.

The second story reminds me of the importance of turning to those who can help me in times of discernment. Faced with a momentous decision, Francis realized the question was too big for him to find his way through alone. He sought the insight of those who knew both him and God well. When their mutual answer came, Francis trusted it to be the voice of God, and he moved forward without hesitation.

### BLESSING

When the way is convoluted
and confusing,
when the choice is not clear
and uncertainty presses close,
may there be those through whom
God's longing speaks,
and, speaking, shows you a way.

# 18

## DISCERNMENT IN THE DESERT

The Latin root of the word *discernment* has to do with sifting and separating. When we have much to sort through, it can be, as Brother Masseo found, a dizzying process. The work of discerning one direction or choice from among many may require that we separate ourselves, that we go into a desert: a figurative one, if not actual. Removing ourselves from at least some of our usual routines, for moments or for months, can shift the way that we view our life.

In the Gospels, we see how Jesus does this at the outset of his public ministry. He has just been baptized by John, just been Holy-Spirit-descended-upon, just been named Son and Beloved. We might think he is now raring to get to work. Instead he goes in the opposite direction. With the waters of baptism still clinging to him, Jesus disappears into the desert. Into the wild.

As his Jordan-drenched flesh goes dry, Jesus begins to fast and pray. Forty days. Forty nights. His wilderness experience continues the initiation begun by the ritual of his baptism. Son of God he may be; but here at the outset of his ministry, he needs this liminal space, this in-between place, to deepen his clarity and to prepare him for what lies ahead. In this harsh landscape, bereft of any comforts that might distract him, Jesus confronts the basic questions about who he is and what he is doing.

We don't know precisely what Jesus learns there, what he comes to know about himself in that Forty-Day Place. We do know that when Satan shows up, Jesus is ready. He meets the chaos of his tempter with clarity. The baptismal waters may have evaporated from his skin but not from his soul. A river of knowing runs through him. He is drenched with discernment.

The Gospels tell us that at the end of Jesus' desert time, angels came and ministered to him. Mercy, I love that image. I imagine them showing up with armfuls of bread and plenty of wine after the tempter has tucked tail and split. I like to think maybe they looked a little like Francis's friends Masseo, Clare, and Silvester.

So here I am, come to ask you the question I asked David on that road many years ago: What's discernment like for you? When you have a choice to make, when something needs sorting and sifting, what do you do? Is there a place, a person, a practice that helps you see what you need to see? Do you have friends like Clare and Silvester who listen so well to you and to God that they help you hear God's longing for you? How are you keeping your eyes open for the sustenance that comes in even the deepest wilderness?

In every desert, let clarity come.
Let discernment drench you.
Let angels attend you.
Let them give to your hunger
their sweetest delights.

# 19

## A CLARIFYING WAY

When Jesus leaves the wilderness, he takes clarity with him as a treasure of the desert, a sign of the sustenance that always comes to those who survive that landscape. Baptized in the Spirit, named by the Creator, attended by the angels, Jesus walks out of the desert and into the life that has been prepared for him. He is an initiate, ready, going in the company of all who know what it means to walk through the wilderness and find the gifts God hides there.

Sometimes it takes going into the wilderness to learn who we are and what we need. From time to time, God draws us toward a terrain where the familiar contours of our lives disappear, where we leave our landmarks behind, where we let go the people and patterns and possessions that orient us. It doesn't often require taking ourselves to a literal wilderness in the manner that Jesus did. But his sojourn there reminds us there is wisdom in knowing when to turn toward a place, a person, or a practice that can help us see what we cannot always see under our own power.

Jesus knew that going into the barren and uncomfortable places isn't about proving how holy we are or how tough or how brave. It's about letting God lead us into a landscape where we don't know everything, don't *have* to know everything, indeed may be emptied of nearly everything we think we know. Giving ourselves to that place frees us to receive the word, the wisdom, the clarity about who we are and what God is calling us to do.

BLESSING

In this and every season,
may you travel toward the place
God desires for you.
May you walk in the company
of those who know the way.
May you go well.

# 20

## HONEY FROM THE ROCK

Although Jesus will never again make such a lengthy trip into the wilderness, as far as we know, he does persist in his habit of going into places of lack. Again and again we see Jesus hanging out with people who live and struggle amid the daily wildernesses of body and soul.

Jesus challenges his hearers—and us—to go into those same places. In Matthew 25, he tells his disciples of a time when blessing will come to those who give food to the hungry and drink to the thirsty; welcome to the stranger and clothing to the naked; care to the sick and company to the prisoner, for "'just as you did it to one of the least of these who are members of my family, you did it to me.'"

Jesus gets awfully specific in telling us where we can find him. Each of the habitations he lists is marked by lack: lack of food, lack of water, lack of hospitality, lack of clothing, lack of health, lack of freedom. Christ chooses these places, inhabits these spaces, waits for us to show up.

He waits too for us to recognize these places in ourselves. He knows that if we haven't recognized the poverty within our own souls, the places of desert and desolation and emptiness, and if we haven't recognized how he dwells there, then it's hard for us to truly see him and serve him in others.

Christ calls us to those desert places to find what we can find only there. Yet what he knew, what the desert mothers and fathers knew, what the people of God have known for millennia, is this: the wilderness is the place where God provides manna. Wellsprings. Angels. Honey from the rock.

Is there a wilderness you need to enter—with your body or with your soul or with both—in order to gain clarity as this point in your life? What might this look like? Whose stories could you draw on, lean on, take heart from as you contemplate this possibility?

## BLESSING

From every hardship, let there come honey.
From every struggle, sweet.
Let angels. Let manna.
Let wellsprings. Let rest.
To the hungry, let food.
To the thirsty, let drink.
Clothes to the naked, care to the sick.
To the stranger, let welcome.
To the prisoner, let company.
Let honey. Let honey. Let honey.

# 21

## VICTORIOUS OVER THE DEMONS

Amid all the practices that drew the desert mothers toward God, one quality, one disposition, one habit of being surpassed all others and every other practice depended on it. In *The Sayings of the Desert Fathers* we read that Amma Theodora stated, "Neither asceticism, nor vigils nor any kind of suffering are able to save, only true humility can do that." She went on:

> There was an anchorite who was able to banish the demons; and he asked them, "What makes you go away? Is it fasting?" They replied, "We do not eat or drink." "Is it vigils?" They replied, "We do not sleep." "Is it separation from the world?" "We live in the deserts." "What power sends you away then?" They said, "Nothing can overcome us, but only humility." "Do you see how humility is victorious over the demons?"[23]

The desert folk, however, understood humility in a different way than we tend to in the twenty-first century. In *To Love as God Loves*, Roberta

Bondi points out, "Humility did not mean for them [the ammas and abbas] a continuous cringing, cultivating a low self-image, and taking a perverse pleasure in being always forgotten, unnoticed, or taken for granted. Instead," she writes, "humility meant to them a way of seeing other people as being as valuable in God's eyes as ourselves. It was for them a relational term having to do precisely with learning to value others, whoever they were. It had to do with developing the kind of empathy with the weaknesses of others that made it impossible to judge others out of our own self-righteousness."[24]

At the root of *humility* is the Latin word *humus*. Earth. The earth that God made and called good; the earth from which, as one of the Creation stories goes, God fashioned us. Humility is our fundamental recognition that we each draw our life and breath from the same source, the God who made us and calls us beloved. Humility not only prevents us from seeing ourselves as *more* deserving or graced or better than another; it compels us to recognize that we are no *less* deserving or graced than another. For women, so often conditioned to take on roles and attitudes of subservience, this is a point that the desert mothers would have us understand. Humility draws us into mutual relation in which we allow no abuse, no demeaning, no diminishment of others *or of ourselves*.

And when we bungle it or see others bungle it, humility gives us a break. "When it comes to living together," Bondi writes, "humility is the opposite of perfectionism. It gives up unrealistic expectations of how things ought to be for a clear vision of what human life is really like. In turn, this enables its possessors to see and thus love the people they deeply desire to love."[25]

BLESSING

That you will see others
with the humility
that has the power to save.
That you will see yourself
with the humility
that has the power to save.
That you will see.
That, seeing, you will love.

# 22

## THE NOONDAY DEMON

The ammas and abbas experienced the desert as a place to wrestle with the passions. Their understanding of the term *passion* differed from ours. They viewed the passions as dispositions, habits, emotions, and ways of seeing that distort perceptions of God, others, and ourselves. The passions hinder us from experiencing those relationships fully in freedom and love.

Roberta Bondi writes,

> A passion may very well be a strong emotion, but it need not be. A passion can also be a state of mind, or even a habitual action. Anger is usually a passion, but sometimes forgetfulness is called a passion. Gossip and talking too much are also regularly called passions in this literature. Depression, the very opposite of a passion as we usually use that term in our modern world, is one of the most painful passions.[26]

A passion that surfaces repeatedly in the desert literature is *acedia*, a finely nuanced word whose meaning is difficult to capture. Its Greek root refers to a lack of concern, a state of care-lessness that threatens to overpower the person whom it visits.

The fourth-century writer Evagrius Ponticus called acedia "the noonday demon" and described how it "makes it seem that the sun barely moves, if at all, and that the day is fifty hours long."[27] Amma Syncletica described it this way:

> There is grief that is useful, and there is grief that is destructive. The first sort consists in weeping over one's own faults and weeping over the weakness of one's neighbours, in order not to destroy one's purpose, and attach oneself to the perfect good. But there is also a grief that comes from the enemy, full of mockery, which some call *accidie*. This spirit must be cast out, mainly by prayer and psalmody.[28]

Bondi points out that although acedia has sometimes been called sloth—laziness—it is not the same thing. "Acedia," she writes, "is a restless boredom that makes our ordinary tasks seem too dull to bear. . . . Nothing seems right; life has lost its savor and it all seems somebody else's fault, so that the only alternative is to leave everything and go off somewhere else."[29]

Bondi identifies two sources of acedia. "First, acedia often comes from one degree or another of exhaustion from too little sleep or not enough leisure."[30] Of its second cause, she writes,

> We often try to find meaning in life from things that do not give ultimate meaning: work, marriage, friendships, hobbies, material possessions. . . . All of these things are good and important, but they are not ultimate. Of course we cannot find our deepest self in them. We are not made that way. Only God, finally, can satisfy our bored and restless hearts so that we are able to love.[31]

BLESSING

When your heart grows
restless, care-less,
weary and bored,
may God meet you and rest you
and stir you toward love.

# 23
## ANTIDOTES TO ACEDIA

In her book *Acedia & Me*, Kathleen Norris observes, "The person afflicted by acedia refuses to care or is incapable of doing so. When life becomes too challenging and engagement with others too demanding, acedia offers a kind of spiritual morphine: you know the pain is there, yet can't rouse yourself to give a damn."[32]

Norris acknowledges the similarities between acedia and depression and seeks to describe the subtle distinctions between the two. Where depression often has a physiological or environmental source that may respond well to treatment, acedia arises within the soul, oftentimes out of the blue. Though acedia and depression are kindred, what heals one may not heal the other.

The desert mothers understood that acedia often finds its remedy in the practices the monastic tradition gives us—practices designed to foster endurance that overcomes the distortions and lethargy that acedia can induce. The difficulty lies in the fact that acedia tries to lure us away from these very practices. The ammas responded by persisting in their practice. Amma Theodora said,

> It is good to live in peace, for the wise man practises perpetual prayer. It is truly a great thing for a virgin or a monk to live in peace, especially for the younger ones. However, you should realize that as soon as you intend to live in peace, at once evil comes and weighs down your soul through *acidie*, faintheartedness, and evil thoughts. It also attacks your body through sickness, debility, weakening of the knees, and all the members. It dissipates the strength of soul and body, so that one believes one is ill and no longer able to pray. But if we are vigilant, all these temptations fall away.[33]

What sustains you when acedia comes to call?

BLESSING

When you cannot
summon them on your own,
may vigilance and peace
come as gift, as grace,
as remedy from the hand
of the Healer of Souls.

# 24

## DREAMING IN THE DESERT

It must be at least
eighty degrees already this morning.
Spring has barely begun,
which bodes ill
for the summer to come.
I can already feel
my energy leaking out
into the heat;
air conditioning barely stems

the lethargy that steals in and
pins me to my bed
most of the morning,
lulls me into reading
the next page of a book,
and the next
and the next
as I linger over breakfast
and then,
shortly after,
lunch.

I have read the desert mothers
and fathers
and so I know this is what
they called *acedia*:
weariness, listlessness,
lack of care.

Abba Evagrius called it
the noonday demon.

Amma Syncletica said
it was a spirit that must be cast out
mainly with prayer and psalmody.

And so I keep to my psalms
morning and night,
a thread in the fabric
of my fluid days,
though it will feel,
as summer oozes forward,
more and more like trying
to stitch water together.

What would they have done,
I wonder,

those ammas and abbas
blazing in the desert,
if they had known of
mint juleps and
wraparound porches,
ice cream and
swimming pools?

What would they have made
of ceiling fans
while cool jazz plays,
of Southern tea,
of chocolate shakes?

If the desert folk
had dreamed these things,
as I do
in these draining days,
would they have
uttered exorcisms,
chanted prayers for deliverance,

or
with the wisdom burned into them
by sun and desert sand,
would they have
for a moment
licked their lips,
closed their eyes,
and breathed
one low and longing
sigh?

BLESSING

In the desert,
in the draining days

and wearying nights,
     may delight find its way to you.

# 25

## IN THE REALM OF THE SPIRITS

In describing the spiritual forces that run contrary to the purposes of God, the desert mothers and fathers often referred to them as *demons*. Whatever we may think of that term, the ammas and abbas possessed a clear, desert-born understanding of the many forces that seek to lure us from the holy.

> [Amma Syncletica] also said, "We must arm ourselves in every way against the demons. For they attack us from outside, and they also stir us up from within; and the soul is then like a ship when great waves break over it, and at the same time it sinks because the hold is too full. We are just like that: we lose as much by the exterior faults we commit as by the thoughts inside us. So we must watch for the attacks of men that come from outside us, and also repel the interior onslaughts of our thoughts."[34]

At one time I didn't give much thought to what it meant to confront evil and suffering in the realm of the spiritual world. I'm mainline Protestant, after all. Spiritual warfare, as some call it, was something best left to the charismatics and others who dealt in such things.

Then I began to live and work within systems and organizations that have given me cause to think again about the notion that evil can coalesce as a force and inflict itself in discrete ways. In my professional ministry and in my personal ecosystem, the years have afforded plenty of occasions to witness the ways in which chaos that exists in the spiritual world can manifest itself in the physical realm. It's stunning, how a single individual in spiritual disarray can distribute pain and discord among an entire body of people. And the reverse: how the diffuse chaos that often lurks so easily within a system can erupt in acts of harm against individuals.

In confronting the destructive forces that he encountered in those around him, Jesus offers a model for how we can reckon with the forces that work against God's desire for wholeness. We see this, for instance, in Mark's story of a man with an unclean spirit who approaches Jesus in the synagogue. Interesting, isn't it, that this encounter takes place in a holy space? It's a great example of what I've seen time and again: that places meant for worship and seeking after God often attract the most chaotic folks. That which is opposed to God is often most drawn to those places devoted to God.

In Mark's story, Jesus responds to the spirit with calm authority. Jesus addresses the spirit from the core of who he is. He is not exhibiting a display of magic or seeking to dazzle the crowd with a show. Rather, Jesus demonstrates his willingness to confront and call out what is contrary to God. Acting from that fiercely calm and centered place, he releases the man from the force that has tormented him.

The healthy spiritual practices of the Christian tradition give us tools to do the necessary work at the level of spirit. These practices, when undertaken with the humility to which the desert mothers encourage us, cultivate within us the grounded, centered authority that enables us to confront spiritual brokenness as Jesus did. Such practices keep us calm amid chaos and deepen our ability to respond to disorder that manifests itself in the world.

BLESSING

In the presence of evil,
may God so protect you, calm you,
center and surround you
that chaos falls before you
and peace reveals its face.

# 26

## A PRAYER OF ENCOMPASSING

In my own spiritual practice, I have taken to opening my day by offering the prayer known as "Saint Patrick's Breastplate." It's also called "Deer's Cry," due to its association with the legend that Saint Patrick prayed it when he and his companions were in peril, and the prayer caused them to take on the appearance of deer and thereby elude their attackers. Though the prayer originated some time after Saint Patrick, it is an old, old prayer of encompassing—what the Celtic folk call a lorica—that in a poetic and profound way calls upon God to protect us from the forces that work against God.

I'm particularly fond of the version that Malachi McCormick offers in his book *Deer's Cry*. Published by his small press, The Stone Street Press, *Deer's Cry* offers McCormick's translation of the prayer (alongside the Old Irish version), handwritten with his charming calligraphy. I gradually committed the prayer to memory several years ago. I pray it not as some kind of magic charm but rather as a reminder that I go into my day and into the world in the encompassing of God who bids me rely completely on the power of God rather than on my own devices. It's a prayer that, honestly prayed, cultivates humility, an awareness of how we depend entirely upon God. This humility in turn fosters the type of calm authority by which Jesus confronted spiritual chaos.

The desert mothers, who spoke of the importance of balance, would remind us not to give more power to the presence of evil than is warranted; obsessing over chaos can breed it. Rather, God calls us to confront evil where we find it. The demons—by whatever form or name we know the presence of disorder—fight hardest when we, like Jesus, and like the ammas, look them in the face. But this is what depletes evil of its power. It cannot bear being named, challenged, called out.

Where do you personally witness the forces that work against God? What do you think about those forces, and how do you reckon with them? How do you seek God's protection against them? In what ways do you feel called to confront the presence of chaos? What practices help keep you centered in and reliant upon the power of God?

### BLESSING

May you go
with the encompassing of Christ
who does not abandon us to chaos
but instead accompanies us
in every realm.

# 27

## OTHER MOTHERS OF THE DESERT

The readings this month have focused primarily on the earliest women of the desert, those who went into the wilderness in the early centuries of the church and whose words are gathered in *The Sayings of the Desert Fathers*. Yet Christian history, both East and West, teems with the stories of other women who came to be known as desert mothers.

In her article "The Desert Mothers: A Survey of the Feminine Anchoretic Tradition in Western Europe," Margot H. King observes, "When I first began my research into this area of studies—despite my limited access to primary materials—I was able to locate in somewhat less than eighteen months approximately 1100 named Desert Mothers and 900 anonymous female recluses who lived from the sixth to the fifteenth centuries. It was clear," she goes on to write, "that I had only scratched the surface."[35] She speculates that women solitaries in medieval western Europe numbered in the tens of thousands.

King, along with others, understands the term *desert mother* to include not only the women who dwelled in the wilderness in the early centuries of Christianity; the title extends as well to women who found other ways to devote themselves to the service of Christ in a monastic fashion. This includes women who lived in the cities as solitaries or in community, deaconesses, and also married women who remained wedded to their husbands but gave up their sexual relationship as an ascetic practice.

We know the names of some of these women. The details of their lives, though often sketchy, are tantalizing. King tells, for instance, of "the sisters Nymphodora, Menodora and Metrodona, recluses in a tumulus at Pythiis" in the fourth century.[36] King writes that between the mid-fifth century to the mid-sixth century "we find, among others, Anastasia, Apollonaria, Athanasia, Euphrosyne, Hilaria, Theodora, Matrona, Eugenia, Marina, Eusebia Hospitia, Pelagia, as well as Marana and Cyra who lived in chains in a small half-roofed enclosure for forty-two years and who were visited by Theodoret, Bishop of Cyprus."[37] She names Tygria, who "barely qualifies as a recluse since she did not conceal herself to pursue a solitary life but in order to hide the thumb and two fingers of John the Baptist which she had stolen from his shrine in Alexandria."[38]

Over time, this impulse toward the eremitical life spread beyond the Middle East and the Mediterranean. It found a special foothold in Celtic lands such as Ireland. The literature gives us stories and hints of some of these women who left their homelands as pilgrims, taking up a monastic way of life elsewhere. This form of exile became a way of entering the desert.

King tells of three sisters who left Ireland and took up the hermit life on the banks of the Marne. Posenna, Prompta, and Fracla were their names. These women, along with all the others who left what they knew, haunt my imagination. What prompted them to leave their homeland? What did the sisters find on the banks of the Marne? What sustenance—what manna, what wellsprings—did God provide in their wilderness? What did they come to know in that place?

BLESSING

Wherever you make your home,
may your heart be a habitation for God.

# 28
## BROTHERS IN THE DESERT

The records of the desert are marked by stories of monks who perceived women as a source of temptation and sin. At the same time, there exist wondrous stories of monks who came to the aid of women, who helped them find their path, who became allies and friends in their solitary way of life. Laura Swan writes, for instance, that when Syncletica of Palestine (not the same as the Amma Syncletica we've already met) sought to become a monastic, "One of the old desert dwellers she had met clothed Syncletica in simple attire and gave her his books, including a two-volume Bible."[39]

When Euphrosyne of Alexandria, a fifth-century Christian, left home, "A hermit from Scete shaved her head, gave her a monastic robe, prayed with her, and departed."[40]

One of the most famous desert women was Saint Mary of Egypt. Said to have been a prostitute, Mary had an experience of transformation on a pilgrimage to Jerusalem. Thereafter she lived for many years as a hermit in the wilderness, clad only in her hair—one of the details that suggests that aspects of her story may have been conflated with legends of Mary Magdalene, of whom a similar tale is told. The *Life of St. Mary of Egypt*, probably composed in the seventh century and falsely attributed to a theologian and writer named Sophronious, tells of Mary's extraordinary friendship with a priest named Zosimas. They met but twice, yet she entrusted him with her life story at their first meeting—though not with her name.

At Mary's request, Zosimas returned a year later and served her Communion, which she had not received since her trip to Jerusalem decades earlier. She asked him to return and do the same the following year. When he did, Zosimas found Mary dead, facing the east with her hands folded across herself. Beside his friend, Zosimas found a message written in the dust. "Father Zosimas," it said, "bury the body of the humble Mary in this place. Return *dust to dust*, and pray always to the Lord for me. I died . . . on that very night of the Passion of our Savior, after I received the holy Last Supper." Mary's *Life* relates, "When the monk read these words he was overjoyed, for he had learned the name of the blessed woman."[41]

Who are the men who have helped you on your way—who have provided support, shelter, communion, friendship? How do they wear the face of God for you?

BLESSING

Bless the brothers, O God,
who show us your face,
who by their love and by their lives
offer us communion
and sustain us on our way.

# 29

## BREAD IN THE WORD

In many cases we know the desert women because of men who wrote to them or about them: men who were their teachers, relatives, colleagues, and sometimes students; men whose lives and writings were formative of the Christian church and who acknowledged the influence of these women. Gregory of Nyssa, a famed bishop of the fourth century, wrote an account of his sister titled *The Life of Saint Macrina*, in which he referred to Macrina as "my teacher." He describes how, from a young age, Macrina gave herself to the study of the scriptures as part of her devotion to God. Gregory writes that as a child, "There was none of the psalms which she did not know since she recited each part of the Psalter at the proper times of the day, when she rose from her bed, performed or rested from her duties, sat down to eat or rose up from the table, when she went to bed or got up to pray, at all time she had the Psalter with her like a good travelling companion who never fails."[42]

In addition to Gregory, Macrina had two other brothers who became bishops, Basil of Caesarea and Peter of Sebaste. Leaders in the development of the monastic movement, they drew their inspiration from Macrina and her ascetic way of life.

In accounts such as Gregory's, we find fascinating hints of the literary culture in which many women of the early church participated. Laura Swan writes that Marcella, born in 325 CE and who established one of the first household communities in Rome, "knew Greek and gained a reputation for her detailed, literal biblical exegesis. . . . Marcella debated significant points of scripture with Jerome [an early church father famed for translating the Bible into what is known as the Vulgate], who later credited her with much of his own learning." Marcella also became a mentor to others in the study of the scriptures, including notable women such as Paula and her daughter Eustochium as well as Melania the Elder, a Roman woman of Spanish descent who founded a monastery in Jerusalem.[43]

Writing about Melania the Elder, Paulinus describes her as a "woman who finds restoration in fasting, repose in prayer, bread in the Word, clothing in rags. Her hard couch (it is a cloak and a patchwork quilt on the ground) is made soft by her scholarly work, because her delight in reading mitigates the insult of the inflexible bed, and it is rest to her holy soul to keep vigil in the Lord."[44]

Melania the Elder's granddaughter, Melania the Younger, inherited her grandmother's love of learning and ministered alongside her husband,

Pinianus. Melania and Pinianus, who had considerable wealth, sold their possessions, using the money to support monks and other ascetics, to minister to the poor, and to secure the release of prisoners.[45] They traveled widely to such places as Africa, where they sold the estates they owned there, provided endowments for African monasteries, and came under the guidance of Saint Augustine. Melania the Younger's actions found their grounding in the Word to whose study she devoted herself. Her biographer, Gerontius, relates that Melania "wrote elegantly and faultlessly in little notebooks. She mentally decided how much she should write each day, how much in the Canonical Books [of Scripture] she should read, and how much in the collections of homilies. After she had had her fill of these writings, she went through the lives of the Fathers as if she were eating a cake."[46]

BLESSING

May the love of the Word
that inhabited these women
dwell also in you,
drawing you into its mysteries
and inspiring your actions
for the life of the world.

# 30

## A LIVING PALIMPSEST

In 1892, the Scottish-born scholar Agnes Smith Lewis traveled to Egypt to make her first visit to Saint Catherine's Monastery. Established in the sixth century at the foot of Mount Sinai, the Greek Orthodox community is famed for the many treasures it holds from the early centuries of Christianity. In the company of her twin sister, Margaret Dunlop Gibson, also a scholar, Lewis made the journey to Saint Catherine's in hopes of studying some of the ancient manuscripts in its library.

Lewis, who along with her sister made a life in the academic community of the University of Cambridge, writes that among the ancient books placed into their hands by the librarian of Saint Catherine's "was a thick volume, whose leaves had evidently been unturned for centuries, as they could be separated only by manipulation with the fingers."[47] In some cases, they had to separate the leaves with a steam kettle.

Immediately Lewis recognized the book as a palimpsest, a manuscript whose text had been effaced and overlaid by a later text. Such a practice was common in times when vellum was scarce. Looking closer, she saw that the more recent text was "a very entertaining account of the lives of women saints."[48] Desert mothers.

Looking closer still, beneath the lives of these women saints, Lewis recognized the more ancient writing, still legible, as belonging to the Gospels. The manuscript proved to be what was then the oldest Syriac version of the four Gospels, dating to the fourth century. It was a stunning discovery.

In the eighth century, a monk had taken the Gospel text, rubbed its words pale, and begun to write. "By the strength of our Lord Jesus Christ, the Son of the Living God, I begin, I the sinner, John the Recluse of Beth-Mari Kaddisha, to write select narratives about the holy women, first the book of the Blessed Lady Thecla, disciple of Paul, the Blessed Apostle. My brethren, pray for me."[49]

John the Recluse would go on to write about other women saints of the Eastern Church, including Eugenia, Mary (Marinus), Euphrosyne, Onesima, Drusis, Barbara, Mary, Irene, Euphemia, Sophia, and Justa: women who gave up safety, security, convention, and finally their lives in order to follow Christ.

"Here we find in sober fact," writes Lewis, "what happened only metaphorically in the middle ages—the Word of God completely obscured by the legends of the saints."[50]

Yet not obscured. The lives of these women—on the page and in the world—preserved the gospel message. By their devotion, they became living palimpsests, Christ the Word shimmering through their own sacred text.[51]

BLESSING

May you be a living palimpsest,
the Word of God visible
through the sacred pages of your life.

# 31

## THE BOOK OF THE DESERT

Page by page it was
written into their flesh
not by addition
but instead by what
they gave away

the emptiness inscribed
itself upon them
until all the text
that remained of them
was a thin track
lingering
in the dust

until even that
blew away
and was carried off
by a vast silence.

### BLESSING

In the lives of these
women of the wilderness,
among the lines that God inscribed
onto their hearts and souls and minds,
may you find words
to sustain and to challenge,
words to comfort and to call.
May these be bread for the journey;
may they be manna for your way.

## FURTHER READING

*Acedia & Me: A Marriage, Monks, and a Writer's Life* by Kathleen Norris. New York: Riverhead, 2008.

*The Forgotten Desert Mothers: Sayings, Lives, and Stories of Early Christian Women* by Laura Swan. New York: Paulist Press, 2001.

*Handmaids of the Lord: Contemporary Descriptions of Feminine Asceticism in the First Six Christian Centuries* trans. Joan M. Petersen. Kalamazoo, MI: Cistercian Publications, 1996.

*Harlots of the Desert: A Study of Repentance in Early Monastic Sources* by Benedicta Ward. Kalamazoo, MI: Cistercian Publications, 2006.

*The Holy Way: Practices for a Simple Life* by Paula Huston. Chicago: Loyola Press, 2003.

*Holy Women of Byzantium: Ten Saints' Lives in English Translation* ed. Alice–Mary Talbot. Washington, D.C.: Dumbarton Oaks, 2006.

*Joy Unspeakable: Contemplative Practices of the Black Church* by Barbara Ann Holmes. Minneapolis, MN: Augsburg Fortress, 2004.

*Lectio Divina: Contemplative Awakening and Awareness* by Christine Valters Paintner and Lucy Wynkoop. Mahwah, NJ: Paulist Press, 2008.

*Praying with the Desert Mothers* by Mary Forman. Collegeville, MN: Liturgical Press, 2005.

*Sacred Reading: The Ancient Art of Lectio Divina* by Michael Casey. Ligouri, MO: Ligouri/Triumph, 1996.

*The Sayings of the Desert Fathers: The Alphabetical Collection.* Rev. ed. Trans. Benedicta Ward. Kalamazoo, MI: Cistercian Publications, 1984.

*To Love as God Loves: Conversations with the Early Church* by Roberta C. Bondi. Philadelphia: Fortress Press, 1987.

*To Pray and to Love: Conversations on Prayer with the Early Church* by Roberta C. Bondi. Minneapolis, MN: Fortress Press, 1991.

*Silence, Solitude, Simplicity: A Hermit's Love Affair with a Noisy, Crowded, and Complicated World* by Sister Jeremy Hall. Collegeville, MN: Liturgical Press, 2007.

*Women at Prayer* by Mary Collins. New York: Paulist Press, 1988.

## NOTES

1. Laura Swan, *The Forgotten Desert Mothers: Sayings, Lives, and Stories of Early Christian Women* (New York: Paulist Press, 2001), 10.

2. Mary Forman, *Praying with the Desert Mothers* (Collegeville, MN: Liturgical Press, 2005), 33. [Quotation about the desert as "the region of the tombs . . . " is her translation from Antoine

Guillaumont, *Aux origenes du monachisme chrétien: Pour une phénoménologie du monachisme,* Spiritualité orientale, 30 (Maine & Loire: Abbaye de Bellefontaine, 1979), 77-78.]

3. Wendy M. Wright, "Desert Listening," in John S. Mogabgab, ed., *Communion, Community, Commonweal: Readings for Spiritual Leadership* (Nashville, TN: The Upper Room, 1995), 123.

4. Swan, *Forgotten Desert Mothers,* 23.

5. Benedicta Ward, trans., *The Sayings of the Desert Fathers: The Alphabetical Collection,* rev. ed. (Kalamazoo, MI: Cistercian Publications, 1984), 233–34.

6. Ibid., 84.

7. Ibid., 231.

8. Swan, *Forgotten Desert Mothers,* 47.

9. Ward, *Sayings of the Desert Fathers,* 139.

10. Swan, *Forgotten Desert Mothers,* 28.

11. Father Luke Dysinger, "Accepting the Embrace of God: The Ancient Art of *Lectio Divina,*" http://www.valyermo.com/ld-art.html.

12. Ibid.

13. Michael Casey, *Sacred Reading: The Ancient Art of Lectio Divina* (Ligouri, MO: Ligouri/Triumph, 1996), 7.

14. Ibid., 8.

15. Swan, *Forgotten Desert Mothers,* 28.

16. Ward, *Sayings of the Desert Fathers,* 175.

17. Kathleen Norris, *The Cloister Walk* (New York: Riverhead Books/Penguin Putnam, 1996), xiii.

18. Thomas Moore, "Neither Here nor There: Allies of Transitional Places," *Parabola* 25, no. 1 (February 2000): 36.

19. Wright, "Desert Listening," 122–23.

20. Ibid., 125.

21. Related in Robert H. Hopcke and Paul A. Schwartz, *Little Flowers of Francis of Assisi: A New Translation* (Boston: New Seeds Books, 2006), 38–39.

22. Ibid., 53–55.

23. Ward, *Sayings of the Desert Fathers,* 84.

24. Roberta C. Bondi, *To Love as God Loves: Conversations with the Early Church* (Philadelphia: Fortress Press, 1987), 18.

25. Roberta C. Bondi, *To Pray and to Love: Conversations on Prayer with the Early Church* (Minneapolis, MN: Fortress Press, 1991), 101.

26. Bondi, *To Love as God Loves,* 58.

27. Evagrius Ponticus, *The Praktikos,* as quoted in Kathleen Norris, *Acedia & Me: A Marriage, Monks, and a Writer's Life* (New York: Riverhead Books/Penguin Putnam, 2008), preface.

28. Ward, *Sayings of the Desert Fathers,* 235.

29. Bondi, *To Love as God Loves,* 74.

30. Ibid., 75.

31. Ibid.

32. Norris, *Acedia & Me*, 3.

33. Ward, *Sayings of the Desert Fathers*, 83.

34. Ibid., 234–35.

35. Margot H. King, "The Desert Mothers: A Survey of the Feminine Anchoretic Tradition in Western Europe," http://www.peregrina.com/matrologia_latina/DesertMothers1.html.

36. Ibid.

37. Ibid.

38. Ibid.

39. Swan, *Forgotten Desert Mothers*, 102.

40. Ibid., 83.

41. Maria Kouli, trans. "Life of St. Mary of Egypt," in Alice-Mary Talbot, ed., *Holy Women of Byzantium: Ten Saints' Lives in English Translation* (Washington, D.C.: Dumbarton Oaks, 2006), 91.

42. Gregory, Bishop of Nyssa, *The Life of Saint Macrina*, trans. Kevin Corrigan (Eugene, OR: Wipf and Stock Publishers, 2001), 23.

43. Swan, *Forgotten Desert Mothers*, 136–37.

44. Paulinus's description of Melania the Elder is from his Epistle 29 to Sulpicius Severus, found in the *Corpus Scriptorum Ecclesiasticorum Latinorum*. This English translation is from Elizabeth A. Clark, *Women in the Early Church* (Collegeville, MN: Liturgical Press, 1983), 220.

45. Gerontius, "The Life of the Holy Melania," in Joan M. Petersen, ed. and trans., *Handmaids of the Lord: Contemporary Descriptions of Feminine Asceticism in the First Six Christian Centuries* (Kalamazoo, MI: Cistercian Publications, 1996), 326.

46. Ibid., 327.

47. Agnes Smith Lewis, *A Translation of the Four Gospels from the Syriac of the Sinaitic Palimpsest* (New York: Macmillan and Company, 1894), xi. Downloaded from http://www.archive.org/details/atranslationfou00lewigoog.

48. Ibid., xii.

49. John the Recluse, in Agnes Smith Lewis, trans., *Select Narratives of Holy Women from the Syro-Antiochene or Sinai Palimpsest* (London: C. J. Clay and Sons, 1900), 1. Downloaded from http://www.archive.org/details/selectnarratives017362mbp.50. Lewis, *A Translation of the Four Gospels*, xix.

51. As this book neared completion, a book about Agnes Smith Lewis and Margaret Dunlop Gibson was published. See *The Sisters of Sinai: How Two Lady Adventurers Discovered the Hidden Gospels* by Janice Soskice (New York: Knopf, 2009). [Paperback edition to be published August 2010.]

# SAY WHAT YOU SEE

## *The Book of Hildegard of Bingen*

### INTRODUCTION

It's been half a lifetime since I sat in the opening session of a college course on women and religion. As the professor made her way through an overview of the semester, she said that we would be studying some of the medieval women mystics. I didn't know what a mystic was, but the word seized my imagination. I wanted to find out.

One of the mystics I met during that semester was Hildegard of Bingen, the famed German abbess, visionary, and writer who lived from 1098 to 1179. She was the last of ten children born to a noble family. Hildegard's parents offered her to God as a tithe and placed her in the hermitage of Jutta, a family friend, when Hildegard was eight. Jutta taught Hildegard a monastic way of life, and, with a group of other women who joined them, they formed a community that followed the Benedictine Rule. Hildegard became abbess of the community after Jutta's death in 1136.

Hildegard's work as writer did not begin until she was forty-two years old. Her first and most famous book is the visionary work called the *Scivias*, which means "Know the Ways." Although she had experienced visions since the age of five, Hildegard had kept them private for nearly four decades. She writes that she took up the work in response to a voice that called to her in the midst of a vision; the voice said to her, "Say and write what you see and hear,"[1] and, with a voice more insistent, "Cry out therefore, and write thus!"[2]

Having begun, Hildegard wrote with a vengeance, her curiosity leading her across a diverse range of disciplines. She produced two other visionary works, an encyclopedia of natural science titled *Book of Simple Medicine*, and a companion book titled *Book of Composite Medicine*. Animals, herbs, trees, gems, moral symbolism, healing charms, physics, cosmology, ethics, and doctrine were among the subjects that, with the scribal assistance of others including her friend and secretary, the monk Volmar, Hildegard wrote about with curiosity and authority. Nearly a millennium later, she is perhaps most widely remembered as a composer; she wrote more than seventy liturgical songs, many of which remain in use today.

Hildegard was also a prolific correspondent, communicating with abbesses, abbots, priests, kings, bishops, the pope, laywomen, and laymen. Several hundred of her letters survive, and in them we see with particular clarity Hildegard's strength and her relentless courage in confronting brokenness within the church and the people she believed were contributing to that brokenness. In her time, she became known as "the Sybil of the Rhine" and was sought after for her counsel on all manner of affairs from personal to political to medical. She did not hesitate to offer her opinions unsolicited; she could be fierce in upbraiding those who incurred her displeasure, and no one, not even the emperor Frederick Barbarossa, who was her patron, was exempt.

In the Middle Ages and beyond, Hildegard and other women mystics went to extraordinary lengths to find a rhythm of life that enabled them to seek God and to leave behind some words describing what they found in their searching. They did this with great sacrifice and often at great risk to themselves: the Spanish mystic Teresa of Ávila, for instance, was brought before the Inquisition; the Beguine Marguerite Porete was burned at the stake as a heretic; and Hadewijch, another Beguine, was forced out of her community.

Hildegard and her kinswomen remind us that seeking God is not a luxury. It's not something we pursue only if we have the time for it, the leisure for it, the resources for it, the disposition toward it. The mystical life does not depend, either, on grand visions; nor is it something we seek out only for ourselves. The kind of life to which these women point us is one that is as simple and as complicated as opening our eyes to the presence of God who is always with us, opening our hearts to receive the wisdom that God has to offer us, and opening our hands to participate in the healing of the world.

More than two decades since I first began to meet them, Hildegard and her sisters continue to inspire and challenge me. These mystic women, who remained intimately entwined with the institutional church while claiming a visionary place within it, remain wise traveling companions as I continue to make a creative home for myself along the edges of the church, making it up as I go along.

Hildegard and other visionary women invite us to ask, How do we seek God? Where do we perceive the presence of the holy? How far are we willing to go to find it? What feeds our minds and imaginations in our searching? How does our hunger for God impact our other relationships—with institutions and systems and other people? How do we claim and create our own visionary spaces in the church and in the world?

In the coming days, may these women of vision inspire your way.

# PRAYER FOR THE MORNING

With this new day,
we open our eyes
and we pray:
God, inhabit our seeing.
Live in our looking.
Be our vision and our sight.
Illumine us, that we may perceive you,
know you, welcome you
in all the ways you go hiding
in this world.

# PRAYER FOR THE EVENING

Now be rest for our eyes,
God of the evening.
In these dark hours,
repair us, renew us,
restore and redeem.

# 1

## LIVING BY VISION

I pull my copy of the *Scivias* from the bookshelf, run my finger down its battered spine, and remember. The spine gained its creases during a time, more than a decade ago, when I used the book as a source for *lectio*. It had been about a year since I had moved from a congregation to the retreat center where I served as artist-in-residence. I was still settling into my new skin, still discerning what it meant to pursue a call to a ministry that intertwined art and writing.

I found myself drawn once again toward the women mystics I had first encountered in college. These women had found a way to live by their visions, and their vision; these women had figured out how to remain connected with the church while claiming their own visionary and creative space within it. I thought they might have a powerful word for me as I worked to carve out a path where there was no path.

I took up the *Scivias*—hardly the easiest material for *lectio*—not solely for the content of Hildegard's words, though her writing offered a plenitude of material for reflection and prayer. More than this, I sought her words as a way to be in the company of a woman who had been fierce in finding her own way and had also, beyond this, chosen a path that gave credence to the imagination as a place for meeting God. Vision by vision, image by image, Hildegard offered—and offers still—a world in which words are not the only currency, and what meets our waking eyes is not all there is.

Who serves as a touchstone for you? Are there writers you return to time and again? What do you find in their company?

### BLESSING

When there is no way,
no path, no road made plain,
may there be wise ones
who inspire you to see
where the way could begin.

# 2

## HOW IT WORKS

The *Scivias* works like this: Hildegard offers a series of twenty-six visions, which she divides into three books having to do with creation, redemption, and salvation history. In the course of this, she explores a range of topics including the nature of the universe, the relationship of body and soul, the Incarnation, the redeeming work of Christ, the Trinity, the end of the world, and the new heaven and new earth.

Hildegard recounts each vision, then offers reflection and interpretation of the vision's meaning. She clearly understands that the visions are not solely for her benefit. Nor are they primarily devotional material. Hildegard is doing theology here. She approaches each vision as a text for theological reflection that has import for the church. She works to interpret and convey, vision by vision, God's desire for order and wholeness not only in the life of the church but also in the world and throughout the entire cosmos.

So, for instance, Hildegard will briefly convey the content of a vision, such as this one:

> Then I saw a bright light, and in this light the figure of a man the color of a sapphire, which was all blazing with a gentle glowing fire. And that bright light bathed the whole of the glowing fire, and the glowing fire bathed the bright light; and the bright light and the glowing fire poured over the whole human figure, so that the three were one light in one power of potential.[3]

Hildegard then goes on to offer an interpretation of the vision. In this vision, for instance, the sapphire man designates the Trinity, with the bright light signifying the Father, the sapphire man the Son, and the glowing fire the Holy Spirit. Beyond this, she describes how we should not forget to invoke God "in these Three Persons." As she continues to explicate the vision, she draws from scripture, the natural world, and its phenomena to describe the unitive nature of the Trinity. Hildegard even likens the Trinity to human speech. "How?" she writes.

> In a word there is sound, force and breath. It has sound that it may be heard, meaning that it may be understood, and breath that it may be pronounced.

In the sound, then, observe the Father, Who manifests all things with ineffable power; in the meaning, the Son, Who was miraculously begotten of the Father; and in the breath, the Holy Spirit, Who sweetly burns in Them. But where no sound is heard, no meaning is used and no breath is lifted, there no word will be understood; so also the Father, Son and Holy Spirit are not divided from one another, but do Their works together.[4]

BLESSING

May the God
who works together
as Three-in-One
work also in you
with power and with grace.

# 3

## CAVEAT

I should say, before we go further, that Hildegard can be a bit much and then some. Even as I'm drawn to her work, it sometimes overwhelms. As Hildegard's visions go, the sapphire man is pretty tame and soothing. Elsewhere, her visions can daunt with their intensity and complexity. Blood and smoke and circles within circles. Fire and whirlwinds, hairy beasts and winged beings. Celestial wonders and complex architectural forms. A maze of characters belonging to the realms of heaven or hell, come to grace or to plague the beings of earth.

*Shhh*, I sometimes want to say to her. *Easy there. Take a breath.*

Hildegard works to see and explain the things of God and their import in the redemption of creation, and she clearly desires to be comprehensive in her attempt. Reading her, I think sometimes of Picasso, how in his paintings he worked to expose every angle. Hildegard wants to expose what we have missed of God, to reveal all the angles of the Divine.

Humans are not meant to see this way all the time. We cannot sustain this seeing for long stretches. Even one step removed, reading what Hildegard sees rather than receiving it firsthand ourselves, is best taken slowly, in small doses. *Shhh, easy.*

And still, amid my caution, something in the sheer force of Hildegard's seeing, the wildness of its intensity, the way she abandons herself to it and to the One who gives it, tugs at me. Makes me want to look and look harder and look completely. Calls me not to turn away.

BLESSING

May God bless your seeing,
inhabit your reading,
draw you to look deeper,
remind you to breathe.

4

WISE SIFTER OF ALL THINGS

When I made my prayerful way through the *Scivias* years ago, I kept a journal. I did this in part as a strategy against losing myself amid the density of the book. Writing provided a way to be in conversation with Hildegard's words, and it helped me navigate my way through them: an Ariadne's thread, say, through Hildegard's maze.

Looking back through the journal, I am struck by how often the small details among Hildegard's visions captured my imagination and gave me something I needed. As is typical with *lectio*, the doorways into prayer came not in trying to take in an entire passage or a whole swirling vision but rather in opening my attention to the small, subtle details tucked in amongst the whole: a portion of an image, a phrase turned just so.

In a vision in which Hildegard describes an array of women gathered nearby the wall of a building, what drew my eye was not the meticulous way she set forth her explication of the building as symbolizing the history of salvation; nor even, in that moment, the wondrous diversity of the women, who symbolize Virtues—qualities that God seeks to cultivate in human souls. Among this virtuous gathering of Truth, Peace, Beatitude, and their friends, the one who commanded my gaze that day was the one Hildegard identifies as Discretion. "She is the wise sifter of all things," Hildegard says of her, "holding what should be held and cutting off what should be cut off, as the wheat is separated from the tares."[5]

*The wise sifter of all things.* In a time when I was deep into discerning where my path lay, this kind of image could set me to pondering and lead me into prayer. This ongoing work of choosing, of trying to figure out what our choices are, of weighing and measuring and sorting and occasional wild guessing: this is often so intangible and so trackless. Amid this, Hildegard provided a picture that helped orient me. It struck me that *the wise sifter of all things* not only described a Virtue; it was a name for God. As I sifted among the choices—the choices that I knew and those I had yet to see and name—this image went with me, haunting me, bidding me turn toward God for wisdom to find my unfolding path. Hildegard's image reassured me that even at its most mundane, this sifting and sorting and choosing is holy work, and we are not meant to do it alone.

BLESSING

In every choosing, every sorting,
every deciding, every guess,
may you go in the company
of the Wise Sifter of All Things.

# 5

## PATIENCE AND LONGING

The Virtues are a compelling aspect of Hildegard's visions. A dazzling and varied group including Humility, Charity, Hope, Wisdom, Fortitude, and Celestial Desire, these womanly figures populate the final book of the *Scivias*, occupying the building that signifies the history of salvation. They speak in their own voices, as when Wisdom cries out, much as she does in the Bible, "O slow people, why do you not come? Would not help be given you, if you sought to come?"[6]

The Virtues are crucial to Hildegard's visions and to the theology she creates from them. In describing the importance of the Virtues, Barbara Newman notes that the Latin word *virtus* can be translated not only as "virtue" but also as "energy" or "power" and that Hildegard draws on both of these meanings. The Virtues are aspects or qualities of God that invite the participation of humans; they inspire us to act for good in the world.[7] Hildegard herself clarifies, "not that any virtue is a living form in itself, but a brilliant star given by God that shines forth in human deeds. For humanity is perfected by virtues, which are the deeds of people working in God."[8] Although depicting the Virtues as women was not original to Hildegard, as Newman notes, Hildegard was intentional about depicting them as feminine figures "because in Hildegard's symbolic theology the feminine represents the sphere of synergy in which divinity and humanity work together for salvation."[9]

It was among the Virtues that I found, doing *lectio* with the *Scivias* years ago, another small detail that opened a doorway into prayer. In a vision titled "The Tower of Anticipation of God's Will," Hildegard describes seeing an "iron-colored tower" in the middle of the outer wall of the building of salvation. In the tower she sees and describes five figures—women, again—who are the Virtues of Celestial Love, Discipline, Modesty, Mercy, and Victory. She also describes seeing two more Virtues inside the building—Patience and Longing. "Longing stands next to Patience," Hildegard writes.[10] Noting this detail in my journal, I wrote, *Oh yes she does!* Amid the wonderings and siftings that attended my path in those days, not only with respect to my vocation but elsewhere in my life, I thought, *Yes, Patience and Longing stand together.* And I, with all the yearning I held amid mysteries that were slow to unfold, thought, *Yes, and I am wedged in between them.*

How do Patience and Longing live together in you?

### BLESSING

That you will know your longings,
that they will show you their face,
that you will be graceful toward them
and the slow wisdom they bear.

# 6

## "LONGING STANDS NEXT TO PATIENCE"

Longing would sometimes
like to be assigned
a different spot.
Would like to be less near
this one who approaches everything
with such equanimity.
Would like some distance
from the measured way
that Patience marks time,
holds herself with such politeness
toward its passing.

Patience knows this
about Longing.
Accepts it,
even loves it about her.

This makes Longing
crazy.

Patience has not told her
she has some envy
of Longing's perfect ache
or that she thinks
it must be an art
to hold oneself
so perpetually poised
toward the horizon.

For her part,
Longing has not confessed
that there are days
she finds Patience restful.
Soothing. A relief.

Meanwhile,
by little
and by little,
so slowly its appearance
will startle them both,
a horizon is drawing near.

## BLESSING

May Longing and Patience
teach you by turns:
not just the fire but the tending of it,
not just the well but the digging;
not just the vision but the enduring it asks,
by day and by darkness drawing us on.

# 7

## MANIAC

"All should trust in Me to feed them in all their needs," God says through Hildegard.[11]

That phrase, *all their needs.*

*I am struggling mightily these days with my hungers and needs,* I wrote in my *lectio* journal. *Yesterday was a day of feeling overwhelmed and frustrated and angry with all the unknowing.*

Hildegard's words prompted me to return to Annie Dillard and her book *Pilgrim at Tinker Creek*. In the chapter "The Waters of Separation," I found these words:

> There is not a guarantee in the world. Oh your needs are guaranteed, your needs are absolutely guaranteed by the most stringent of warranties, in the plainest, truest words: knock; seek; ask. But you must read the fine print. "Not as the world giveth, give I unto you." That's the catch. If you can catch it it will catch you up, aloft, up to any gap at all, and you'll come back, for you will come back, transformed in a way you may not have bargained for—dribbling and crazed. . . . You see the needs of your own

spirit met whenever you have asked, and you have learned that the outrageous guarantee holds. You see the creatures die, and you know you will die. And one day it occurs to you that you must not need life. Obviously. And then you're gone. You have finally understood that you're dealing with a maniac.[12]

*A maniac, indeed,* I wrote. *I am searching for the mercy of a maniac who seems to delight in outrageous possibilities and maddening timing and in opening the ground beneath our feet, carving a fissure, breaking open a gap from which we will not exit the same way that we entered.*
*Mercy, mercy, mercy.*

### BLESSING

May the mercy
of the maddening,
outrageous, outlandish God
meet you and feed you
in every need.

# 8

## FRIENDS OF JESUS

The mystics across history seem, by and large, to understand Annie Dillard's assertion that she is dealing with a maniac, though they perhaps would not have used this word. They comprehend that the God in whose grip they live does not operate entirely by reason. This God has a passion for order that often, to our eyes, wears the face of chaos; works within our deepest desires to draw us toward places we would never venture on our own; meets our resistance with grace that does not always feel graceful. The mystics are those who understand this about God, and yet desire God nonetheless.

The mystics have a fierce kind of seeing and knowing about God that enables a depth of intimacy with God that sometimes baffles. They speak to God as to one with whom they are familiar, as indeed they are; there is not always room or need for politeness or circumspection.

The story is told from the life of Saint Teresa of Ávila, the great Spanish nun, mystic, and reformer of the Carmelite order, that on a day when she is struggling through muck and mire—and stories vary as to whether this is literal muck encountered on a journey or the figurative muck through which she had to wade much of her life—she hears Jesus say, "See, Teresa, this is how I treat my friends."

Teresa, not one to mince words, shoots back, "No wonder you have so few."

BLESSING

When your devotion draws you
down a difficult way,
may you know
the friendship of Christ,
who goes with you.

9

THE LIVING LIGHT

In describing the origin of the visions that gave rise to the *Scivias*, Hildegard writes, "Heaven was opened and a fiery light of exceeding brilliance came and permeated my whole brain, and inflamed my whole heart and my whole breast, not like a burning but like a warming flame, as the sun warms anything its rays touch." With fire came illumination: "And immediately I knew the meaning of the exposition of the Scriptures," she writes, "namely the Psalter, the Gospel and the other catholic volumes of both the Old and the New Testaments." Along with the visions she experienced a voice from heaven, which said to her, "I am the Living Light, Who illuminates the darkness."[13] This Living Light permeates Hildegard's visionary experience.

In our own time, some have speculated that Hildegard's visions had a physiological origin; that her descriptions of the light and visual patterns she saw, combined with the pain she felt, suggest she may have experienced migraine auras that contributed to the images she perceived. However, as

Barbara Newman points out, while migraines may have played a role in Hildegard's visions, they cannot account for all of them; such a condition "no more 'explains' her prophetic vocation than Dostoevsky's epilepsy explains his literary genius."[14]

Hildegard herself understood her visions as gifts from God that she received with clarity and consciousness. She writes that "the visions I saw I did not perceive in dreams, or sleep, or delirium, or by the eyes of the body, or by the ears of the outer self, or in hidden places; but I received them while awake and seeing with a pure mind and the eyes and ears of the inner self, in open places, as God willed it."[15]

Whatever the cause of the visions, Hildegard knew that their significance lay in discerning their meaning. Hildegard devotes far more time to explaining the visions than to describing them. Whatever the medium, whatever its cause, its import came in the message it conveyed.

### BLESSING

The light of God to illumine you,
the fire of God to warm you,
the brilliance of God to wake you
in mind and ear and eye.

# 10

## OUR MYSTIC, OURSELVES

Living as we do nearly a millennium after Hildegard, it's crucial to recognize that Hildegard was, as are we all, a creature of her times. However groundbreaking and visionary she was, Hildegard was also embedded in a medieval psychology and in a culture that tended to hold clear views regarding the structures of class, religion, and gender. Like many monastic leaders, Hildegard allowed only wealthy women into her community. Her writings indicate that she shared the prevailing narrow views regarding people of non-Christian faith. And for all the ways that she called into question gender stereotypes in her ministry as a charismatic leader, preacher, and visionary, Hildegard held a largely traditional perspective on the role of women. The powerful imagery of female figures such as the Virtues in Hildegard's visions did not always correspond to similar roles for human females. In the *Scivias*, for instance, Hildegard conveys that God prohibits women from serving as priests, "for they are an infirm and weak habitation, appointed to bear children and diligently nurture them."[16]

Though we might prefer to tidy up the problematic aspects of Hildegard's life and thought, we do well to resist such an urge. Better instead to let Hildegard stand in her complicated and flawed brilliance, and pray that whatever faults our twenty-first-century eyes may perceive in her, God would heal our own faults this day, this time. We do well also to tread with caution in trying to fashion Hildegard into a figurehead for agendas she might not have claimed for herself—would not have had the framework to claim for herself—so many centuries ago. Better to pray that this remarkable woman who provided the vision needed in her own age would inspire us to seek and proclaim the vision we need in our own lives, in our own age, for the life of the world.

Hildegard's life finally prompts us not to wish we could change aspects of her story; rather, her story leads us to turn our attention toward our own story and our own seeking after God. As with each of the women in this book, Hildegard's life invites us to ask questions of our own lives. Where do her struggles intersect with your own? How do her gifts help you think about yours? How do her fierce devotion and vision inspire you and call you? What questions does Hildegard stir up for you?

BLESSING

In the light and complexity
of Hildegard's life,
may you see your own life
more clearly.

# 11

## ILLUMINATED

Part of Hildegard's enduring fame lies in the artwork—illuminations—that accompany her visions. Some scholars have speculated that Hildegard created the illuminations herself. There is little evidence to support this; it's more likely, as Barbara Newman suggests, that the artist was one of the nuns of Hildegard's community or a monk from one of the monasteries associated with Hildegard. We can presume, however, that even if she didn't wield the paintbrush, Hildegard oversaw the creation of the illuminations and so was intimately involved in their production.

More than merely illustrating the content of Hildegard's visions, the illuminations offered viewers a doorway, an invitation to walk into her visionary world and to see it for themselves. What Hildegard describes in words takes on its own life in the space of the illuminated page. Hildegard can describe a vision of a man in sapphire blue or the cosmos in the shape of an egg or the choirs of angels ranked in circles. But to see the images whose making she directed opens a new world of perception and multisensory experience.

Barbara Newman writes that, with the presence of the artwork, this already multifaceted book "may be considered as a multimedia work in which the arts of illumination, music and drama contribute their several beauties to enhance the text and heighten the visionary message."[17]

For centuries, the earliest surviving illuminated version of the *Scivias* was the one created sometime around 1165 in the scriptorium of the convent that Hildegard founded at Rupertsberg, near Bingen. Newman notes that this manuscript contained thirty-five "remarkable" miniatures incorporating gold and silver leaf and that they were quite distinct from other illuminated manuscripts of the day, both in style and form. Sadly, Newman notes also that this manuscript disappeared in World War II during the bombing of Dresden in 1945. It has not been seen since. She tells, however, of a providential photocopy made in 1927, from which a group of nuns of Eibingen, the daughter-house that Hildegard founded, prepared a facsimile that took them seven years to replicate by hand.[18]

BLESSING

Between the words,
beneath the words,
beyond the words,
may God meet you
in the places
where words cannot go.

# 12

## BELOVED

In her preface to the *Scivias*, Caroline Walker Bynum points out that Hildegard was atypical of the women mystics of the medieval period. Where much of the writing of other mystics is marked by intimate, ecstatic experiences of union with God, Hildegard's visions are broader in scope and serve primarily as a source for theological reflection. "A visionary who took her revelations as a text for exegesis," Bynum writes, "not an experience for reliving, Hildegard was not, technically speaking, a mystic at all. She wrote not about union but about doctrine."[19] Bynum continues, "If one pauses for a moment while reading and looks beyond the elaborate and often confusing details of Hildegard's revelations, one realizes one has been shown the structure of salvation. With Hildegard one does not feel; one sees."[20]

Although Hildegard's visions lack the more affective qualities present in many other mystical accounts, the God whom Hildegard encounters is one who, if less intimately effusive, clearly knows her as beloved. At one point, Hildegard relates that she hears God say to her, "Oh, how beautiful are your eyes, which tell of divinity when the divine counsel dawns in them!"[21]

While Hildegard is sparing in her use of the bridal imagery that pervades the work of other medieval mystics, she does not abandon it entirely; one might even suspect that she so assumes an intimate relationship with Christ that she does not harp on it. And indeed such imagery makes an appearance at the very end of the *Scivias*—after the climax, as it were, where Hildegard wants to press home the point of writing the book in the first place. As she closes, she draws from the sensual imagery of both the Song of Songs and the book of Revelation as she writes, "And whoever tastes this prophecy and fixes it in his memory will become the mountain of myrrh, and of frankincense, and of all aromatical spices, and the diffusion of many blessings; he will ascend like Abraham from blessing to blessing. And the new spouse, the Bride of the Lamb, will take him to herself, for he is a pillar in the sight of God."[22]

In turning to such images at the last, Hildegard lets us know—we who have made with her the visionary journey that took her ten years to write down—that the point of all this is to draw us deeper into the God who counts us as beloved. The God whom Hildegard has seen, the Living Light who becomes known to her in dazzling complexity: this God longs for us. Desires us. Seeks us out. And not only for ourselves—though God seeks us in our singularity, to be sure—but also as part of the whole beloved creation that God—stubborn, maniacal God—is working to redeem.

BLESSING

May you know yourself
beloved and blessed
by the God who
seeks you,
desires you,
calls you by name.


# 13

## THE OTHER WAY AROUND

This, perhaps, is the enduring gift of the mystical tradition: it acknowledges the presence of a God who desires us and seeks to become known to us in whatever way we can understand. In the writings of the medieval mystics, this knowing often carries with it, as in the Hebrew sense of "to know," an erotic element. We see this, for instance, in the work of Hadewijch, who in the thirteenth century lived in what is now Belgium. In describing an experience at Eucharist—a sacrament that often opened a doorway into mystical encounter—Hadewijch writes of a vision of Christ:

He came in the form and clothing of a Man, as he was on the day when he gave us his Body for the first time; looking like a Human Being and a Man, wonderful, and beautiful, and with glorious face, he came to me as humbly as anyone who wholly belongs to another. Then he gave himself to me in the shape of the Sacrament, in its outward form, as the custom is; and then he gave me to drink from the chalice, in form and taste, as the custom is. After that he came himself to me, took me entirely in his arms, and pressed me to him; and all my members felt his in full felicity, in accordance with the desire of my heart and my humanity. So I was outwardly satisfied and fully transported. Also then, for a short while, I had the strength to bear this; but soon, after a short time, I lost that manly beauty outwardly in the sight of his form. I saw him completely come to nought and so fade and all at once dissolve that I could no longer recognize or perceive him outside me, and I could no longer distinguish him within me. Then it was to me as if we were one without difference.[23]

Reading such accounts, some have chalked them up to frustrated sexual desire, more horny than holy in their origins. Yet such a view poses as narrow an understanding of mysticism as it does of sexuality.

Talking with an acquaintance one day, a monastic woman well versed in mystics such as Hadewijch, I asked her what she made of the erotic language present in their writings. "These were women," she said, "who gave themselves wholly to God. In trying to describe their utter love of God, this was the only language that even came close." Where some would see such eroticism as extreme, it actually pales, she suggested, in its ability to convey the depth and fullness of what the mystics experienced.

I wonder if these women, had they heard the suggestion that mysticism was a substitute for sex, might have suggested that the truth was the other way around: that for those not called to lives of celibacy, sex offers but a glimpse of what the mystics had found.

What do you make of imagery and language such as Hadewijch used? Does it challenge you? comfort you? Does it raise questions? invitations? What words, what language, what images would you use to describe what you know of Christ?

BLESSING

May you know
the God who knows you.

# 14
# INTO THE WORLD

What the mysticism-as-substitute-for-sex assessment risks missing is that ecstatic union with Christ was rarely seen as the goal; it was, rather, a gift and a grace that helped inspire and sustain the work to which God had called the mystic. Hadewijch's experience of union with Christ in the Eucharist, for instance, prepares her for another vision in which, after she is shown further wonders, she hears a voice telling her, "Return again into your material being, and let your works blossom forth."[24] She is not to remain in a perpetual unitive ecstasy intended only for herself. She is to get to work.

True mysticism does not consist of eternal bliss. It doesn't even depend on the experience of visions and ecstatic union with the Divine. Though some few may experience visions and ecstasies, the mystical life does not find its center in this. Such occurrences come as a gift, a grace, and—most important—a by-product of seeking after God. They are not the goal. God provides them for the purpose of sustaining us for our work in the world that God loves and calls us to enter and engage.

In their book *Inviting the Mystic, Supporting the Prophet: An Introduction to Spiritual Direction*, Katherine Marie Dyckman and L. Patrick Carroll write, "The person deepening in prayer and growing in faith is not called *out* of the world to be with God, but is more profoundly immersed *in* that world's heart." They cite Teresa of Ávila, "who was not in some ivory tower feeling good with Jesus. In fact," they write, "out of her own darkness of many years, she remained balanced and witty, founded several new monasteries, and reformed her entire congregation. She found time to advise many priests and to do a great deal of writing. Somehow the great heroes of prayer became great because their prayer immersed them in life."[25]

The true mystic path does not offer an escape from the world; it offers a doorway for entering more deeply into it. It calls us to look at our ordinary lives and to see into the gaps, the possibilities, the painfulness of the world, the beauty of it. It means not closing our eyes to the world to seek only our own bliss but rather turning our gaze toward the world and to the God who calls us here.

### BLESSING

That you will go into the heart of God
and find the heart of the world.
That you will go into the world
and find the heart of God.

# 15

*The Secret Room*

## TESTIMONY

Some years ago, sitting in a small group, I glanced at a friend just as she opened her mouth to speak. Something in her manner—the tilt of her head, perhaps, or the briefest pause she took as she gathered herself—caused the thought to flash through my mind: *She looks like a woman about to testify.* At the same moment, an idea was planted: a character, a story. A tale about a woman who sees things, things that others cannot, and must learn to say what she sees.

I carried the seeing woman around with me for a while, thinking of her from time to time, waiting. I spent a fine season of summer mornings sitting at my drafting table with a notebook, listening to her, listening into her story, writing down the bits and pieces that came. I discovered that fiction comes from a different place, a neighborhood near but other than where my usual writing lives. It is more like prayer in the kind of listening and waiting it invites: an act of contemplation. It stirred memories of the first book I undertook, a long story written when I was perhaps eight. I remembered the utter absorption of inhabiting a story, of being part of its creation. Taking up this novel, the one about the woman who sees, is the closest I have ever come to recapturing that sense of abandoning myself to a story.

It's been a long while since I've taken up that summer notebook in which I began to set down what I heard in my listening. Though I haven't worked on the book in several years, I think it's been working on me. I don't know if it will ever find its finish, at least not in the form that I first began to imagine. But I can show you its beginning. Maybe it's something meant for you to take up yourself, something that will waken the beginnings of a story of your own. Something about a woman who sees.

It's called *Testimony*. It begins like this:

*I cannot give you any doctrine, only testimony. Places have spirits; they haunt us as they are haunted by the lives that have been lived in their shelter, on their ground.*[26]—George Ella Lyon

The grace in this is that I'm not the only one, not the only woman ever to have seen things that I can't explain. I've read some of the stuff written by women who had visions, and some of it scared me because it all seemed so big. Like Hildegard, with all these people everywhere, circles within circles of heavenly host or all the virtues standing around in a huge build-ing that's supposed to symbolize the church or figures with brilliant lights radiating in rings from them. Or like St. Teresa, with her huge castle and all its rooms that are the places a soul journeys through. I got lost some-times, trying to keep track of what happens in every part.

What I see seems so small by comparison, so tiny; sometimes all I get are pieces, just scraps and shadows of images. How can you call a shadow a vision? Maybe there's not visions at all. Just flotsam and jetsam crashing around my brain. Leftover shreds of dreams, old imaginings, things I saw or read or dreamed once and forgot.

But I read Julian, too, what she wrote there in her cell in Norwich with her cat and her three windows, one into the church and one into her garden and one out onto the world. I liked her. God showing her the whole world in something the size of a hazelnut, so small she could put it in the palm of her hand. A little thing.

I said that maybe these aren't visions at all, but maybe what I mean is that they *are* visions, really, but they're nothing special—that everyone has some way of seeing or imagining or hoping, of intuiting some part of the whole, getting a glimpse of the holy, and this is mine. Maybe it's all revelation, everything that passes through us, every piece of the landscape around us that becomes that much more *there*, becomes more itself and rooted and part of a place because we've seen it—really *seen* it—and touched it and loved it and maybe even left it.

BLESSING

That you will see in the way
God longs you to see.
That you will be given vision
that speaks precisely to
and through who you are.
That the holy will reveal itself,
unhide itself,
divulge itself in you.

# 16

## ALL THAT

Wading among the words of Hildegard and her visionary sisters, still I come back around to wondering, *do I want God to be so present to me?* All that knowing. All that wisdom. All that love. All that power. All that immanence. All that. I think again of Annie Dillard's words from *Teaching a Stone to Talk*, which I shared back in the Book of Eve, how she confronts us with the question of what it is we're doing when we call upon God. Just how much do I want God to know me anyway?

It's questions like these that give rise to poems like this:

*Chops*

There is something of God
that is consuming,
and I am starting to wonder
if what wakes me in the night
is the sound of her

sitting in the corner
calmly licking her chops.

BLESSING

May you abide
the longing of God
who yet stands back,
holds back,
waits.

# 17

## ORDINARY MYSTICISM

What the medieval mystics found is our invitation too. Not to seek out dramatic experience for the sake of dramatic experience. But to look at what is around us, to look again, to look more closely, to open ourselves to the God who lives among all this and who invites us to see differently.

In her essay on mysticism in *Amazing Grace*, Kathleen Norris writes, "I find that I appreciate mysticism best in its most ordinary manifestation, as a means for tapping into the capacity for holiness that exists in us all."[27]

BLESSING

In the midst of your life:
the daily of it,
the ordinary of it,
the noontime and night of it,
let there be moments
that open to you
the hallowed and holy of it.

# 18

## LEARNING TO SEE

The mystics invite us to remember what we all too often forget: God is everywhere present in the world, suffusing creation with the being of God. Once in a while, if we keep our eyes open, if we look closely enough, something amid the familiar reveals itself, offers itself to us in a new way. What we know, what we have learned, is taken apart. Is remade. Remakes us.

Our work and our call is to keep washing our eyes again and again, like the blind man whom Jesus sends to the pool of Siloam after smearing his eyes with mud. How do we cultivate these habits of seeing, these practices of perception that enable us to recognize God in this world?

I think of Annie Dillard's book *Pilgrim at Tinker Creek*, in which she describes reading Marius von Senden's book *Space and Sight*. Dillard recounts von Senden's descriptions of what happened when eye surgeons began to perform the first successful operations to remove cataracts. For many born with blindness, the experience of sight was terrifying in the beginning. Their brains had never learned how to process and make sense of the images that now confronted their eyes. Shapes appeared flat, meaningless, fearsome. One young man, raised in what was then called an asylum for the blind, threatened to tear his eyes out if they refused to return him to the asylum. A newly sighted young woman walked around for two weeks with her eyes closed.

Gradually, Dillard says, many passed through their fright and began to work with what their eyes were trying to tell them. She describes one man who, trying to develop his depth perception, would toss a boot out in front of himself. He would estimate how far away the boot was, walk toward it, pick it up, toss it again. Slowly, boot by boot, he learned to see.

What are you looking for this day? How do you stretch yourself to see with greater clarity and keener insight? Where do you look for God among the commonplace occurrences of this world?

### BLESSING

May God,
who comes to us
in the things of this world,

bless your eyes
and be in your seeing.

May Christ,
who looks upon you
with deepest love,
bless your eyes
and widen your gaze.

May the Spirit,
who perceives what is
and what may yet be,
bless your eyes
and sharpen your vision.

May the Sacred Three
bless your eyes
and cause you to see.

# 19

## THE SECRET OF SEEING

Annie Dillard writes that the influence of von Senden's book affected her
vision for weeks. She sees differently, as she looks differently: patterns of
light and texture appear to her; the hidden reveals itself under the intensity
of her gaze. She discovers too what comes when she loses her focus, when
she sees without agenda, when she allows her eyes to blur. "When I see this
way, I see truly." She goes on to observe,

> But I can't go out and try to see this way. I'll fail, I'll go mad. All I can do
> is try to gag the commentator, to hush the noise of useless interior babble
> that keeps me from seeing just as surely as a newspaper dangled before
> my eyes. The effort is really a discipline requiring a lifetime of dedicated
> struggle. . . .

The secret of seeing is, then, the pearl of great price. If I thought he could teach me to find it and keep it forever I would stagger barefoot across a hundred deserts after any lunatic at all. But although the pearl may be found, it may not be sought. The literature of illumination reveals this above all: although it comes to those who wait for it, it is always, even to the most practiced and adept, a gift and a total surprise.[28]

Amid your seeking, what practices help you remain open to the surprises that come unsought? How do you leave spaces in your looking to perceive what you never expected to find?

BLESSING

That you will learn to look
and not to look.
That you will focus your attention
and let your focus fade.
That you will give everything to see,
then give it up
finally to be surprised
by the treasure at your feet.

# 20
## WHERE THE QUESTION IS BORN

For some few—John the Revelator, Hildegard of Bingen, Julian of Norwich, and the like—the mystic life takes vivid, dramatic form. Fire and wheels and wings. For most others, the mystic path is more quiet. It is a life in which we remember the root of the word *mystic* is the Greek *mystes*, "to keep silence." It is the same root that gives us *mystery*. It means shutting up long enough to notice God shuffling around in the daily events that make up our lives.

But this path requires us not only to know God but also to be willing to live with our not-knowing of God. It invites us to be present to the vast mystery of God who often seems to keep silence toward us and who speaks to us in questions more often than in answers.

In her book *The Vigil: Keeping Watch in the Season of Christ's Coming*, Wendy Wright notes, "A novice master of a Trappist monastery I once visited offered this observation: To be a Christian does not mean knowing all the answers; to be a Christian means being willing to live in the part of the self where the question is born."[29]

What questions are you carrying?

### BLESSING

Let mystery.

Let silence.

Let questions

and where they are born.

## 21

## WHEN NIGHT IS YOUR MIDDLE NAME

I am a night owl. I love the dark hours. Periodically I work on going to bed earlier, but it feels like entering alien territory, trying to make sense of a landscape and a language that I have a hard time fathoming. A friend, knowing my dark ways, once asked me, "So what do you do at night?" Oh, what there is to do at night! "I read," I told him, "or perhaps write, or pray, or soak up the quiet, or unwind in front of the TV." I take time to gather up the threads of the day; it is a period in which interruptions are rare and intrusions are few, a space where my soul can catch up with me. If I have spent the day around people, my inner introvert needs quiet time before sleep. If I have not had enough solitude by day's end, insomnia ensues.

Even my name denotes darkness. My middle name, Leila, means "night" in Hebrew. My parents did not know this at the time—the name belongs to a great-grandmother—but it proved a felicitous choice.

I'm inclined to link my fondness for night and my level of comfort with mystery. Perhaps because my path in life has taken some unusual turns, I have become fairly adept at living with a sense of unknowing. I have had plenty of occasion to develop skills that help keep me grounded as the conundrums of my life unfold. Being connected with a Benedictine community has been a great help in this regard. When you hang out with folks who are part of a tradition that has been around for nearly a millennium and a half, you learn a few things about taking the long view and about practicing in the midst of mysteries that can take years and decades and centuries to reveal themselves.

Still and all, I sometimes find myself wondering, *What illumination might God be calling me toward? Are there any mysteries I have become too willing to live with, any space in my soul that needs to be brought out of the shadows?*

It is one thing to live with the mysteries that attend our human lives, to enter into the rhythms of the sometimes strange ways that God works with us. The older I get, the more I think of God as the Ancient of Days, the Holy One of the Long Haul, who seems so deeply fond of working things out over vast expanses of time. This aspect of God calls us to trust, to step out without seeing what's ahead.

It is another thing, however, to allow the shadows to enthrall us. Mystery has its own enchantments; without spiritual practices and habits of discernment to ground us, those enchantments can lull us into becoming overly comfortable with the shadows and the places of unknowing that we find in our journeys. If I'm willing to live in a ceaseless process of discernment that never leads to action, if I cannot see a place of brokenness in my own soul or in the soul of the world, then I don't have to do anything about it.

That's called denial.

With her fiery visions, her hunger for illumination, her willingness to fling herself into the flames of God, Hildegard asks me to ponder how I'm seeking illumination in these days. Has some corner of my soul lived too long in shadow? Of the mysteries I have been content to live with, is there one that God might be ready to solve? Am I ready to receive the clarity that might come? How will I meet the God who longs to shine God's face not only on me but through me as well? How will you?

### BLESSING

May you have the courage
to turn your face to the God

who meets you in darkness
and in daylight.

# 22
# A VISIONARY VOCABULARY

Across the Christian tradition, the writings of the mystics reveal how steeped they were in the scriptures. In Bible study, in *lectio*, and in liturgy, the Word of God pervaded the rhythm of their days and the layers of their souls. The scriptures provided a visual vocabulary, a matrix of images that seeded their visions and gave them a language for their experience of God.

It's fair to say that the Christian mystical tradition holds no truly new, original visions. The visions that John relates in the book of Revelation, for instance, frequently echo those of the Hebrew prophet Daniel. We're not discussing plagiarism here; John is not merely cribbing from his mystic forefather. He uses images that influenced and nourished those who went before, experiencing and reconstituting them for a new time and a different need. And so for the visionary folk who would follow. Later mystics drew from this shared matrix, this wellspring that finds its source in both testaments of the Bible.

From generation to generation, the mystics engaged this visionary matrix according to their experiences and dispositions as well as according to their desired impact on their readers. We see this in Hildegard, who frequently used structural images as she wrote about the ordering of the church and creation. Architectural forms fill her visions: pillars and buildings and towers and columns line the landscape she evokes. She wants people to pay attention to God's desire for right relationship within the church and creation.

Other mystics employed more domestic imagery—for the most part neither better nor worse than Hildegard's but distinct from it. Christ as bridegroom, lover, mother, child: with bridal or maternal imagery that conveys an intensely intimate experience of Christ, such mystics challenge us to reckon with a God who desires us not just corporately but specifically, as individual people whom God has created and loves.

With the diversity of mystical experience and the range by which they expressed it, the medieval mystics offer a rich weave, a stunning tapestry of descriptions of God. Rather than conflicting with one another, the variety among these visionary experiences underscores how God speaks to us in ways we can understand, with distinctive words and images that engage who we are. An African proverb says, "One hand cannot cover the face of God." Across time, vision by vision, image by image, the mystics invite us to peek through.

What images, depictions, and descriptions of God do you find in you and in your own experience? Have these images changed over time? If so, what evoked those changes? Where do you find the face of God in the world?

BLESSING

That one image of God
will never appease you.
That one word for the holy
will never suffice.
That by uncountable names
and limitless forms
the infinite God
will find and delight you.

# 23

## HOLY FEAST, HOLY FAST

In the literature by and about the medieval women mystics, we see how their devotion to God could take extreme forms. Stories abound of hair shirts, body chains digging into flesh, rolling in glass or nails, and an array of other forms of self-mortification that impress and disturb with their diversity and creativity.

Such mortifications of the flesh can be deeply unsettling to our twenty-first century sensibilities, and we may find it tempting to be judgmental; I do. And yet, when we go deep into the literature, it becomes more difficult to dismiss such practices as evidence that the women (as well as the men who undertook such disciplines) hated their bodies. The meanings of self-mortification are more complex than this.

Perhaps the most widespread form of severe asceticism revolved around food. Food—its absence, its presence—was a way to share in both the suffering and the sustenance of the Christ who gave himself as body, as bread, as wine. In her book *Holy Feast and Holy Fast: The Religious Significance of Food to Medieval Women*, which focuses on women in religious orders, Caroline Walker Bynum describes what she calls the "rich and paradoxical meanings of eating and not eating" among these women.

> To religious women, food was a way of controlling as well as renouncing both self and environment. But it was more. Food was flesh, and flesh was suffering and fertility. In renouncing ordinary food and directing their being toward the food that is Christ, women moved to God not merely by abandoning their flawed physicality but also by becoming the suffering and feeding humanity of the body on the cross, the food on the altar. However absurd or vulgar some medieval practices and language may seem to casual modern observers, we do well . . . not to take offense. Deeper study of these "simple things" suggests that food and body can be powerful ways of encountering suffering and fecundity—aspects of the human condition from which even we in the twentieth century cannot hide completely.[30]

Many authors suggest that the mystics sometimes became more attached to their ascetical practices than to the object of their devotion. I think again of the desert mothers and fathers who cautioned against seeking austerities for austerities' sake; that we must instead seek Christ and let him lead us in our practices.

And yet I cannot help but wonder: *What might the wild hunger of these mystic women teach us?*

BLESSING

May the love of Christ
be your center, your focus,
your practice, your feast.

# 24

## THE CURE FOR MYSTERY

So how are you holding up with Hildegard and with the places she and her sisters are leading us? What's stirring for you, both in the illumination and in the shadows of mystery that the mystics offer? Where do you find Hildegard's intricate labyrinth leading you in these days?

Hildegard and her companion mystics can sometimes overwhelm with their intensity, with the density of their work, and with their challenge to us to hold the paradoxes that come in following Christ. As I ponder the places where their words, their lives, their passions, and their questions intertwine with my own path, I discover much to discern, sort through, sift.

In the midst of this, I find myself thinking of the mystic poet who asked, "What's the cure for love? More love." The formula holds true elsewhere. The cure for mystery? More mystery. The cure for paradox? More paradox.

Much like Jesus, whom they devoted their whole selves to following, the mystics dare us not to shrink from what besets and befuddles and daunts us but instead to look deeper into those very places and find the treasure that God has placed there.

In John's Gospel, not long before his crucifixion, Jesus says to his hearers, "'Very truly, I tell you, unless a grain of wheat falls into the earth and dies, it remains just a single grain; but if it dies, it bears much fruit'" (12:24). Go into the things you shrink from, Jesus tells his hearers—and us—in this passage. Go into the questions, the mysteries, the paradoxes, the seeming contradictions. Go into the dying that is not dying after all. We work so hard at letting go, trying to train ourselves to release our grip on all that is not God. But what if it is not about giving up but giving in? Falling into dirt, as Jesus says here. Going where grain is supposed to go. Following the spiral within the seed that takes us deeper into the dark but also—finally, fruitfully—out of it.

After Jesus finishes this discourse, he "departed and hid from them." And perhaps this is what Jesus expects us to do from time to time: hide. Not to focus on figuring everything out but rather to let at least some part of ourselves, for some space of time, withdraw. To cease from wrestling with the questions and mysteries and simply rest with them and give in to them. To secret our souls like a seed in the earth. To see what grows.

## BLESSING

Into love. Into mystery.
Into paradox. Into questions.
Into the seed and the ground
that holds the seed.
May you go. May you go.

# 25

## SAINT CATHERINE'S LABYRINTH

One day a friend handed me a quote from Saint Catherine of Siena, the fourteenth-century Italian nun and mystic who was widely known and sought out for her wisdom and miraculous gifts. "I want a piece of artwork that contains these words," my friend told me. "Can you do this?"

I pondered the quote for months, tried various artful approaches, set it aside, took it up again. Finally, as I contemplated the words at my drafting table one day, more than a year after the quote had come into my hands, the idea of a labyrinth arrived, its path made up of Saint Catherine's words. More days, more weeks, more discerning and experimenting; but this time with focus and vision. Finally I took up the materials that had presented themselves as fitting. Midnight black paper. Calligraphy pen. Shimmering gold gouache paint.

On the expanse of midnight black, I laid out a golden labyrinth, its path not a continuous line but rather dots shouldered close to one another. Tiny dots. Hundreds of dots. Within the path of the labyrinth, letter by letter, word by word, I wrote the quote from Saint Catherine that my friend had tucked into my hand all those months ago. And at last, in the center of the labyrinth that I had traveled toward for so long, I placed a collage, a circle filled with leaves of painted paper. Leaf after leaf after leaf.

Shortened so that it wouldn't spill over the borders, this is the passage that leads to the center of the labyrinth:

Imagine a circle traced on the ground, and in its center a tree sprouting with a shoot grafted into its side. The tree finds its nourishment in the soil within the expanse of the circle, but uprooted from the soil it would die fruitless. So think of the soul as a tree made for love and living only by love. . . . The circle in which this tree's root, the soul's love, must grow is true knowledge of herself, knowledge that is joined to me, who like the circle have neither beginning nor end. You can go round and round within this circle, finding neither end nor beginning, yet never leaving the circle. . . .

So the tree of charity is nurtured in humility and branches out in true discernment. . . .

. . . To me this tree yields the fragrance of glory and praise to my name, and so it does what I created it for and comes at last to its goal, to me, everlasting Life.[31]

BLESSING

May you sink
the roots of your soul
deep and deeper still
into the love of God,
who encompasses and encircles you
without beginning, without end.

# 26

## PENNIES IN YOUR SHOES

Perhaps what we call mystics are persons who have become thin places within themselves. They live fully open to the things of heaven and the things of earth. In their own being, they have become a place of meeting.

It takes continual work to approach such equilibrium. It is hard to keep our eyes open to the things of heaven while attending to the things of earth, and vice versa. How do we sort through these competing claims?

There are days I long to escape the mundane, days I want to flee from dealing with dishes, with laundry, with phone calls, with taxes, with errands, with paperwork, with institutions, with broken systems, with all that tries my patience and wears me out. Yet at the same time I recognize that even at their most maddening, these recurring activities help ground me, keep me from tilting off the planet, root me in this world where God lives. Where God hides. Where God waits for me to look for the holy not beyond my daily life but in the very midst and sometimes mess of it.

In her book *The Fruitful Darkness: Reconnecting with the Body of the Earth*, Joan Halifax writes of her journey that leads her far, far into the nether realms of spiritual experience. She tells of a dream she has, one she perceives to shimmer with spiritual import. "I am in a longhouse of native peoples of Canada," she recounts. "I look out the door and see to the west a great circle of men and women from all races and all nations sitting on a meadow of brilliant green. I go to join them, and as I approach, I rise into the air. I am at first afraid and incredibly self-conscious, but soon others join me. I awaken ecstatic."

At the time of the dream, she was working with Joseph Campbell, widely known for his work as a mythologist. After she tells him of her dream, Campbell responds, "Joan, you should put pennies in your shoes."

"Joe, in fact, was being more than polite when he recommended that I 'put pennies in my shoes,'" writes Halifax. "Though I felt that I was exploring the edge, Campbell was convinced that I had gone over it. He was right."[32]

As you open yourself to the things of heaven, as you seek to go deeper into the things of God, what keeps you tethered to this life, this earth, this world that God has given as a place to find the holy?

## BLESSING

May you give your devotion
to the things of heaven.
May you give your attention
to the things of earth.
May they find a place of meeting
in you.

# 27

## BEGIN THE BEGUINES

When I consider how mysticism engages us with the world, I think of the Beguines, a movement of women that began to take hold near the end of the twelfth century. The Beguines, for various reasons, had chosen not to enter the convent but instead created their own lives of simplicity, devotion, and ministry in the world. In the early days of the movement, Beguines lived in their own homes and pursued largely independent religious lives. Later they began to organize themselves into communities that shared spiritual practices and work that ranged from domestic arts such as weaving and embroidery to nursing, caring for lepers, and preparing the bodies of the dead for burial.

As the thirteenth century unfolded, many of the Beguine communities took physical form as the women acquired houses and other buildings. Ernest W. McDonnell notes that by the beginning of the fourteenth century, one such community, the Great Beguinage at Ghent, included "two churches, eighteen convents, over a hundred houses, a brewery, and an infirmary."[33] Centered primarily in the Low Countries, northern France, and Germany, the beguinages offered thousands of women the opportunity to live in autonomous communities that respected and encouraged their religious experiences.

In time, the autonomous nature of the beguinages and the independent lives of the Beguines aroused suspicion and accusations of heresy. Many beguinages came under the authority of the Catholic Church, while others disbanded in the wake of persecution or other stresses. By the end of the Middle Ages, few communities remained.

### BLESSING

In work, in worship,
in service, in prayer,
may you go in the good company
of the lovers of God.

# 28

## O YOU POURING GOD

The Beguine movement produced extraordinary mystics and writers whose works have survived the centuries. These Beguine writers are distinctive in part because they were among the first to write in the vernacular. While this may not strike us as unusual today, to write a book, particularly a theological work, in one's own language rather than in Latin was a radical act in their time.

One of these mystic writers was Mechthild of Magdeburg, born in Germany in the early thirteenth century. With her book, *The Flowing Light of the Godhead*, Mechthild offers a stunning work in which her visions, poetry, and theological reflections flow into one another. She completed the book after moving around 1270 to Helfta, the site of a great Cistercian convent that became an influential center of women's spirituality during the medieval period. Mechthild relates that her mystical experience began in her twelfth year, when she was "greeted by the Holy Spirit" with a great "outpouring" that transformed her. Thirty-one years later, Mechthild wrote, "This precious greeting occurred every day and lovingly spoiled for me all worldly sweetness, and it is still increasing day by day."[34]

Mechthild had an agile imagination, coupled with a remarkable facility for language that she uses to describe God and God's relationship with the soul. She draws from a variety of literary genres to create a distinctive style that moves from prose to poetry and back again. As with other Beguines, Mechthild suffuses her writing with imagery. *O you burning Mountain*, she addresses God in one of her poems. *Chosen Sun*, she goes on to describe the Divine; *full Moon, bottomless Well, unscalable Height, Brightness without measure, Wisdom without ground.*[35] *O you pouring God in your gift*, she writes in another poem. *Flowing God*, she calls out. *Burning God, melting God, resting God.*[36]

### BLESSING

May the God
who dwells within and beyond
greet you this day.

# 29

## ON THE PILGRIMAGE OF LOVE

The Flemish Beguine Hadewijch lived in the thirteenth century. Beyond this, we have scant details about her life. From her writings we know that she either founded or joined a group of Beguines and became their leader. Her leadership met with opposition, and she left the community, perhaps evicted by her sister members. Mother Columba Hart, who translated Hadewijch's works into English, notes that it's generally held by scholars that Hadewijch was forced from the community "because of her doctrine that one must live Love."[37] Hart writes, "It may perhaps be conjectured, considering how often Hadewijch urged her Beguines to care for the sick, that when she finally became homeless she offered her services to a leprosarium or hospital for the poor, where she could nurse those who suffered and sleep at least part of the night in some corner, with access to the church or chapel always attached to such establishments in her time."[38]

All the more remarkable, then, that at least some of Hadewijch's work survived, including a collection of letters, two series of poems, and an account of her visions. Caroline Walker Bynum calls Hadewijch "the first great poet in the Flemish language."[39] Her poetic sensibility extends to her prose works, including the letters, most likely to her community, that she composed with such artful care.

In one of these letters, "The Pilgrimage of Love," Hadewijch offers her readers nine points that "are fitting for the pilgrim who has far to travel."[40] In beginning this journey, she makes clear that those who want to follow Christ need to go in the company of those familiar with the way. She writes,

> Ask about the way from his saints, those he has taken to himself, and those who still remain here below, who are following after him in perfect virtues, who have followed him up the mountain of the noble life from the deep valley of humility, and have climbed the high mountain with strong faith and perfect confidence in the contemplation of the Love so sweet to our heart.
>
> And further, ask about the way from those who are close to you, and who you see are now going his ways in the manner most like his, and are

obedient to him in all works of virtues. Thus follow him who himself is the way, and those who have gone this way and are now going it.[41]

Who helps you know the way? Are you asking anyone who has traveled the way before you? In whose company are you going—or long to go—these days?

BLESSING

When you have far to travel,
may God grace you with companions
who know the way.

# 30

## A VESSEL FILLED WITH HOLY OIL

Mystical experiences are not limited to those who have a measure of freedom to choose lives that help foster these experiences. We read accounts of mystical experiences during and after the time of slavery in the United States. These accounts remind us that God seeks out God's people in every circumstance and that God's power is available in conditions of oppression and horror.

In the visions that came to those living in slavery, we see God assuring them of the presence of another landscape, a terrain of hope at hand. This landscape does not merely exist in another place in some distant future; rather, with these visions God offers the possibility of healing and freedom in *this* world, in *this* circumstance, in *this* life, not just for the recipient of the vision but for the community as well.

We find such an account in the *Memoir of Old Elizabeth, a Coloured Woman*. Born into slavery in 1766, Elizabeth was sent, at the age of eleven, to a farm some miles from her family. She tells of how she thought she would die if she didn't see her mother, of her master's refusal to allow Elizabeth to visit her, and of the fierce lashing she received after going to visit her mother anyway. Recounting her loneliness and sorrow, Elizabeth goes on to say,

I continued in this state for about six months, feeling as though my head were waters, and I could do nothing but weep. I lost my appetite, and not being able to take enough food to sustain nature, I became so weak I had but little strength to work; still I was required to do all my duty. One evening, after the duties of the day were ended, I thought I could not live over the night, so threw myself on a bench, expecting to die, and without being prepared to meet my Maker; and my spirit cried within me, must I die in this state, and be banished from Thy presence forever? I own I am a sinner in Thy sight, and not fit to live where thou art. Still it was my fervent desire that the Lord would pardon me. Just at this season, I saw with my spiritual eye, an awful gulf of misery. As I thought I was about to plunge into it, I heard a voice saying, "rise up and pray," which strengthened me. I fell on my knees and prayed the best I could the Lord's prayer. Knowing no more to say, I halted, but continued on my knees. My spirit was then taught to pray, "Lord, have mercy on me—Christ save me." Immediately there appeared a director, clothed in white raiment. I thought he took me by the hand and said, "Come with me."

Elizabeth describes how the director leads her to the edge of a fiery gulf. As she prays and wrestles in this place, fearful she will fall into the fire, she has a vision of Christ. With hand outstretched, he says to Elizabeth, "Peace, peace, come unto me."

"At this moment," Elizabeth says, "I felt that my sins were forgiven me, and the time of my deliverance was at hand. I sprang forward and fell at his feet, giving Him all the thanks and highest praises, crying, Thou hast redeemed me—Thou hast redeemed me to thyself. I felt filled with light and love."

Elizabeth's vision finally leads her to a place where she

was shown the world lying in wickedness, and was told I must go there, and call the people to repentance, for the day of the Lord was at hand; and this message was as a heavy yoke upon me, so that I wept bitterly at the thought of what I should have to pass through. While I wept, I heard a voice say, "Weep not, some will laugh at thee, some will scoff at thee, and the dogs will bark at thee, but while thou doest my will, I will be with thee to the ends of the earth."

I was at this time not thirteen years old. The next day, when I had come to myself, I felt like a new creature in Christ, and all my desire was to see the Saviour.

I lived in a place where there was no preaching, and no religious instruction; but every day I went out amongst the hay-stacks, where the presence of the Lord overshadowed me, and I was filled with sweetness and joy, and was as a vessel filled with holy oil.[42]

Elizabeth's vision did not release her from struggle; she goes on to tell of the "deep sorrows and plungings" that yet lay ahead of her. The vision, however, helped her survive her continuing captivity. Eventually sold to a Presbyterian man who released her after a term, "as he did not think it right to hold slaves for life," Elizabeth gained her freedom when she was about thirty. At forty-two, she realized it was time to undertake the call to preach that she had received as a child.[43]

BLESSING

In struggle and in suffering,
in bondage and despair,
may God offer vision and freedom,
redemption and release.

31

WHAT THE BONES KNOW

She thinks of saints
legendary for their levitation.
She knows their secret,
that there is small miracle
in the physics of longing
turning bone to ash,
of consumptive love
that hollows out the skeleton,
disintegrates the marrow.

Still, she thinks there is something to be said
for gravity,
for the nearerness of earth,
for the richness of the oxygen
closer to the ground.

These days
she feels the blessed weight
of her bones:

the smooth planes of her skull,
the hollow of her clavicle,
the solidity of sternum,
her staccato'd, repetitive ribs,
arch of back,
cradle of pelvis,
long bones of legs
splintering into the feet
that hold the bulk of
her body's bones.

It takes every one
to keep her rooted to the earth,
to stabilize her soles,
to hold her to the ground that meets
her solid, blessed flesh.

## BLESSING

May the company of
the saints,
the mystics,
the beloved of God
in body and in soul,
bless and go with you
and help light your way.

## FURTHER READING

*Brides in the Desert: The Spirituality of the Beguines* by Saskia Murk-Jansen. Maryknoll, NY: Orbis Books, 1998.

*Enduring Grace: Living Portraits of Seven Women Mystics* by Carol Lee Flinders. New York: HarperCollins Publishers, 1993.

*Hadewijch: The Complete Works* trans. Mother Columba Hart. New York: Paulist Press, 1980.

*Hildegard of Bingen: Scivias* trans. Mother Columba Hart and Jane Bishop. New York: Paulist Press, 1990.

*Maps of Flesh and Light: The Religious Experience of Medieval Women Mystics* ed. Ulrike Wiethaus. Syracuse, NY: Syracuse University Press, 1993.

*Mechthild of Magdeburg: The Flowing Light of the Godhead* trans. Frank Tobin. New York: Paulist Press, 1998.

*Medieval Women's Visionary Literature* by Elizabeth Alvilda Petroff. New York: Oxford University Press, 1986.

*Sister of Wisdom: St. Hildegard's Theology of the Feminine* by Barbara Newman. Berkeley, CA: University of California Press, 1998.

*Voice of the Living Light: Hildegard of Bingen and Her World* ed. Barbara Newman. Berkeley: CA: University of California Press, 1998.

## NOTES

1. Mother Columba Hart and Jane Bishop, trans., *Hildegard of Bingen: Scivias*, introduction by Barbara J. Newman, preface by Caroline Walker Bynum (New York: Paulist Press, 1990), 59.

2. Ibid., 61.

3. Ibid., 161.

4. Ibid., 164.

5. Ibid., 405.

6. Ibid., 452.

7. Barbara J. Newman, introduction to *Hildegard of Bingen: Scivias*, 37.

8. *Hildegard of Bingen: Scivias*, 345.

9. Newman, introduction to *Hildegard of Bingen: Scivias*, 37.

10. *Hildegard of Bingen: Scivias*, 352.

11. Ibid., 338.

12. Annie Dillard, *Pilgrim at Tinker Creek* (New York: Perennial Library/Harper & Row, Publishers, 1988), 269–70.

13. *Hildegard of Bingen: Scivias*, 59–60.

14. Barbara Newman, "'Sibyl of the Rhine': Hildegard's Life and Times," in Barbara Newman, ed., *Voice of the Living Light: Hildegard of Bingen and Her World* (Berkeley, CA: University of California Press, 1998), 10.

15. *Hildegard of Bingen: Scivias*, 60.

16. Ibid., 278.

17. Newman, introduction to *Hildegard of Bingen: Scivias*, 25.

18. Ibid., 25–26.

19. Caroline Walker Bynum, preface to *Hildegard of Bingen: Scivias*, 2–3.

20. Ibid., 5.

21. *Hildegard of Bingen: Scivias*, 310.

22. Ibid., 536.

23. Mother Columba Hart, trans., *Hadewijch: The Complete Works* (New York: Paulist Press, 1980), 281.

24. Ibid., 284.

25. Katherine Marie Dyckman and L. Patrick Carroll, *Inviting the Mystic, Supporting the Prophet: An Introduction to Spiritual Direction* (New York: Paulist Press, 1981), 81.

26. George Ella Lyon, "Voiceplace," in *Bloodroot: Reflections on Place by Appalachian Women Writers*, ed. Joyce Dyer (Lexington, KY: University Press of Kentucky, 1998), 172.

27. Kathleen Norris, *Amazing Grace: A Vocabulary of Faith* (New York: Riverhead Books/Penguin, 1998), 285.

28. Dillard, *Pilgrim at Tinker Creek*, 32–33.

29. Wendy M. Wright, *The Vigil: Keeping Watch in the Season of Christ's Coming* (Nashville, TN: Upper Room Books, 1992), 166.

30. Caroline Walker Bynum, *Holy Feast and Holy Fast: The Religious Significance of Food to Medieval Women* (Berkeley, CA: University of California Press, 1987), 5.

31. Suzanne Noffke, trans., *Catherine of Siena: The Dialogue* (Mahwah, NJ: Paulist Press, 1980), 41–42.

32. Joan Halifax, *The Fruitful Darkness*, xxvi.

33. Ernest W. McDonnell, *The Beguines and Beghards in Medieval Culture* (New York: Octagon, 1969; reprint of 1953 ed.), 479, cited in Elizabeth Alvilda Petroff, *Medieval Women's Visionary Literature* (New York: Oxford University Press, 1986), 172.

34. Frank Tobin, trans., *Mechthild of Magdeburg: The Flowing Light of the Godhead* (New York: Paulist Press, 1998), 139.

35. Ibid., 45–46.

36. Ibid., 48.

37. *Hadewijch: The Complete Works*, 4.

38. Ibid., 5.

39. Bynum, *Holy Feast and Holy Fast*, 153.

40. *Hadewijch: The Complete Works*, 77.

41. Ibid., 78.

42. *Memoir of Old Elizabeth, A Coloured Woman* (orig. printing: Philadelphia: Collins, 1863) in *Six Women's Slave Narratives* (New York: Oxford University Press, 1988), 4-7.

43. Ibid., 8–9.

# THE MYSTERIES OF MAKING

*The Book of Harriet Powers*

## INTRODUCTION

Born in the southern United States in 1837, Harriet Powers grew up in slavery and spent much of her life near Athens, Georgia. We know that she had children, she was emancipated, she and her husband purchased a farm, and she worked as a seamstress. We have these pieces of her story primarily because of two of her stitched creations that have survived: a pair of quilts.

Known as Bible quilts, Powers's creations captivate with their style and the stories they tell. Using the technique of appliqué and perhaps drawing on the long tradition of appliqué found in the West African country of Benin, Powers stitched her quilts with bold, colorful figures of humans, animals, and celestial bodies: sun, moon, stars. Frame by frame, her quilts tell stories that Powers absorbed, pondered, and reconstructed in an intensely personal and artful fashion. Not only did she include biblical stories such as Adam and Eve, Jonah and the whale, the crucifixion of Jesus, and John's vision of the angels with their trumpets and censer, Powers also stitched local legends and references to astronomical and climatological events that she had heard of or experienced. Her stitched stories included "The independent hog that ran 500 miles from GA to VA"; "the falling of the stars on November 13, 1833"; and "a man frozen at his jug of liquor" on Cold Thursday in 1895.[1]

We know some of Powers's thoughts about her work because two women recorded her reflections. Describing her first Bible quilt, now in the Smithsonian Institution (her second quilt resides in the collection of the Museum of Fine Arts in Boston), Powers said it was "a sermon in patchwork" and that she desired to "preach de Gospel in patchwork, ter show my Lawd my humbility."[2]

Powers's quilts are not the size of typical bed covers; they are significantly wider than they are long. This fact, together with Powers's own words about her work, suggests that she created them as a form of proclamation. The quilts were her way of preaching, of telling the good news of the Word that had taken flesh in her own life.

The little we know about Harriet Powers's life reminds us of how the histories of so many women have disappeared. It reminds us too that mystery always attends the process of making. No matter how much we may know about an artist, what an artist creates can never be fully explained. This is both a gift and a challenge of the creative process: there is a tension between what is revealed and what is concealed.

The work of our hands bears the imprint of its maker and of the One who moves within its making. What we create contains a measure of who we are. Even as it carries our secrets, it also has messages and meanings to convey. The striking quilts that Harriet Powers fashioned are the primary texts she left behind. As with Hildegard of Bingen and others whose written words have come down to us, the visual artistry of Harriet Powers provides a sacred text for reflection and interpretation.

The life and work of Harriet Powers invites us to ponder the mysteries of making and to discern how the Spirit seeks to create in and through us. Creativity, after all, is God's first language. It is our mother tongue, a way to converse and commune with God and with the world. Our journey through this chapter will invite us to ask, What does God the Creator desire to make known in the world through the work of our hands? To what forms of creativity are we called? What practices sustain our creative work?

In the company of Harriet Powers, may these days draw you deeper into the God who has designed us to share in the ongoing act—and art—of creation.

# PRAYER FOR THE MORNING

With the dawning light
let us turn our faces
toward the One
who fashioned us,
and let us give thanks
to the God who
knits us together
with each new day:
bone to bone
breath to breath
beautiful and
blessed.

# PRAYER FOR THE EVENING

God of the night,
now we turn toward the dark
in which all things
have their beginning
and find their form.
Bless the seeds
and tend what grows
in the dark of the womb
in the dark of the earth
in the dark of the soul.
Be with us,
dream in us,
create us anew
in the hours of this night.

# 1

## MY REAL LIFE

Years ago, when I moved from serving as a pastor in a congregation to become the artist-in-residence at San Pedro Center, it aroused a fair measure of curiosity. During my first few years at San Pedro, many folks—most often my clergy colleagues—would ask me, "So are you still on that sabbatical?" Although my bishop had appointed me to this ministry, some people thought I was taking a break from my vocation. The question grated at first. Yet I came to welcome it as an opportunity for conversation about what ministry is and where it happens. I learned to love responding, "No, I'm not on sabbatical; this is my real life!"

A dozen years since moving into the form of ministry to which I feel most called, I no longer receive the sabbatical question. However, I continue to encounter the perception that the arts are extraneous to who we are as the body of Christ. In some quarters, art is considered a luxury, a needless extravagance that is tangential to what it means to be the church. Or, in church communities that do give attention to the arts, creative expression is often approached in an overly cautious, watered-down fashion that gravitates toward work that is "pretty" but does not move us to see differently.

We in the church too often forget that the first face that God shows us—there, at the beginning of Genesis—is of God as Creator, who labors with artful passion and imbues each creative gesture with a wild and extravagant love. This God calls creation good but does not proclaim it finished on the sixth day. This Creator God calls us, who bear the image of God, to participate in the ongoing creation of the world, with every art we can muster.

"Poetry is not a luxury," writes Audre Lorde.[3] We can say the same of other artful acts, those daring leaps by which we take the pieces of our lives and turn them into something new. Not a luxury, but rather an action both essential and wild.

### BLESSING

In the work of your hands,
in the desires of your heart,
may the God of creation

draw you more deeply
into your real life.

# 2

## IN PIECES

For most of my life I did not consider myself an artist. One of my earliest memories, in fact, is of tearing up all my paintings and drawings that my mother had saved. I was about five years old. When my horrified mother found me with the pile of scraps and asked me why I had done it, I replied, "Because they weren't any good!" How early the inner critic starts rising.

Although I considered myself creative in other ways, only in my last year of seminary did I begin to pursue visual art seriously. It was the medium of paper collage that compelled me. I had believed that an artist needed to be able to paint and draw; obviously, since the age of five, I had not thought of myself as someone who could do either of these things well. Yet I found that transformation happened in playing with paper, in taking those skills, picked up in kindergarten, of cutting and tearing and pasting and piecing together. Years later, I found myself wondering if my passion for collage had anything to do with that early memory of destroying my artwork. Perhaps for me, collage is a way of putting those shredded drawings and paintings back together.

Collage became a powerful spiritual practice for me; the drafting table is one of the places where I pray best. It provides a space between and beneath and beyond words, a thin place where memory and hope meet. The practice of collage also provides an image for understanding my work and my life. In much the same way that I sit at my drafting table and take the scraps to piece together a new creation, God does this within me. God takes every-thing: experiences, stories, memories, relationships, dreams, prayers—all those pieces, light and dark, rough and smooth, jagged and torn—and cre-ates anew from them. I have learned to think of God as the consummate recycler: in God's economy, nothing is wasted. Everything—*everything*—can be used. Transformed. Redeemed.

BLESSING

From all that is broken,
let there be beauty.
From what is torn, jagged,
ripped, frayed,
let there be
not just mendings
but meetings unimagined.
May the God in whom
nothing is wasted
gather up every scrap,
every shred and shard,
and make of them
new paths,
doorways,
worlds.

# 3

## A SERMON IN PATCHWORK

At my ordination as a minister in the United Methodist Church, I took a vow to proclaim the Word. As I have grown in my understanding of my call, I have learned that proclamation occurs in many ways. Sometimes it takes place in the pulpit; other times it comes through the art that I create. Paint, paper, charcoal, pen: each tool and medium offers a way of giving flesh and form to the Word.

And so one of the pieces of Harriet Powers's story that I find most fascinating is her description of her quilt-making as a "sermon in patchwork." In her hands, scrap by scrap and stitch by stitch, art became a form of proclamation, her testimony to the Word.

In an essay in *African Americans and the Bible: Sacred Texts and Social Textures*, Richard J. Powell observes that "Harriet Powers's quilts were platforms for speaking her mind and professing her intimate knowledge of the Bible, in the face of restrictions on women in the secular and sacred arenas."

Powell goes on to write,

> In her culture, Powers's only outlet for voicing her beliefs and senti-
> ments—both at home and in a religious context—were her Bible Quilts.
> Her choices of narratives—Adam and Eve, Cain and Abel, Noah's Ark,
> Jonah and the Whale, Jacob's Ladder, the Crucifixion and Resurrection
> of Jesus Christ—were not just standard, biblical recitations rendered here
> in cloth: they embodied biblical discourse filtered through Powers's criti-
> cal mind and visual imagination. Stories that became sermons and spiri-
> tuals in the mouths of others, she transformed into personal images of
> faith, betrayal, grace, testing, and divine intervention. Stories that were
> often shrouded in arcane languages and ministerial jargon, she rendered
> in stark, clear, silhouette forms. Stories that were part and parcel of the
> Sunday church services and other orthodox religious settings, she brought
> to the county fair.[4]

Again and again in the lives of women in the scriptures and across the
generations we see this impulse to proclaim the good news by the means
at hand. Although often limited in the public roles they could take on,
women found ways to give voice to what they had found in Christ. Using
the vernacular language of daily life—not only in their speech but also in
their actions—these women testified to the presence and power of Christ
in their lives.

We see this in the Gospel story of the healing of Simon's mother-in-
law (Mark 1:29-34). Having just come from the synagogue, where he had
healed a man with an unclean spirit, Jesus enters Simon's home and learns
that Simon's mother-in-law is in bed with a fever. Jesus goes to her, takes
her by the hand, lifts her up. In his gesture of reaching toward the woman,
touching her, Jesus crosses with great intention into her condition, her
realm, her world. In this sacred domestic space, no less than in the holy
space of the synagogue, Jesus extends his healing.

In response, Simon's mother-in-law rises and begins to serve Jesus and
his companions. Where other stories of healing sometimes end with the
recipient offering an oral testimony to what Jesus has done, this story does
not ascribe any words to the woman. Whatever she may have said, if anything, the act of her serving Jesus and his companions, her ministering to
them in this basic, bodily way, provides eloquent testimony in the vocabu-

lary that she has at hand. It is a sermon in supper: she is lavish with the language that she knows, using it to proclaim and give praise for what Christ has done. That her creative act falls squarely in the realm of what society sometimes, wrongfully, belittles as "women's work" does not minimize its grace. Rather, it unveils the holiness present—and sometimes hidden—in the dailiness of domestic life.

BLESSING

With everything you have at hand,
may you proclaim
the good news of the Christ
who crosses into your daily life.

# 4

## A WOMAN'S WORK

Reflecting on the story of Simon's mother-in-law, Mary Ann Tolbert offers insight into how some translations and interpretations of this story have reflected and reinforced views of women and women's work as having lesser value. Such interpretations undercut the power of what this woman does for Jesus and his companions, and they compromise our ability to hear the eloquent proclamation that her hospitality contains.

Tolbert points out that the word denoting the woman's action (from the Greek verb *diakoneo*, related to the word for deacon) is the same word used to describe what angels do for Jesus at the end of his forty days in the wilderness. Yet some translators who render the action of the angels as "minister"—a more overtly sacramental act—have chosen to translate the same word as "serve" when it applies to this woman, casting her action in a more subservient light. "The author of Mark," Tolbert observes, "by using the same word for the action of angels and the action of the healed woman, obviously equated their level of service to Jesus. What the angels were able to do for Jesus in the wilderness, the woman whose fever has fled now does for him in her home." Tolbert goes on to note that the door of the woman's house "becomes the threshold for healing for all in the city who are sick."[5]

What Jesus later says of a woman who blesses his body with an anointing, we can say of this woman who blesses his body with her domestic gesture: "She has done what lay in her power" (Mark 14:8, NEB).

Freed from slavery, from illness, and from myriad other forms of bondage, women such as Harriet Powers and Simon's mother-in-law have each, in her own medium, found the power to tell what Christ has done. How about us? How do we offer our testimony about the one who has freed us? What medium do we have at hand to proclaim the news of how Christ has worked and works still to release all people from every form of captivity and bondage? What is the unique vocabulary that God has given you to articulate how God takes shape in your life? How willing are you to use this vocabulary in ways that only you can express?

## BLESSING

In every word,
with every gesture,
by every art,
through every means,
may you be
a living gospel
for the life of the world.


# 5

# PRACTICES

In the course of working as an artist, I have learned that I encounter many of the same difficulties in my creative work as I do in my life of faith. Fatigue, loss of inspiration, isolation, the acedia that the desert mothers and fathers have taught us about: in my creative journey, as in my life of faith, these and other struggles have become familiar companions. I have found that the practices that sustain me as an artist and writer are the same kind of practices that sustain me as I seek God. These are some of them:

- *Living and working with intention*
  What are the rhythms of life that enable me to live with mindfulness instead of reacting to whatever comes along?

- *Finding allies*
  Whom do I turn to for support and sustenance? Am I willing to ask for help when I need it?

- *Revisiting my sources*
  Where are the wellsprings that inspire me and to which I need to return?

- *Living with questions*
  How do I recognize and resist my own attitudes of certainty that stifle the creative process?

- *Engaging in discernment*
  How do I sort through the invitations and possibilities that present themselves?

- *Taking leaps of faith*
  Have I become too comfortable in my practices? How might God be asking me to stretch and move with courage in a new direction?

- *Claiming a vision without trying to unduly control the outcome*
  How do I discern and work toward a goal while remaining open to the mysteries and surprises along the way?

### BLESSING

In your working
and in your seeking,
may you know and embrace
all that will nourish you
and sustain your pilgrim soul.

# 6

## IN THE WEEDS

Jesus' parables give us powerful examples of how the creative spirit moved through him. Jesus knew that to widen people's vision, he had to focus it in certain ways. He did this by telling stories that helped his hearers to see anew what was always before them. With these stories, Jesus trained their eyes—and trains ours—to perceive the kingdom of heaven tucked into the midst of this world.

Teaching us to see the kingdom among us requires symbol, myth, metaphor, story. It requires the visual poetry that Jesus uses repeatedly as he turns to the things of the earth to describe the things of heaven: yeast, seeds, dirt, water, fish, lilies of the field, birds of the air. He employs the ephemeral while seeking to explain the eternal. His doing so both comforts and unsettles: he turns the familiar on its head and us with it.

This is the work of the artist.

The images that Jesus offers in his parables, along with the artfulness that imbued the way he walked through this world, have helped me think about how I approach my own creative work. I find wisdom in Jesus' tale of wheat and weeds (Matthew 13:24-30, 36-43), in which Jesus weaves these agrarian images into a parable about the kingdom of God.

Matthew lets us in on Jesus' explanation of this parable, and it seems straightforward on the surface. Jesus offers an interpretive equation in which, not surprisingly, wheat=good and weeds=bad. I'm curious, however, about how Jesus has the householder respond to the slaves who ask him whether they should gather the weeds. The householder tells them to allow the weeds and the wheat to grow together until harvest time, at which point the slaves will gather the weeds and burn them. Removing the weeds too soon would cause harm to the growing wheat.

I have long been aware that my ongoing work needs to include the cultivation of practices that support my work. Part of me needs a measured rhythm of life—like orderly rows of wheat, say. Yet this orderly part of me regularly grapples with the part that needs a strand of something that's a bit wilder, something less domesticated.

Something weedy.

I can grow dismayed by what I allow to creep into my creative life: commitments that distract me, weariness, or plain old resistance to the process. Although being an artist as well as a writer lies at the heart of who I am, I sometimes wrestle with how the work brings my inner self to the surface, confronting me with the raw, unformed stuff I carry around inside. Some days it is easier to let the weeds grow, as if they could provide a bit of wild shelter from the work of cultivating my interior crop.

My spiritual director, Maru, has encouraged me to think about how I experience these times of distraction and discouragement, those occasions when I skirt the demands of the drafting table or the blank page in favor of another activity. Where I have tended to view these times as wasteful, Maru suggests that I see them as part of the process, integral to the creative crop. Wandering among the weeds serves to clear my vision and sharpen my desire. Weeds don't make for a steady diet. Eventually I grow hungry for what will sustain and satisfy, and I will do anything necessary to find my way to that sustenance. In the fullness of time, an interior apocalypse comes around: the weeds fall away and burn in the fire that comes in times of focused creating. The longed-for crop flourishes and feeds.

What is growing in the landscape of your life? How do you discern the difference between the weeds and the wheat? What do you do with the weeds? How might they become part of the work of cultivating your landscape?

### BLESSING

Let the weeds in their season,
and let the wildness in its time.
Let lostness,
and let wandering
and waste.

And then let it not:
let fire
and let burning,
let the destroying
of every extraneous thing.
Let the wheat.

# 7

## SOMETHING OLD, SOMETHING NEW

For nearly a decade, I have regularly visited Saint John's Abbey, a Benedictine monastery in Collegeville, Minnesota, also the home to Saint John's University. Whenever I go, I pay a visit (sometimes several) to the Hill Museum and Manuscript Library, known as the HMML. The monks of Saint John's founded the HMML to preserve the medieval manuscript heritage of Europe, Africa, and the Middle East. For several summers, the HMML has offered exhibitions of original folios from *The Saint John's Bible*, the first Bible in more than five hundred years to be written and illuminated entirely by hand. By the time team leader, Donald Jackson, and his cadre of scribes and artists complete their lavish, monumental work, the Bible will have absorbed about ten years of their lives.[6]

A group was touring the exhibition during one of my visits to the museum. As I took in the folios, with the gold dancing on their pages, I tuned an ear to the comments that the group's HMML guide offered. After her presentation, she fielded questions. "Why," one person asked, "in this age of high-quality printing technology, would someone spend the time to create an entire Bible by hand?" As the guide responded, she spoke about the value of recovering ancient practices of bookmaking as a sacred art and of the beauty that emerges in fashioning something by hand. She pointed out that contemporary technology has played a significant role in *The Saint John's Bible:* a designer used a computer to plan the entire layout of the pages before the team began to lay ink, paint, and gold leaf on the vellum sheets.

It is a treasure that draws from what is new and what is old.

With his storyteller's art, Jesus offers images of such treasures in the Gospel of Matthew (13:31-33, 44-52). Jesus, who is in a parable-telling mood at this point in the Gospel, gives a series of images that describe what the kingdom of heaven is like. He speaks of a mustard seed that grows into a tree, yeast that a woman mixes with flour, a man who discovers treasure hidden in a field, a merchant who finds a pearl of great value, and a net filled with fish. Jesus closes his litany of images by saying, "Therefore every scribe who has been trained for the kingdom of heaven is like the master of a household who brings out of his treasure what is new and what is old."

The scribe about whom Jesus speaks differs from those who have been laboring over *The Saint John's Bible*. Jesus' scribe is one versed in Mosaic Law, a person who knows and draws from the wealth of the law and also recognizes new treasure when it appears. Yet the scribes of *The Saint John's Bible*, and the pages they have created, embody what Jesus' kingdom-images evoke. They remind us of how the holy, which so often seems hidden, emerges when we stretch ourselves into searching for it, seeking it, laboring toward it. The bakerwoman kneading in her kitchen, the man who sells all that he has to buy the field, the merchant who gives up everything to purchase the pearl of great price, the scribe trained for the kingdom of heaven, the householder who brings forth treasure old and new: all of these have given themselves to a process by which treasure emerges. They know what skill it takes, what vision, what devotion. Trained in their art, they possess in their bones the knowledge that tells them what ingredient to use, what tools old or new to employ, what treasure lies before them.

BLESSING

And so may you give yourself:
your skill, your art,
your vision, your life
to the finding of treasure
and to the fashioning of it.

# 8

## A LONG DEVOTION

In offering these kingdom images in Matthew 13, Jesus recognizes that some things are worth a long devotion; there is treasure worth giving ourselves to for a decade, a lifetime. Such treasure might not have an obvious usefulness or be readily comprehended. In a world where technological shortcuts abound (and are useful at times, to be sure)—bread machines, metal detectors, faux pearls, computer printers—we have a different experience when we take the long way around; when we hunt for the holy that often hides in work that takes time, the development of skill, commitment, the long view.

I recall when I was first learning calligraphy a few years ago. There was no getting around the need for practice. Over weeks and months, as I covered page after page with ink, shaky lines steadily grew more sure, and awkwardness began to give way to art.

When we give ourselves to this type of long laboring and searching, it reveals something about ourselves. Submitting ourselves to a process of practicing reveals secret parts of ourselves, drawing us out and unhiding us and the holy that dwells within us. "The kingdom of God is among you," Jesus says in Luke 17:21. Among us and meant to be uncovered, to become visible, to offer sustenance and grace for the life of the world. Like bread. Trees. Pearls. Pages. Treasure born of what is new and what is old.

What treasure have you found or long to find in the hidden places of your life? What searching, what seeking might God be guiding you toward, to uncover what has been buried? Do you have a practice that invites you to encounter the holy in a process that takes time, skill, devotion? What of yourself do you find in this, and what do you find of God?

BLESSING

That you will find something worth
a long devotion,
a lifelong laboring,
a slow stretching of yourself
into the secret places
where God watches and waits.

# 9

## ART AND JUSTICE

In 2009, Krista Tippett featured the work of the Hill Museum and Manuscript Library on her *Speaking of Faith* radio show. In conjunction with the program, titled "Preserving Words and Worlds," the *Speaking of Faith* blog provided a link to a short video about the making of *The Saint John's Bible*. I was struck by a comment that a blog reader left in response, stating that "the money would be far better spent feeding the hungry and homeless around the world" and that the Benedictines are "being selfish without realizing it."[7]

The comment illuminates a tension that has pervaded much of Christianity for centuries. We in the church often talk about art and justice as two options that we have to choose between, rather than being aspects of one action: our response to a God of grace and creativity who has placed us in a world that is both broken and beautiful.

We often forget that both the Christian tradition and the Bible itself developed and survived largely because people across the centuries transmitted the sacred stories in a variety of creative forms, not just in written texts but also in other media including drama, music, and liturgy. The stunning array of visual art fashioned over the centuries not only helped proclaim the gospel to those who could not read it (as well as those who could) but also became a gift in return to God: an extravagant offering, a gift that takes us where words alone cannot go, and an act of praise in response to the God who has lavished love, grace, and care upon us.

The fact that we live in the twenty-first century, when hunger, homelessness, and a host of other injustices continue to inflict deep suffering around the world does not diminish—and is not separate from—our need for beauty and the sustenance and hope it provides. I think of the story in which, as Jesus sits at table, a woman comes and anoints him with outrageously expensive oil. Mark tells us that some at the table were angry and said, "Why was the ointment wasted in this way? For this ointment could have been sold for more than three hundred denarii, and the money given to the poor." Jesus, however, receives her lavish act with grace and gratitude. "Let her alone," he tells those who scold the woman; "why do you trouble her? She has performed a good service for me. For you always have the poor with you, and you can show kindness to them whenever you wish, but you will not always have me. She has done what she could; she has anointed my body beforehand for its burial. Truly I tell you, wherever the good news is proclaimed in the whole world, what she has done will be told in remembrance of her" (Mark 14:3-9).

In saying that we would always have the poor with us, Jesus was not suggesting that we neglect to work to end poverty. Rather, he recognized that lavish acts of generosity, grace, and beauty, such as the woman offered to him, must be part of our response to him and to the world. It's not just that art should come alongside our work for justice, but that they are part of the same impulse toward hope, healing, and wholeness. Jesus knew that choosing justice at the expense of beauty is just another form of poverty.

BLESSING

May we offer
bread and beauty
from the same hand.

# 10

## THE ART OF HOSPITALITY

As an ordained minister as well as an artist and writer, I understand my call and my vocation to involve feeding people in both body and soul. One kind of feeding cannot long do without the other. I could not work for justice in this world without the creative acts that others have offered across the centuries and in our present time, not only because I could not live without their sustaining hope and beauty but also because they remind me that God desires us to give lavishly, generously, wantonly from the depths of who we are and who God has created us to be. Such extravagant acts can seem wasteful. By his response to the anointing woman, however, Jesus proclaims that such gestures of grace bring healing to the body of Christ and to the whole world.

Through the exhibitions, books, and Web site devoted to *The Saint John's Bible*, as well as the radio and TV shows that have featured it, people are coming into contact with the Bible who might not otherwise encounter it. *The Saint John's Bible* also summons those who think we are oh-so-familiar with the Bible to engage it in a different, deeper, and renewed way. The work of Donald Jackson and his team reminds us that the Bible is not obsolete but rather is a living, dynamic text. As such, the Bible invites us not merely to read it but to lavish our attention upon it, to grapple and wrestle with it, to question it, to discern how it still speaks to and teaches us in this time, and to illuminate it even as it illumines us.

At the same time, we do well to remember that *The Saint John's Bible* has value not because of what it *does* or accomplishes; the value of art is simply that it *is*. Far more than a tool or a means or even a message that may be laden with our own agenda, the grace and power of authentic art lie in its ability to welcome us into the Creator's presence and there find what we need.

The monks of Saint John's and the host of others who participate in the work of the HMML, including the artists, calligraphers, and financial contributors who make *The Saint John's Bible* possible, are offering the world a gift that is precisely the opposite of selfish. In preserving the sacred texts of the past, in employing ancient methods to offer a sacred text that speaks to us in the present, in drenching us with this audaciously lavish gift, they are offering, in fine Benedictine (and Christian) tradition, a profound act of hospitality.

Amid the brokenness of the world to which we are called to minister, these folks have given a rare gift that reminds us that God desires beauty. They bear witness to the fact that recognizing and offering beauty is part of what heals our brokenness. They show us that God is not yet done with the work of creating and that God calls us to offer our creative gifts for the healing and feeding of the world.

And that is good news indeed.

BLESSING

That we may make
of the sacred text
a table in the wilderness
and a feast for the world.

11

UPON THE ASHES

At the same time that Harriet Powers was preaching her sermons in patchwork, a contemporary of hers named Sojourner Truth was preaching around the United States wherever she could find a place to speak. Born into slavery in New York around 1797 with the name Isabella Baumfree, she had ten or twelve brothers and sisters whom she only knew from stories told by her mother, "Mau-mau Bett"; their master had sold all the children except for Isabella and her younger brother, Peter. In 1828, after being sold and later escaping, Isabella gained her freedom and moved to New York City.

After living there for more than a decade, Isabella experienced a call from the Spirit to travel and lecture. She desired a new name that would reflect her new vocation. Saying that she had left everything behind and wasn't going to keep anything of Egypt on her, she went to the Lord and asked him for a new name. "And the Lord gave me Sojourner," she said, "because I was to travel up an' down the land, showin' the people their sins, an' bein' a sign unto them. Afterward I told the Lord I wanted another name, 'cause everybody else had two names; and the Lord gave me Truth, because I was to declare truth to the people."[8] Sojourner Truth became a fiery preacher, orator, and abolitionist.

One day, while preparing for a speech at the town-house in Angola, Indiana, she heard of a threat that the building would be burned down if she spoke there. "Then I will speak upon the ashes," Sojourner replied.[9] Amid the threat of destruction, she made a promise of proclamation.

*I will speak upon the ashes.* With her words, Sojourner Truth gives an image of the work not only of a preacher but also of an artist: to create even—and especially—amid barrenness, destruction, injustice, and pain. In the presence of hatred and violence, creative work is an act of courage and hope. It claims a place for beauty and the possibility of wholeness that it offers.

Where do you see this creative work taking place? How might you offer or support creation upon the ashes?

### BLESSING

May you speak
where the Spirit calls you to speak;
may you create
with courage and with grace.
Amid the threat of destruction
and in the presence of desolation,
may you bear witness to the God

who knows how to create anew
from fire,
from flood,
from all that lays waste
in this world.

# 12

## MORE THAN EVER

In the wake of the attacks on the United States that took place on September 11, 2001, I exchanged some correspondence with a lifelong friend of mine who lives in New York City. A professional artist who provided my first art lessons as a child, Tom was walking to work when he saw the plane fly into the first tower of the World Trade Center. Writing shortly after the attack, he commented to me, "We need artists now more than ever."

I have thought often about his comment in the years that have followed the devastation of that day. My artist friend, who has witnessed and shared in the grief and healing of the city he calls home, continues to create and to offer his artful gifts to the world. And hundreds of miles away, in a wee studio in central Florida, I continue to work at sharing my own creative gifts. What I fashion in my studio doesn't provide a cure for cancer or an end to poverty or a cessation of terrorism. It is, however, what I have to offer the world: an act of hope, a commitment to creation amid devastation, a practice that is not removed from the brokenness of the world but rather is a tangible, tactile, transforming prayer that arises from within it.

What my friend noted in September 2001 is no less true today: we need artists now more than ever. And not just artists, but everyone who can contribute any form of life-giving creativity. The creative life is not limited to making visible work that we can put on a wall or a stage or a screen. It also encompasses less tangible but equally powerful modes of creativity: forming families, tending friendships, cultivating communities of hospitality and peace.

Now
more than ever
let us be the ones
who will not turn away.
Let us be the ones
who will go
farther into the wreck
and deeper into the rubble.
Let us be the ones
who will enter into the places
of devastation beyond belief
and despair beyond our imagining.

And there let us listen
for the Spirit that brooded
over the formless darkness,
and there let us look again
for the God who gathered up the chaos
and began to create.
Let us be the ones
who will give ourselves
to the work of making again
and to the endless beginning
of creation.

# 13

## FINDING MY TRIBE

As I write this, I am sitting on the porch of a house overlooking a river in Washington State. I have spent much of the day in this spot, writing, drinking tea, visiting with the cat who is the true owner of this porch, and surfacing for meals with the other people who have found their way to this piece of holy ground.

This sacred place is a remarkable retreat center called the Grünewald Guild. Nestled among the Cascade Mountains, the Guild was founded by Richard and Liz Caemmerer thirty years ago as a retreat center devoted to exploring and celebrating the connections between art and faith. For ten weeks each summer, as well as at other times of the year, the Guild offers classes in a wondrous variety of media including stained glass, ceramics, fiber arts, painting, and printmaking. What especially compels me about the Guild is that our creative work takes place in a rhythm of community life, with morning and evening prayer, shared meals, informal gatherings, and many conversations in the in-between places.[10]

As I live out a ministry that requires much explaining about what I do, and how, and why, the Guild offers me the experience of being in my element. In this place I find my tribe. Among this diverse gathering of people from around the continent and beyond, I encounter kinship, a shared language, a camaraderie that is much more difficult to find in my daily life

Although this kind of community is elusive the rest of the year, what I find here at the Guild helps to fuel my creative work at home. The Guild reminds me how crucial it is to seek allies on the creative path. It pushes me to ponder how to find and create an artful community in the place where I live, as daunting as this sometimes seems.

Where do you find people who sustain you on your path? Where do you meet the kinfolk who nourish your spirit and your creative work and whom you can support in turn?

### BLESSING

That we who need each other
will find one another.
That we may follow the lines
that will lead us
to the kindred of our souls.
That our tribe will grow
and prosper
and be a blessing.
That we may be the beauty
in which we long to dwell.

# 14

## THE ART OF HOPE

The Grünewald Guild was named for Matthias Grünewald, the German painter best known for his creation of the Isenheim Altarpiece in the early sixteenth century. Grünewald designed the altarpiece for the chapel of a hospice run by the monks of the Monastery of Saint Anthony in Isenheim, a town near the border between Germany and France. The Antonite monks ministered in particular to those suffering from ergot poisoning, also known as Saint Anthony's Fire, a widespread affliction that caused painful skin eruptions as well as spasms and convulsions. At the time, it was not known that the condition, which frequently led to gangrene, amputations, and eventual death, was caused by a poisonous fungus in rye, a primary source of flour for bread.[11]

The Isenheim Altarpiece is a polyptych; its multiple hinged panels swing open to depict such scenes as the Annunciation and the Nativity. The primary feature of the altarpiece is viewed when closed: the Crucifixion of Jesus, his body devastated not only by the wounds of his crucifixion but also by the sores that Grünewald painted upon him. These sores matched those borne by the people suffering from Saint Anthony's Fire, for whom the altarpiece was created. Grünewald presents an image of a Christ who has fully entered into the suffering of humanity. Yet the Crucifixion does not have the final word: among the other scenes that Grünewald depicted, in the innermost section of the altarpiece, is the resurrection of Christ.

Nearly five centuries later, the Isenheim Altarpiece provided inspiration for a remarkable work of art called the Keiskamma Altarpiece. Created in the South African coastal town of Hamburg, the altarpiece is named for the Keiskamma River Valley in which Hamburg lies, in the Xhosa region of Eastern Cape Province. This largely rural area is marked by rampant poverty and illness. HIV and AIDS are prevalent; some communities in the province report over half of their population as infected with HIV.

Organized by Dr. Carol Hofmeyr, an artist and physician who established the first AIDS medical center in the area, and led by Nosimasile Nokuzola Makubalo (known as Noseti), 120 people, primarily women, created the Keiskamma Altarpiece as an artful act of lamentation and hope in the midst of the HIV/AIDS crisis. Like Grünewald's masterpiece that inspired it, the Keiskamma Altarpiece has three layers that depict major events of the Christian faith through the perspective of a suffering community. With stunning beadwork, appliqué, embroidery, and photography, the panels portray the people of the region: for instance, the closed panels depict not the crucified Jesus but rather Xhosa people who wear the face of the suffering Christ.

A Web site featuring the Keiskamma Altarpiece describes the central panel in this way:

> The crucifixion is depicted from the point of view of people without material resources trying to find meaning in their lives. The somber crucifixion panels show a widow in traditional Xhosa [dress] mourning her husband [who] has died of AIDS. On her right are children orphaned by the disease and on her left is an old lady sitting on a bed.
>
> On either side of this central panel are two Hamburg saints, wise old women chosen for this position because of their love for the community. Lagena Mapuma is dressed in a red Methodist church uniform and Susan Paliso with a white shawl.[12]

The other panels of the altarpiece depict scenes of suffering and hope: Susan Paliso's son at his funeral, his body covered with sores; a prophet in the community; a choir; a vibrant swirl of animals and fish. The panels incorporate photographs of women caring for their grandchildren who have been orphaned by AIDS. They are images of pain, of redemption, of solidarity with those who have suffered in every age. "In making this work," states the Web site of St. James Cathedral in Chicago, which has hosted the Keiskamma Altarpiece, "the community artists hoped to draw a parallel between AIDS and other diseases that seemed hopeless and now no longer exist, thereby offering hope to people living with HIV and AIDS, and indeed to all of us. The artists also wanted to show that, although they feel cut off and alone in their suffering, they are part of the whole of humanity, past and present, who have had to deal with terrible afflictions."[13]

BLESSING

In every place
where we encounter
the Christ of the cross
in the suffering of his people,
may we bear forth
the Christ of the resurrection
with every art
in every age.


# 15

*The Secret Room*

## A NEW LANGUAGE

A few years ago, when I received an invitation to do the artwork for Peter Storey's book of reflections on the seven last words of Jesus, it came as a lovely bit of synchronicity. His editor wasn't aware that Peter and I were acquainted, having crossed paths on a few occasions when he visited the United States from his native South Africa, where his ministry as a Methodist pastor included serving as a bishop of the Methodist Church of Southern Africa and as the chaplain to Nelson Mandela when he was in prison. The catch was that the artwork for Peter's book had to be in black and white. With my having worked primarily in paper collage, black and white was not exactly my first language, artistically speaking. I was so eager to work on the project that I told the editor yes. Then I had to set about to figure out what kind of black and white medium I could manage.[14]

I tried doing collages in black and white but made little headway. After several other experiments, I picked up a piece of charcoal—and fell in love.

Beginning to work with charcoal was like learning a new language, with all the delights and difficulties that come in such a process of discovery. Most of my early sketches were a mess. I could sense that a style was emerging, but in the early stages it appeared so raw and unformed that I began to despair of having anything ready in time for Peter's book.

On the verge of calling the editor to do an embarrassing backing-out dance, I instead called my artist friend Peg to ask if she could either collaborate with me or counsel me on the project. Peg told me to bring her all the sketches I had done: the good, the bad, and the ugly. To my eye they were mostly bad and ugly. But Peg took the smudgy, ashy papers, spread them out, and pondered them. In a fashion that struck me as a form of *lectio divina*, she followed their tangled lines until she began to perceive the beginnings of coherence and form. Moving through what I had viewed as chaos, Peg showed me what she saw and offered suggestions on how to pursue and develop the path that had been obscure to me. Not only did this help to make it possible to complete the project, it also began to open creative doors within and beyond me in ways I never would have imagined.

In large measure, what I came to love about working in charcoal was the dramatic contrast it offered to my colorful, more intricate collage work. Where collage involves a process of accumulation and addition as the papers are layered together, charcoal invites me to an opposite experience. When I do a charcoal drawing, my goal is to find the fewest number of lines necessary to convey the scene. It is a medium of subtraction, involving little more than a piece of blank paper, a stick of charcoal, and an eraser to smudge and then smooth away all that is extraneous. What remains on the page—the dark, ashen lines—is spare, stark, sufficient.

For every artist, a critical habit to develop is staying open to what shows up. In the process of cultivating a unique vision, with the consuming focus this involves, we need to learn how to keep an eye open for the creative surprises that can lead to new pathways or deepen existing ones. If I stay too attached to a favorite medium or familiar technique, I risk shutting myself off to possibilities that take me to new places in my work and my soul.

Taking up a new medium, entering a different way of working, diving or tiptoeing into a new approach: all these can be complex, unsettling, disorienting, discombobulating. Launching into the unknown and untried confronts us with what is undeveloped within us. It compels us to see where we are not adept, where we lack skill, where we possess little gracefulness. Yet what may seem like inadequacy—as I felt in my early attempts with charcoal—becomes fantastic fodder for the creative process and for life. Being present to the messiness allows us to sort through what is essential and clear a path through the chaos. To borrow the words of the writer of Psalm 51, it creates a clean heart within us.

BLESSING

May the Holy One
who never ceases to practice
the art of creating
keep us ever
at the edge of our skills,
our habits,
our vision,
that we may never
grow so content
in our creating
that we miss the God
who is ever about
to do a new thing.

# 16

## THE COMPLICATED PLACES

Simply put, the creative life invites us to envision and discern what God is trying to accomplish in the world. It employs the intellect but also takes us beyond it, down into the deeper levels, to the realms of intuition and imagination. The creative process, in its many forms, involves bringing back the treasures of those realms and offering them to the world.

Here's how Gary put it one day: "Life is too complicated to deal with only in words. If you can only deal with stuff that's simple enough to put into words, you're not going far enough. And that's where God is—in the complicated places."

BLESSING

May you go
into the complicated places
with courage
with wisdom
with the protection of God
who meets you there.

# 17

# FROM A LETTER TO A FRIEND WRITING A THESIS, WHO ASKED ME ABOUT ART AND FAITH IN MY WORK

The poet Jane Hirshfield has a wonderful essay in her book *Nine Gates: Entering the Mind of Poetry.* The essay is titled "Writing and the Threshold Life," but what she says about writers is often true of other creative folks as well. She offers the image of the monk—himself a threshold figure living on the margins of the community—who daily goes out with his begging bowl, receiving scraps of sustenance from the community in exchange for what he has to offer, including wisdom and prayers. Hirshfield writes,

> Monks are recyclers, composters—out of waste and communal labor they create subsistence, beauty, and wealth. This is the work of the threshold: to step into places of seeming barrenness, emptiness, or neglect and bring back an abundance new-coined. For writers, as for monks, to take on this work often means leaving the mainstream in outward ways, abandoning the world of ordinary jobs and housing; the garret life is found up literal stairs as well as within the steep reaches of the psyche. In its deepest sense, though, threshold life for a writer has to do with a changed relationship to language and culture itself. In writing lit by a liminal consciousness, the most common words take on the sheen of treasure—transformed in meaning for the entire community because they have been dipped in the mind of openness and connection.[15]

I connect with what she writes about in a variety of ways, both in my vocation as a writer and also as an artist who works in a couple different media (and who, in my garage apartment, lives the "garret life" she describes!). The medium of collage provides a tactile way for me to experience what Hirshfield describes—taking the scraps and, with the help of the Spirit, transforming them into "an abundance new-coined." This is much the same thing that I experience the Spirit doing with my life—taking the bits and pieces and sometimes ragged-edged scraps, the light and the dark, the rough and the smooth, and piecing them together, transforming them, to create something new.

To cross through the doorway into that threshold space is its own act of faith. As you know in your own life, the creative crucible is not always an easy place to be. Our own layers get exposed in the creative process in ways that are wondrous and sometimes unsettling or scary. And certainly chaotic. I don't think I could do it if I weren't aware of the presence and sustenance of God in the midst of it all, if I didn't feel called and companioned by the One who, in the beginning, hovered over the chaos and began to create from it. So even as art is for me a doorway into faith, the converse is also true. As I open to God's presence, trust God's call, and engage (and struggle) with the Spirit who hovers over my chaos and brings forth creation, then faith is a doorway into art.

### BLESSING

That we may live
on the threshold
where barrenness
becomes beauty
and poverty
becomes plenitude.

# 18

## KINDLING THE FIRE

The kind of threshold life that Jane Hirshfield describes requires a perpetual exposure and openness: openness to God, to the layers of our lives and their sometimes raw spaces, to the world with its beauty and its terrors. That's the deal: we must have all this and reckon with all this in order to create. We can't shut it out and still do the work to which God calls us. Yet dealing with the level of exposure that comes in living in a liminal space can be daunting as well as exhilarating.

When we open ourselves to the God who calls us to live on the creative threshold, we open ourselves to other forces that actively work against creation. These forces can manifest themselves in big ways, but I find they like the subtle approach best of all. They take the form of extraneous commitments that assume precedence over creative work, of busyness that we let creep in; they present themselves as fatigue or boredom with the process; they wear the face of the critic—internal or external—to whom we give power. They come in the guise of systems or individuals that, explicitly or indirectly, tell us there is not enough time, not enough money, not enough reason to give ourselves to the work. These contrary forces may come from outside ourselves or from the inside, in our own resistance to the work and to the continual exposure it involves.

However they come, these forces that ally themselves against the work of creation do come. And so I have learned the importance of praying for the protection and encompassing of God in my creative work. I have sometimes been complacent about this, too prone to operating under my own power or assuming that God's power will be there without my asking for it. Failing to ask for the sustenance and protection that I need is perhaps the fastest route to the fatigue that sometimes dogs my work.

Remembering to pray for our creative work and to engage in the practices that sustain our work can feel like a lot of work in itself. But I think of Amma Syncletica, a desert mother who had a keen understanding of the forces of resistance that come from within as well as from without. Syncletica once said, "In the beginning there are a great many battles and a good deal of suffering for those who are advancing towards God and afterward, ineffable joy. It is like those who wish to light a fire; at first they are choked by the smoke and cry, and by this means obtain what they seek (as it is said: 'Our God is a consuming fire' [Heb. 12.24]): so we also must kindle the divine fire in ourselves through tears and hard work."[16]

How do you seek the protection and the encompassing of God for your work in the world? How do you kindle the divine fire in yourself?

BLESSING

May everything
that keeps you from your work
give way to your work.
May the God who created you
encompass and protect you,
and may you move with joy
deeper and deeper still
into the life that God
has made for you.

# 19
## TRACING THE PATTERNS

For the past year or so, I have found myself noticing patterns. It owes, perhaps, to the textiles magazine that I subscribe to, a gem called *Selvedge* that's produced in England. Drawing from textile traditions around the world, each issue offers a visual feast. Weaving, block printing, knitting, embroidery, tapestry, sewing: in a variety of textile media from nearly every continent, from centuries past to the present day, the patterns among these pages tantalize my eye and tug at my imagination.

Patterns have found their way into my artwork as well as into my home. When I needed a new bedspread—the old one, made by a friend from a fringed sari, having grown worn from years of use—I chose a bedspread from India. Hand blocked in a blue-and-white pattern called "Midnight Lotus," it enfolds me each night within its bower of twining flowers and vines.

Noticing patterns has gotten me thinking about the patterns in my own life and the rhythms of repetition and return. What recurs amid the days, months, years? What contributes to a pattern that makes for wholeness, and what distorts the rhythm of my life?

I am coming to appreciate that patterns, in art and in life, do not always have to do with dullness, with tedium or boredom. I have a temperament that resists stultifying sameness: I need a life in which no two days are quite alike. Yet I also need an underlying sense of order—well, not order, precisely, though perhaps I might work toward that; more like a conscious continuity that holds my days together. In the midst of change and unpredictability, I need routines and practices that help me find my grounding and my way.

What patterns do you notice in your life? What patterns have you inherited? Which ones serve you well? What habits, rhythms, and ways of being do you struggle with? How might they become a place of prayer?

BLESSING

May you find and follow
the rhythms that bring life.
May you let go of the patterns
that confine and constrain.
May your turning and returning
trace pathways of peace,
and each step you take
make a life-giving way.

# 20
## KNOCKING FROM THE INSIDE

Part of what I love best about my vocation is getting to witness what emerges when folks are given time, tools, and space to reflect on their lives. In retreat and workshop settings, I always make collage supplies available as a means of contemplation. Collage is great because anyone who made it through kindergarten has the necessary skills. Cut. Tear. Paste. Voilà! Even those who may freak out in the face of an invitation to be artful often find they can engage the collage process, especially when the papers, with their stunning patterns, textures, and colors, beg to be picked up and played with.

In my favorite collage exercise, I ask participants to think about their lives as a landscape. I suggest that they reflect on their commitments, their relationships, whatever makes up the terrain of their days, and then create a collage that evokes that landscape. Often I give them a small, four-by-six-inch piece of paper for the background, to make it as manageable as possible.

It is amazing what a landscape people can fit into twenty-four square inches.

After folks have created a collage, I often do a quick process of *lectio divina* with them. A little *collagio divina*, if you will. In much the same way that we can read a written text, we can also read the visual text of a piece of art, whether created by us or someone else. I invite them to ponder their collage silently as I offer a few questions. One of the questions I ask is this: "When you turn your collage—your landscape—in a different direction, what do you see?"

Things turn up in collages that we're often unaware of at the time, and changing our perspective helps us notice them. This happens in our own lives too. Sometimes, when we need a shift, we find it by looking at our lives from a different view. Often the shift comes from within ourselves. I think of the poem by Rumi in which the poet describes how he has been making himself crazy, knocking on a door, only to discover, "I've been knocking from the inside!"[17]

Do you feel stuck right now? What might help you gain perspective, a different view of your life? What piece needs turning, considering from another angle, in order to better see what's there and what's possible? Might the needed shift be within your own self?

## BLESSING

That you will see
the landscape of your life
in all its fullness.
That when you are stuck
you will be given eyes
to see your terrain anew.

# 21

## THE ANTIDOTE TO ENVY

One of the cool things about going to the Grünewald Guild each summer is the opportunity to see what other artists are doing. One of the risky things about going to the Guild each summer is the opportunity to see what other artists are doing. Coming into contact with creative folks is a two-edged sword: even as it supplies inspiration and camaraderie in a vocation that requires much solitude, it can also provide an opening for envy to slip in.

Take my friend Gilly. Gilly comes over from England to teach at the Guild. As if having a fabulous accent weren't enough, she is also a fantastic artist. Much of Gilly's work involves painting on fabric. Oftentimes, really big pieces of fabric. In churches, in her local theological school, and in other settings, Gilly creates large-scale pieces that both evoke and invoke a sense of the sacred.

Those who teach at the Guild give evening talks in which we share our work. Last year, Gilly offered a presentation with images of her work, both in progress and completed. I was taken in particular by a series of large painted fabric pieces inspired by Saint Patrick's Breastplate, the remarkable prayer for protection attributed to the patron saint of Ireland. As Gilly described creating the pieces and her use of them with groups, I felt a stab of envy. For nearly two years, my primary artwork has been the collages for my blog, The Painted Prayerbook, which are just three-by-four inches. I love working small right now since completing a commission that was four and one-half by six and one-half feet. It took nearly two years to complete and was a real trick to create in my three-hundred-square-foot studio apartment. So the wee collages have been a powerful way to explore new directions and techniques in a more manageable and intimate fashion. Yet as I listened to Gilly and saw her images, I found it hard not to compare. I envied her talent, her vision, her access to a church and a school where she could explore and offer her gifts. I envied her having a space that enabled her to stretch out and design such large pieces.

At the same time, I knew that focusing on what others are doing and constantly comparing our work to theirs distracts us from our own work. Left unchecked, envy saps our energy, robs our creative focus, and eats us alive. I appreciate the way that Bonnie Friedman writes about this in her book *Writing Past Dark: Envy, Fear, Distraction, and Other Dilemmas in the Writer's Life.* She asks,

> What is this thing that can take the best from us and yet remain unsatisfied? When I think of envy, I think of Pharaoh's lean cows [from Pharaoh's dream in Genesis 41]. They eat up the healthy ones—cannibals, those cows!—yet they remain as skinny as ever, so that, the Bible tells us, "when they had eaten them up, it could not be known that they had eaten them; but they were still ill favored, as at the beginning." I've always felt sorry for those cows. We're told they're poor and lean-fleshed, emaciated and ugly. They feed, but cannot digest. They are unhealthy desire incarnate.[18]

Friedman closes her chapter on envy by writing, "The antidote to envy is one's own work. Always one's own work. Not the thinking about it. Not the assessing of it. But the *doing* of it. The answers you want can come only from the work itself. It drives the spooks away."[19]

## BLESSING

That your eye may draw you
beyond yourself;
that your imagination
may be captured
and quickened;
that your vision
may grow sharper
and more clear;
that your eye
will return to your own work
renewed
and restored.

# 22

## MEETING THE MESSENGER

I am learning to engage envy as I engage any other difficult emotion: as a signal, an invitation, a messenger come to tell me there is something here I need to work on. I find that when envy comes to visit, it offers a couple of possible messages. Envy may be encouraging me to push into a creative terrain I have not yet entered. Conversely, it may be daring me to recommit to my own direction, my creative vision, my call. In the latter case, envy over another person's work becomes the catalyst that sends me deeper into my own work.

Dealing with envy and other demanding emotions that emerge along the path of our practice is, in itself, a form of practice. It is part of the process of sharpening our focus and wrestling with what distracts us. If I give envy a measure of attention, try to hear what it has to tell me, it can deepen my practice; if I ignore it or obsess over it, it can sabotage my practice.

The stab of envy can be painful, but its knife has a way of laying us bare and revealing what we need to see. When I acknowledge the presence of envy and let it do its piercing, paring work for a limited time, it opens room both to explore new directions that other artists inspire me toward and also to renew my commitment to my unique calling.

Maybe one day, under Gilly's influence, I will grow desperate enough to knock out one of the walls of my cozy apartment, unroll a bolt of fabric over the side until it touches the driveway below, and start painting. Until then, I'm keeping my eye on my bits of painted paper, piecing them together inch by inch, following the pathway they make.

How about you? Does envy surface in your own life? What triggers it? What message or invitation might it hold for you? How do you listen to it?

### BLESSING

May God send you
the messengers you most need.
May you abide
the work they come
to do in you:

the piercing, paring labor
of laying bare.
May you move
with freedom
in the direction of the path
the messengers
make within you.
May you walk
with desire and delight
along their welcoming way.

# 23

## THE ART OF OBEDIENCE

In her book *Walking on Water: Reflections on Faith and Art*, Madeleine L'Engle writes about Mary, the mother of Jesus—a woman who, like Harriet Powers, knew what it meant to proclaim the good news with the creative means she had at hand. For Mary, proclamation came not only in the form of a song that we have come to know as the Magnificat; it came also in her own being, in giving her own self, her own body, to bear God into the world. L'Engle writes,

> What would have happened to Mary (and to all the rest of us) if she had said *No* to the angel? She was free to do so. But she said, *Yes*. She was obedient, and the artist, too, must be obedient to the command of the work, knowing that this involves long hours of research, of throwing out a month's work, of going back to the beginning, or, sometimes, scrapping the whole thing. The artist, like Mary, is free to say *No*. When a shoddy novel is published the writer is rejecting the obedient response, taking the easy way out. But when the words mean even more than the writer knew they meant, then the writer has been listening. And sometimes when we listen, we are led into places we do not expect, into adventures we do not always understand.
>
> Mary did not always understand. But one does not have to understand to be obedient. Instead of understanding—that intellectual understand-

ing which we are so fond of—there is a feeling of rightness, of knowing, knowing things which we are not yet able to understand.[20]

The word *obedience* can—and should—be a difficult one for us. This is especially true for many women, of whom obedience has often been demanded, expected, and wrested by those who fail to understand that when forced or given without mindfulness, it is not true obedience.

Monastics, who promise obedience as one of their vows, generally have a much richer understanding of the word. In this context, I learned that the root of the word *obedience* means "to listen to." Obedience involves placing ourselves in a context where we are surrounded by people who know us well and who seek to know God well. As a result, they bring wisdom and perspective that we may be unable to summon on our own. Obedience asks that we give ourselves to what can be trusted: a person, a community, a practice, a way of life.

In the creative process, being obedient to the work, as L'Engle describes, calls us to trust that the work knows more than we ourselves know. Exerting too much control over the process can damage the work and us as well. Artful obedience requires intention and discernment. It requires attention to the demands of the work, to its rhythms and needs, and to the mystery that lies at its heart.

### BLESSING

May you listen into the work
and around it;
may you listen within it,
behind and
beneath it.
May you let
your true work lead you
into the places
that only it knows.

# 24

## A KIND OF FIERCENESS

True art, good art, authentic art arises from the depths of one's self. It emerges from the dark, mysterious, and sometimes chaotic interior waters—the place where the Spirit hovers and broods over the formless void as it did at the beginning of Creation.

It requires enormous focus and a kind of fierceness to do the listening involved in this process, to be obedient to the work and to the God who leads us to it. Because of this, others may mistake our fierce focus for selfishness.

This creative work, however, is neither selfish nor self-indulgent. Art is a form of service, an act of hospitality, an offering back to the One who labored with absorbed devotion to the creation of the universe. Our art invites others to encounter this God who persists in entering the chaos of our world with anguish and delight and who calls us to share in creating anew.

### BLESSING

May the God of the heavens
and of the earth
enter into the place
within you
that holds the keenest chaos,
the deepest mystery,
the most intense darkness

and there
may the God of
sun and moon
stars and seasons
breathe the words
that will bring forth
a new world.

# 25

## THE ONLY MAGIC

While I was in seminary, the artist and writer Meinrad Craighead came to Atlanta for a speaking engagement. Craighead, a writer and artist known for such books as *The Mother's Songs: Images of God the Mother*, spent time responding to questions after her talk. Many members of the audience wanted to talk about the creative process—how it happens, what it involves. One woman told Meinrad about her longing to spend more of her life being creative, then listed the obstacles that hindered her from that kind of life. She asked Meinrad how she could be more creative in the midst of these pressing commitments.

In her typically forthright manner, Meinrad told the woman that if being creative was important to her, she would do it. It was an abrupt response, bordering on harsh, yet it offered a stunning clarity that I have carried with me ever since.

There is no magic that will give us more time. The only magic comes in making choices about how we enter into time and how we discern what is most important. We will always encounter resistance to choosing a creative life: if not from outside ourselves, then from within. Often the inner resistance—even to the life we think we most want—manifests itself in commitments and obstacles that become excuses from pursuing what we long for. "That which hinders your task is your task," says actor and teacher Sanford Meisner.

I have found it important to remember that life unfolds in seasons. At times other commitments necessarily take precedence over artful pursuits. In such times, we need either to postpone our creative desires and make peace with this (and make a plan for when we will pursue these desires again) or find other ways to attend to these desires.

An artful life is a *sacrifice*, in the root meaning of the word: it is an act of making sacred, and it requires something of us. This life continually confronts us with questions about our priorities. It presses us to choose and to abide the choices that we make. It demands a continual process of giving: giving up illusions and distractions, giving in to the God who calls us here, giving away all that hinders us from the life that God desires for us. We do this to make the sacred and the holy more visible in this world. When this truly happens, we have moments when this seems no sacrifice at all. Somehow, in the holy magic that lies at the heart of creating, there comes a point where everything we have let go of—everything we have given up, given away, and chosen against—returns to us in a form we never could have predicted or contrived on our own.

BLESSING

That you will be wise
to each season and time;
that every hour
will open its purpose to you;
that you will know
the need of the moment
and give yourself to it
with abandon
and with grace.

# 26

## BEAUTY BEFORE BED

Of late I have taken to going through my old *Selvedge* magazines. Just before entering sleep each night, I'll pick up an issue and take in a few pages, visiting with something beautiful as I prepare for sleep. One night, it's textiles made by Amish and Mennonite women in the nineteenth century, their homespun work elegant and reverent in its simplicity. Another night, the vivid block-printed designs of Brigitte Singh, a Frenchwoman who went to India as an art student three decades ago and never left. Funky tea towels by South African designer Heather Moore. Cloth made by Hiroko Karuno, a Japanese textile artist who puts her own spin on the intricate, labor-intensive, centuries-old tradition of paper weaving known as *shifu*.

Something beautiful before bed: it is a benediction on the day, a blessing for the night to come. It is a prayer that in the coming hours, when evil is making its way in the world, there will yet be beauty to meet it, to confront it with healing, with transformation, with hope.

BLESSING

May it be
that beauty will attend you
in your waking,
in your working,
in your resting,
and in your dreaming.

# 27
## THE RED CIRCLE

In his book *The Lives of the Artists*, the sixteenth-century painter, architect, and writer Giorgio Vasari tells the story of how Pope Benedict IX, in search of someone to create several paintings for St. Peter's Basilica, dispatched an assistant to collect samples from various artists. The candidates included Giotto di Bondone, the Italian painter who was a harbinger of the Renaissance. Of the visit to Giotto, Vasari tells this:

> Having gone one morning to Giotto's shop while the artist was at work, [the courtier] explained the pope's intentions and how he wanted to evaluate Giotto's work, finally asking him for a small sketch to send to His Holiness. Giotto, who was a most courteous man, took a sheet of paper and a brush dipped in red, pressed his arm to his side to make a compass of it, and with a turn of his hand made a circle so even in its shape and outline that it was a marvel to behold. After he had completed the circle, he said with an impudent grin to the courtier: "Here's your drawing." The courtier, thinking he was being ridiculed, replied: "Am I to have no other drawing than this one?" "It's more than sufficient," answered Giotto. "Send it along with the others and you will see whether or not it will be understood."[21]

Giotto got the job.

The image of Giotto's crimson O particularly grabbed me because of a small, abandoned collage that had been lying on my drafting table for a couple of weeks when I encountered the story. The collage began, and finally ended, with a red circle on a gold background. After a long struggle to develop it, I gave up and turned my attention in another direction. A collage artist, however, is reluctant to throw anything away; and I did like that red circle, so I kept it around, hoping it might become the basis for another piece. Reading Vasari's story, I began to think perhaps I had stalled out because I was trying too hard to add to something that was already complete. I have become aware that although I'm no Giotto, there is something very satisfying in the spareness of that circle. It is sufficient.

Vasari's story and that red circle set me to pondering the amount of time and energy we give to explaining, justifying, or selling who we are. We catalog and calculate our qualities in order to impress others and persuade them to hire us or love us or include us in their circle.

Plenty of situations call for demonstrations of competence and expertise. Walking into a doctor's office, a day care, a church, you want to know that the people who work there are qualified to care for your body, your child, your soul. But in a culture that sometimes pushes us to accumulate credentials and qualifications without developing the character that will sustain our expertise, it can be disarming to encounter someone who bows to simplicity instead of doing backflips to win us over.

One of the clearest examples I've seen of the power of a gesture like Giotto's came at a gathering of clergy that I attended early in my ministry. The design team had invited a potter to be the artist-in-residence during our conference and to offer a few words at our opening session. In a room full of clergy who live and minister in a system that has its own complicated culture of credentials and rewards, the potter stood before us, a small piece of pottery cupped in her hands. Gazing into the O of her bowl, she began to tell us what she had come to offer. Watching her, listening to her, I had the sense that we were encountering a woman whose life and creative work had worn away the impulse to impress, to prove, to convince. In her years of working with clay, the clay had also worked on her. Shed of pretense, the potter held out to us what she had to give.

It was more than sufficient.

In a culture that bases so much on evaluation and competition, there's often little room to squeeze around the need to demonstrate and display who we are. Whether we are selling ourselves for a job, a promotion, a membership, a mate, we live with the pressure to appear polished. That's not wholly a bad thing. Yet, in the midst of this, where might we trace a red circle of our own? What gesture or unadorned offering can we make that arises from the core of who we are? Where might we be called to make this offering, knowing others may not understand it but need it? What support and sustenance will help us do this?

BLESSING

That God will
make of your life
a circle,
an offering,
a gift
sufficient and
whole.

# 28

## PATRON DREAMS

Much of what we know about Harriet Powers and her work, especially the Bible quilt now at the Smithsonian, we owe to Jennie Smith. An artist herself, Smith headed the art department at the Lucy Cobb Institute, a school for young women in Athens, Georgia. Smith saw Powers's first known Bible quilt on exhibit at a cotton fair and contacted Powers in hopes of purchasing the quilt. Powers held her off for five years, but when her economic situation became perilous, Powers offered in 1891 to sell Smith the quilt for ten dollars. Smith told her she could only pay half that amount; after consulting her husband, Powers agreed to this. Smith spent time with Powers and recorded Powers's descriptions and interpretations of the story panels in the quilt she had created. Smith also wrote a letter that included her own elaboration of the descriptions and an account of the quilt's acquisition. She mentions that Powers returned to Smith's home several times to visit the "darling offspring of my brain."[22]

Like so many who had lived in slavery, Harriet Powers and her family encountered keen struggles in working for economic freedom. In her distinct and complex social setting, Powers illuminates a challenge that artists across the ages have encountered in some form: finding financial sustenance to support the work.

In my off-the-beaten-path ministry, I have a remarkable degree of autonomy to pursue my calling. Having this freedom also means that, for more than a decade, I have lived without the institutional security that I had when I worked for a congregation. I raise my own income. I take care of my own housing. I pay for my own health insurance. The trade-off is completely worth it, and I am grateful for those who have helped sustain this ministry.

Many days, however, I find myself wishing that someone would just come along and take care of everything. As a woman who prizes her independence and who values not being beholden to another, it occasioned a fair measure of cognitive dissonance when I first began to get in touch with the powerful yearning for someone else to take care of things—food, shelter, all that. I've gotten over the dissonance but not the desire.

I remember reading Mary Gordon's novel *Spending* some years ago. It's about an artist who, to her surprise and considerable delight, acquires a patron. I thought, *Ooohh, yeah, that sounds great.* I would not wish myself back to the era when the patronage of artists was at its height—it wasn't exactly the best of times for women in religious leadership—but I wouldn't mind seeing a resurgence (a renaissance, shall we say?) of folks with a commitment to supporting individual artists.

In the midst of longing for a patron, I have found myself pondering and praying with the question, *How might God be calling me to be the deliverer I am longing for?* Not just *How do I find support for myself*, but also *How do I support others who are working to make their creative way in this world?*

How about you? Where do you find support for your work? How do you provide sustenance for others or how might you be led to do so?

BLESSING

May the God of
manna in the desert,
wellsprings in the wilderness,
honey from the rock,
wine from water:
may this God provide
what you most need
for the work
God most desires for you.

# 29

## WONDERS AND POSSIBILITIES

One spring day I went with my sweetheart to the Morse Museum of American Art in Winter Park, not far from where I live. The primary draw of the Morse is its collection of works by Louis Comfort Tiffany, the artist famed for his stained-glass designs. I have always liked Tiffany well enough—a poster of one of his windows accompanied me through a succession of dorm rooms and apartments in college—but in more recent years I found I had a somewhat limited affinity for this kind of work. It was pretty, in an ornamental fashion, but didn't go much beyond that.

I had, however, changed as an artist since the last time I had walked through the museum's doors, had begun to work in ways that—I came to realize—altered how I saw Tiffany's work. And so I found myself in front of one of his windows, leaning in close, pulling back, leaning in again. I was amazed by his line work, the loose style so markedly different from the stained-glass designs of previous centuries. His lines captivated the part of me that had begun to work in charcoal since I had last been to the museum, and I had become fascinated with how the lay of a line—how it turns this way, then that—can convey a whole world.

And between the lines lay the remarkable glass, so distinctive of Tiffany, who radicalized the manufacture of stained glass and turned each fragment into an art form in itself. I spent a long moment at a table that offered pieces of Tiffany glass to touch. Every piece a different texture—smooth, coarse, rippled, ridged. A fragment that so looked like flame that its coolness seemed incongruous. I ran my hand over the pieces, each an embodiment of its maker's vision and daring, each a window onto the mysterious crucible that gives rise to art, each a threshold leading me deeper into my own creative path and reminding me why I set out on it in the first place.

Being an artist alters the way I see. It changes not merely how I view the work of other artists but also how I view the world. To give ourselves to a creative life does not mean simply producing. It means committing ourselves to looking for possibilities, connections, potential. It means seeing things as they are, how they could be different, looking for where the fragments and pieces might come together. This kind of seeing is risky, because we cannot always control how change will come. We can only give ourselves to the process. Audre Lorde writes, "Once you live any piece of your vision it opens you to a constant onslaught. Of necessities, of horrors, but of wonders too, of possibilities."[23]

BLESSING

That you will know your vision
and live into it.
That you will withstand
the onslaught that comes.

That places of necessity
and places of horror
will give way to
wonders and possibilities.

That you will see.
That your seeing will change you.
That your seeing
will change the world.

# 30

## THE LOST SUPPER

In her book *This I Accomplish: Harriet Powers' Bible Quilt and Other Pieces*, Kyra E. Hicks brings to light a recently discovered letter, written in Harriet Powers's own voice, which relates new biographical details about the quilter's life. Composed when she was fifty-eight years old, the letter reveals that Harriet was the mother of nine children—"6 dead and 3 living." She tells how, at age eleven, she was taught by white children to read "by sound on a poplar leaf" and also did her own studying. "In 1882," Powers states, "I became a member of Mt. Zion Baptist church.

"Then," Powers relates in an arresting detail, "I composed a quilt of the Lord's Supper from the New Testament."[24] *A Lord's Supper quilt.* It tantalizes the imagination—the possibility that a quilt that Harriet Powers created may still exist; and perhaps more than one, as other scraps of evidence suggest.

Thinking of Powers's lost quilt, I think too of the lost Gospelbook of Kildare, created during Saint Brigid's lifetime, and of all the other traces of women's lives that have gone missing. Relics in reverse, there is some place these lost creations hallow by the hollow they leave, a space that shimmers with their absence. It is a place of loss and lamentation, yet its emptiness allows room for the imagination to enter, to wonder, to ask not only, What did it look like? What went into its making? What does it reveal of the woman who created it? But also to ask, Among the absences, what is yet possible? Within the gaps, what might we dream? What does the vision of this woman inspire us to create in our own day?

### BLESSING

Let us lament
what has been lost.
Let us grieve
in the gaps
and reach into the absence
and hold the emptiness
with both hands.

Let us mourn
the sisters, mothers, grandmothers
whose work has been
devalued or destroyed.
Let us go in sorrow
for the stories
we will never know.

Yet let us also make
an offering of gratitude
for those whose work
made a way for us.
And then let us take up
the work that is ours.
And let us move
with the grace
of the generations
gone before us
whom we will never know
but whose stories still sing
within our making.

## 31

## PRAISE POEM FOR THE TOOLS OF A SEAMSTRESS

*History begins with needlework.*
—Pamela Norris, *Eve: A Biography*

Let us give praise
to the scissors
for they are elegant
in their stainless sharpness.

Let us give praise
to the pins

for they are precise
in their piercing art.

Let us give praise
to the needle,
praise to the thread,
praise to the meetings
their marriage makes.

Thimble and chalk
tape measure and gauge
seam ripper, pincushion, bobbin:

let us give praise to these
and to the blessed utility
of all things
that give themselves
to the art for which
they were made.

### BLESSING

May you know the work
that is yours to do.
May you give yourself
to the doing of it.
May the Spirit who has
inhabited creation
from generation
to generation
move through you
with power
and with grace.

## FURTHER READING

*The Artist's Way: A Spiritual Path to Higher Creativity* by Julia Cameron. New York: Tarcher/Putnam, 1992.

*A Communion of the Spirits: African-American Quilters, Preservers, and Their Stories* by Roland L. Freeman. Nashville, TN: Thomas Nelson, 1996.

*The Creative Call: An Artist's Response to the Way of the Spirit* by Janice Elsheimer. Colorado Springs, CO: Shaw/Doubleday Religious Publishing, 2001.

*Harriet Powers's Bible Quilts* by Regenia A. Perry. New York: Rizzoli International Publications, 1994.

*Learning by Heart: Teachings to Free the Creative Spirit* by Corita Kent and Jan Steward. New York: Bantam Books/Random House Publishing, 1992.

*Living Color: A Writer Paints Her World* by Natalie Goldberg. New York: Bantam Books/Random House Publishing, 1997.

*The Substance of Things Seen: Art, Faith, and the Christian Community* by Robin M. Jensen. Grand Rapids, MI: William B. Eerdmans Publishing, 2004.

*Walking on Water: Reflections on Faith and Art* by Madeleine L'Engle. New York: North Point Press/Farrar, Straus and Giroux, 1980.

## NOTES

1. Harriet Powers, description of her Bible quilt now in the Museum of Fine Arts, Boston; related to an anonymous writer in 1898. Regenia A. Perry, *Harriet Powers's Bible Quilts* (New York: Rizzoli International Publications, 1994), index to illustrations.

2. Lucine Finch, "A Sermon in Patchwork," in Kristen Frederickson and Sarah E. Webb, eds., *Singular Women: Writing the Artist* (Berkeley, CA: University of California Press, 2003), 95-96.

3. Audre Lorde, "Poetry Is Not a Luxury," in *Sister Outsider* (Freedom, CA: Crossing Press, 1996), 37.

4. Richard J. Powell, "Conjuring Canes and Bible Quilts: Through the Prism of Nineteenth-Century African American Spirituality," in Vincent L. Wimbush, ed., *African Americans and the Bible: Sacred Texts and Social Textures* (New York: Continuum International Publishing, 2003), 350–51.

5. Mary Ann Tolbert, "Mark," in Carol A. Newsom and Sharon H. Ringe, eds., *The Women's Bible Commentary* (Louisville, KY: Westminster/John Knox Press, 1992), 267.

6. To learn more about *The Saint John's Bible*, visit http://www.saintjohnsbible.org.

7. http://blog.onbeing.org/post/70369866.

8. Quoted by Harriet Beecher Stowe in her article, "Sojourner Truth, The Libyan Sibyl," in *Narrative of Sojourner Truth* (New York: Oxford University Press, 1994), 164.

9. *Narrative of Sojourner Truth*, 140.

10. For information about the Grünewald Guild, visit http://www.artfaith.com.

11. Fred S. Kleiner, Christin J. Mamiya, and Richard G. Tansey, *Gardner's Art Through the Ages*, 11th ed. (Fort Worth, TX: Harcourt College Publishers, 2001), 692–93.

12. http://www.keiskamma.org/art/major-works/keiskamma-altarpiece.

13. http://www.saintjamescathedral.org/keiskamma.asp.

14. See Peter Storey, *Listening at Golgotha: Jesus' Words from the Cross* (Nashville, TN: Upper Room Books, 2004).

15. Jane Hirshfield, *Nine Gates: Entering the Mind of Poetry* (New York: Harper/Perennial, 1998), 209.

16. Benedicta Ward, trans., *The Sayings of the Desert Fathers: The Alphabetical Collection*, rev. ed. (Kalamazoo, MI: Cistercian Publications, 1984), 230–31.

17. Rumi, *The Essential Rumi*, trans. Coleman Barks (Edison, NJ: Castle Books, 1997), 281.

18. Bonnie Friedman, *Writing Past Dark: Envy, Fear, Distraction, and Other Dilemmas in the Writer's Life* (New York: HarperCollins Publishers, 1993), 1 2.

19. Ibid., 8.

20. Madeleine L'Engle, *Walking on Water: Reflections on Faith and Art* (New York: North Point Press/Farrar, Straus and Giroux, 1995), 22–23.

21. Giorgio Vasari, *The Lives of the Artists*, trans. Julia Conaway Bondanella and Peter Bondanella (New York: Oxford University Press, 1998), 22.

22. Perry, *Harriet Powers's Bible Quilts*, introduction.

23. Lorde in "An Interview: Audre Lorde and Adrienne Rich," in *Sister Outsider*, 107.

24. Kyra E. Hicks, *This I Accomplish: Harriet Powers' Bible Quilt and Other Pieces* (Arlington, VA: Black Threads Press, 2009), 38.

# IN THE
# GARDEN OF DELIGHTS

*The Book of the Bride*

## INTRODUCTION

I AM SITTING by a garden. It is a small patch of earth, a beautiful tangle, and perhaps my favorite garden in all the world. On this bright afternoon at the Grünewald Guild in Washington State, it is a portion of loveliness. I hear the sound of the sprinkler in one direction, the river in another, crows above. The garden is a vision of sunflowers, marigolds, poppies, and the vegetables that have graced our table the past two weeks: zucchini and yellow squash, cabbages, tomatoes, golden beets and crimson ones. My sweetheart sits beside me at the edge of the garden, reading, drinking coffee. I didn't plan it this way, but this is the setting through which I am entering the landscape of this chapter, which we will travel in the company of the woman from the Song of Songs.

For all its wisdom, the Bible provides comparatively little insight into what it means to be in intimate relationship. The Hebrew scriptures present a range of configurations by which marital and sexual relationships take place. Both testaments offer potent images of love in the context of community. Yet when it comes to navigating the mysteries of what it means to be in intimate relationship with another person, the Bible provides no clear road map.

One of the gifts that it does offer us, however, is landscape. When the Bible wants to make a point about relationships, it chooses sometimes to conjure a garden or a vineyard. Drawing us into a space both cultivated and somehow wild, such a landscape provides a setting that compels us to consider how the rhythms of the natural world—growth and fruitfulness, decay and renewal—take place in the space between two people. We find the most famous example, of course, in the Song of Songs.

With its eight brief chapters tucked between the poetic book of Ecclesiastes and the prophetic book of Isaiah, the Song of Songs—also known as the Song of Solomon for the long-held belief that King Solomon composed it—reveals to us a world at whose center is a community of two: a woman and a man, lovers who move from landscape to landscape, each setting suffused with longing and delight.

Dramatic and intimate, the Song offers extravagant sensory images. The text finds its grounding and language within the created world. With its persistent imagery of food and feasting, the Song acknowledges our human hunger for one another. It offers us wine, raisins, apples, pomegranates, nectar, honey and milk, spices of saffron and cinnamon . . .

It is a book good enough to eat.

Across the centuries, the Song of Songs, which makes no explicit mention of God within its verses, has been a locus of contention as well as inspiration. In the Middle Ages, the Song attracted the greatest number of biblical commentaries, and it continues to stir debate about its origins and purpose. In her commentary on the Song, Marcia Falk acknowledges the ways that interpreters across the centuries have sought to classify the enigmatic Song: as an allegory of love between God and Israel or between Christ and the church or the individual soul, a drama, a cycle of wedding songs, a liturgy with roots in an ancient fertility cult, or a love poem that its author or authors designed as a unified whole. Falk, along with others, views the Song as a collection or anthology of love poems that were brought together to become the Song that found its way into the Bible.[1]

Although the Song was most likely crafted for a secular setting, its inclusion in the scriptures, along with its rich and inspired history, has made of it a sacred and beloved text of Jews and Christians alike. Within its lines, theologians, mystics, writers, artists, and musicians have found fertile ground by which to describe and enter into the mysteries of love and desire. In our own day, the Song continues to bid us wander through its sacred and sensual terrain.

Within this terrain, we find a woman who compels our imaginations with the power and poetry of her presence. The text identifies her only as the *Shulammite*, itself a mysterious term whose meaning has been debated; Falk translates the word as "princess," while others suggest the term describes her simply as a woman of Jerusalem. Whoever she may be, the woman of the Song has a voice that is rare in the scriptures. She speaks freely and with abandon, exulting not only in her lover but also in herself. She possesses an autonomy that we do not often see in the Bible. "Nowhere else in scripture," writes Renita Weems, "do the thoughts, imaginations, yearnings, and words of a woman predominate in a book as in the Song of Songs."[2] Although more of the speeches in the Song are ascribed to her than to the man, making the woman the primary character of the book, the authors of the Song have created a setting where we find remarkable mutuality between a woman and a man, a shared space in which each may freely seek, desire, name, take their delight.

Within the landscape that the Song offers to us, the woman—this lover, this bride—confronts us with questions about our loving and our desire. For what and whom do we long? How do we acknowledge and name our own hungers? Do we seek places and relationships in which we can live, move, and speak with freedom and abandon? How do we find God's presence and love in our human relationships?

As you travel with the woman of the Song, may love and delight attend your days.

# PRAYER FOR THE MORNING

O God my beloved,
may I walk into this day
as into your arms
and be a cause
for your delight
in these hours,
this world.

# PRAYER FOR THE EVENING

Lay me down, O God,
and lie with me
this night.
Spread your cloak
over my worries and fears;
gather up
my desires, my dreams.
Bless everyone
beloved to me.
Be comfort,
be rest,
be close
in this dark.

# 1
## ENTERING THE LANDSCAPE

Let us begin here: with the landscape. To see the woman who inhabits the Song of Songs, we must see what surrounds her. Like the young man who is her lover, she is not static; she does not remain fixed in one place while the poem unfolds around her. She covers much ground in the short space of the Song: either in imagination or in actual presence, she moves through domestic spaces of house and home as well as populated spaces of city streets and squares.

We find the primary landscape of the Song, of course, in spaces less populated, less domestic, and more wild: the garden, the vineyard. For those hearing the Song in the first centuries following its composition, these spaces would have conjured images not only of the real gardens and vineyards so prevalent and familiar in the land of the Song's origin; these landscapes would have tapped also into their collective imagination with a constellation of meanings and associations.

Both the garden and the vineyard appear throughout the Bible not only as real places but also as ones that have entered into the mythic memory of the people of God, from the garden of Eden to the garden tomb where the risen Jesus meets Mary Magdalene, and from the story of Noah's planting of a vineyard to Jesus' vineyard parables. These settings symbolize the people of Israel, as in Psalm 80, where the psalmist writes of how God brought a vine out of Egypt, and Isaiah 5, where, in a passage called "The Song of the Unfruitful Vineyard," the prophet laments, "For the vineyard of the LORD of hosts is the house of Israel, and the people of Judah are his pleasant planting; he expected justice, but saw bloodshed; righteousness, but heard a cry!" (v. 7). Gardens and vineyards recur, especially in the Prophets, as images for the restoration and peace that God promises: "For the LORD will comfort Zion," the prophet Isaiah sings; "he will comfort all her waste places, and will make her wilderness like Eden, her desert like the garden of the LORD; joy and gladness will be found in her, thanksgiving and the voice of song" (51:3).

These landscapes can be places of danger, as in Judges 21, which offers the chilling story of how men of the tribe of Benjamin hide themselves in the vineyards of Shiloh, emerging to capture the young women who have come out to dance and carrying them off as wives. Yet more often gardens and vineyards offer a terrain where redemption and right relation become possible: between lovers, between God and the people of Israel, and between Jesus and his followers ("'I am the vine, you are the branches'"). Each is, at heart, a place meant for sheer delight, a space that offers a remedy to what was lost in Eden. They give us a glimpse of what it means to know and to be known instead of hiding ourselves and turning away from one another and from God. This is nowhere as evident as in the exuberant, sensual poetry of the Song: "Come, my beloved," the bride sings in chapter 7, " . . . let us go out early to the vineyards, and see whether the vines have budded. . . . There I will give you my love."

BLESSING

May the God
who created the world
from love and from pleasure
draw you into places
of desire and delight.

2

HER OWN

The gardens and vineyards to which the Bible invites us offer elemental metaphors of fertility and fruitfulness. They are often profoundly feminine images. Within the Song of Songs, the bride does not simply inhabit the spaces of garden and vineyard; these places become identified with her own body. She becomes a landscape within herself: a sacred terrain, a holy ground.

This identification between the bride and her surroundings happens in many ways. One comes in the form of a literary device called a *wasf*. Found in Arabic literature from ancient times, the *wasf* is a praise song or poem that draws from the imagery and sensations of the natural world in describing one who is beloved. "The images are not literally descriptive," note Ariel and Chana Bloch in their commentary on the Song; "what they convey is the delight of the lover in contemplating the beloved, finding in the body a reflected image of the world in its freshness and splendor."[3]

And so within the Song we hear the woman's lover borrowing from the landscape as he sings, "Your cheeks are like halves of a pomegranate," and, elsewhere, "You are stately as a palm tree, and your breasts are like its clusters. I say I will climb the palm tree and lay hold of its branches. O, may your breasts be like clusters of the vine, and the scent of your breath like apples" (7:7-8).

We find this identification between the garden and the bride's body not only in her lover's speech but also in her speech about herself: for instance, in chapter 4, where she sings, "Awake, O north wind, and come, O south wind! Blow upon my garden that its fragrance may be wafted abroad. Let my beloved come to his garden, and eat its choicest fruits" (v. 16).

For all the generosity of the landscape and its lovers, one thing is clear: although the bride gives herself—her body, her earth—to her lover with freedom and delight, she does not exist solely for him: "My vineyard, my very own, is for myself," she exults near the close of the Song (8:12). Her body is ever her own.

## BLESSING

May the blessing
that is your body
be ever your own.
May the terrain
that you carry with you—
the terrain that *is* you—
be sacred,
and may you know
your earth
as holy ground.

# 3

## A SACRED STRANGENESS

In structure and in content, the Song of Songs is unlike any other text in the Bible. It does not fit easily into a particular category. I find it intriguing that, in the Christian Bible, it took its place between Ecclesiastes and Isaiah. (Jewish Bibles place it in the section called the Writings.) Like Ecclesiastes, the Song is classified as Wisdom Literature. At the same time, the Song contains imagery that echoes within the text of the prophetic books that follow it, where the prophets borrow from the natural world to describe how God will heal and redeem God's people. A threshold book, the Song offers us a sacred strangeness.

In their commentary on the Song, Ariel and Chana Bloch point out a detail that captures something of the unusual character of this book. They observe that the Song has an unusual number of *hapax legomena*, words that occur just once in a text. Because of their rarity, such words pose a challenge to translators: their meanings remain elusive, difficult to pin down. "Actually," write the Blochs, "the Song itself is a kind of hapax, for it is the only example of secular love poetry from ancient Israel that has survived."[4]

There is something fitting about the rarities *within* the Song and the rarity *of* the Song itself. It comes as a reminder that every love has its own language, that it resists explanation and defies definition. Despite its ubiquity, every love is its own phenomenon, its own mystery, its own species.

For all the barriers it poses to fathoming its mysteries, the Song remains compelling to our imaginations. Perhaps its very strangeness makes it so inviting. Ariel and Chana Bloch write,

> In some respects, the Song seems very accessible to readers now, more so than it has been for some two thousand years. . . . In our day it is the innocence of the Song, its delicacy, that has the power to surprise. Perhaps that very innocence is one source of the poem's continuing attractiveness. To read the Song is to recover, through the power of art, a freshness of spirit that is now all but lost to us. The Eden story preserves a memory of wholeness and abundance from the beginning of time; the prophets look forward to a peaceable kingdom at the End of Days. The Song of Songs locates that kingdom in human love, in the habitable present, and for the space of our attention, allows us to enter it.[5]

BLESSING

Within the space
of human loving—
in the wonder of it,
in the strangeness of it,
in the completely common
rarity of it—
may you find
your healing
and your home.

4

THE WILD CARD

With its distinctiveness, the Song of Songs offers its own irresistible textual terrain. It beckons us in to wander among the words and the imagery within its borders, to wonder at the lushness of its language, to ponder the questions and peculiarities that its text offers, and to wrestle with the persistent metaphors that create wide spaces for contemplation and interpretation.

It is the wild card of the Bible. Its strangeness opens it to many interpretations. Its inclusion in our sacred text provides a potent message about how the framers of the Bible viewed God and God's desire for God's people.

By itself, however, the Song gives no indication that its authors intended it as a theological text. Nowhere within its lines is the name of God uttered. The same is true for the book of Esther. Yet unlike Esther, the Song does not even suggest God's presence by alluding to Jewish festivals or by any other references that give it a religious character.[6]

Seeking to make sense of the seeming absence of God, medieval interpreters, both Jewish and Christian, often chose to approach the Song as an allegory of God's love for the people of Israel or of Christ's love for the church or the individual soul. In this allegorical approach, each character, each landscape, each image and detail within the Song took on spiritual import.

"In the abundance and generosity of the Song," Ariel and Chana Bloch write, "a lily is a lily is a woman's body is a man's lips is a field of desire."

Faced with such a landscape, those who approached the Song allegorically turned over every phrase, every image in an attempt to reveal the spiritual meaning that lay beneath. In doing so, write the Blochs, they "read the Song as if they were decoding a cryptogram. From their perspective, of course, they were not imposing an arbitrary meaning but searching out the hidden soul of the text." The Blochs observe that such a reading "now seems to us constrained and often absurd," and yet it may have helped ensure the preservation of the text. "When we remember how many great works of antiquity have been lost—the poems of Sappho, for example, have come down to us only in fragments—we must be grateful for the protective wrap of allegory, if indeed it helped to preserve the Song intact."[7]

## BLESSING

That the words
that have survived the ages
will find a home in you.

That you will read them
with renewed vision
and receive them
with open hands.

That their power
and their grace will be
a blessing on your days,
fire in the night,
companions on your way.

# 5

## HOLY AMBIGUITY

Allegory calls upon the imagination and can provide a first step beyond a literalism that limits our engagement with a text. Allegory does so, however, in a fairly linear fashion. It sets up equivalencies that ascribe a single spiritual meaning to any given image or character. At the same time that this acknowledges that a text has a deeper meaning, it generally limits that meaning to a single possibility.

Both within and beyond the Bible, searching a text for its sole meaning—allegorical or otherwise—is a habit to which we still often fall prey. I remember being thrilled in a long-ago English class to encounter the suggestion that some poets wrote in a coded fashion, and I approached the assigned poem avidly, poring over each word of the poem, searching the dictionary for alternate definitions that might lay bare the poet's deeper intent. Raised on Nancy Drew mystery books, I hungrily sought clues to a poem's "true" or hidden meaning.

Such an approach acknowledges that a poem—or a biblical text—is more than one layer deep. At the same time, it creates its own fixity and fundamentalism to assume that a text can mean only one thing instead of evoking many possibilities at once. Molly Peacock writes of this in her book *How to Read a Poem . . . and Start a Poetry Circle.* She reflects on entering poetry with loving attention to the wholeness of the text, approaching it with intuition and devotion rather than with the intention of dissecting it into its component parts in an attempt to decipher a solitary meaning. Peacock writes that when we read poetry carefully and mindfully, "we are restoring those wings torn from poems by bullies with low tolerance for ambiguity—the bullies perhaps we ourselves once were."[8]

The Song's ambiguity makes it no less holy. In fact, it gives us something far more sacred than any surety we might seek to impose upon it. The Song invites us, draws us into the text where its lines intersect with our own lives, until suddenly a landscape opens before us, opens within us; and we find ourselves in the field that the Song inhabits. Searching. Sought. Beloved.

BLESSING

May you have
the courage and the wisdom
to wander beyond what you know
to be certain,
to be true,
to be real.

May you tug at the meanings
that have been pinned in place
and look beneath the answers
handed to you.

And there
in shadow
may you know
the certain presence of God
who meets us in mystery
and takes pleasure
in each question we find.

# 6

## A LANGUAGE FOR LOVE

So if not allegory, then what? Why the presence of the Song of Songs in the Bible? What does the book have to teach us?

Although likely originating as secular love poetry, the Song nevertheless offers us rich and sacred text for *lectio*. Approached in a spirit of contemplation, this prayer book encourages us to examine our longings and desires and to find God, our beloved, within them. God's seeming absence from the Song of Songs bids us recognize that God dwells even in places where God is not invoked or acknowledged. We might read the Song, then, as a lyric meditation on the God whom the author of First John would describe, centuries later, in this way: God is love, and those who love, know God (4:7-8). In their loving, in the fullness and delight and desire of it, the lovers within the Song embody and reveal the God who desires a loving relationship with us.

And so the theologians and mystics, both Jewish and Christian, were not wrong to find within the Song a language that we can also use to describe the love between God and Israel, or Christ and the church, or Jesus and the individual soul. One question this ancient text poses is not what shall we make of the Song, how will we classify it, how will we dissect and define its meaning; but rather, what will the Song make of us? How will we enter its story, give ourselves to such a narrative that fairly embarrasses with its riches, and risk the remaking of everything we think we know about love?

BLESSING

May you love.
May you love.
May you love.

# 7

## BLACK AND BEAUTIFUL

Within the Song there is a fluidity to the borders, a blurring between what is human and what belongs to the rest of creation. The lovers, however, possess an integrity: they are ever themselves. We see this especially in the woman who describes herself with a clarity that eludes most women elsewhere in scripture—and sometimes eludes the men as well. The bride of the Song receives her lover's praise of her, from her teeth to her toes, yet she does not accept his words as the only definition of herself. She knows herself, knows who she is, and speaks on her own behalf without reservation.

Early in the poem, the woman says this of herself: "I am black and beautiful, O daughters of Jerusalem, like the tents of Kedar, like the curtains of Solomon" (1:5). Some translations render the text as "I am black *but* beautiful," as if the two states existed in opposition, despite the fact that, as some scholars note, the original Hebrew likely intended the reader to understand the conjunction as "and" rather than as "but." Nonetheless, the bride does seem to be offering some measure of defense of herself to her audience; she goes on to tell them, "Do not gaze at me because I am dark, because the sun has gazed on me" (1:6).

About this passage and its translations, Marcia Falk writes,

> I believe that the woman's assertion of her blackness is affirmative, not apologetic, and that the tension in the poem is the result of conflict between her and her audience. The city women stare with critical eyes, yet

the speaker defies them to diminish her self-esteem. No, she argues, I will not be judged by your standards; I am black *and* I am beautiful. Thus, I read the images in the first stanza as parallel: the tents of the nomadic tribe of Kedar and the drapes of King Solomon are each dark and attractive veils. There is both pride and mystery in these images, as the speaker defies her beholders to penetrate, with their stares, the outer cloak of her skin.[9]

What words do you use to describe yourself and who you are in this world? Where do these words come from?

BLESSING

May you be wise
to your own terrain
and know the lay
of your own land.
May you see who you are
in all the fullness
of your spirit
and your flesh.
May you tell it forth
without shame
or dismay.

# 8

## TO SEE AND LIVE

Unafraid to describe herself, the woman of the Song does not hesitate, either, to describe the man. "My beloved is all radiant and ruddy," she sings in a litany of longing and praise, "distinguished among ten thousand." She goes on to rejoice:

His head is the finest gold; his locks are wavy, black as a raven. . . . His arms are rounded gold, set with jewels. His body is ivory work, encrusted with sapphires. His legs are alabaster columns, set upon bases of gold. His appearance is like Lebanon, choice as the cedars. His speech is most sweet, and he is altogether desirable. This is my beloved and this is my friend, O daughters of Jerusalem (5:10-11, 14-16).

The freedom with which the woman of the Song tells of her lover calls to mind the times when other women of the Bible take on the power to describe and to name. I think in particular of the story of Hagar in Genesis 16. Pregnant with Ishmael, driven away by a jealous Sarai and a hapless Abram, Hagar finds herself—and is found by the angel of God—at a spring in the wilderness. Genesis recounts that after hearing the angel's words about Ishmael's great future, Hagar "named the LORD who spoke to her, 'You are El-roi'; for she said, 'Have I really seen God and remained alive after seeing him?'" (16:13).

In all the Bible, Hagar is one of the only people, female or male, who dares to name the God whom she has seen. The Bible acknowledges that there is power both in seeing and in naming. This power belongs ultimately to God and, where God allows us to participate in this, it comes as a gift and a responsibility: to see and describe truly, to recognize and name the presence of the holy in another being.

Whether with an intimate partner, a family member, or a friend, love calls us to move past our fixed ideas, our expectations, our assumptions about what we want to see, the false visions we construct about who others are. Love requires us to recognize and receive what is really there and to perceive how God dwells in the other. It can be difficult to abide the seeing, not because it is so challenging but because it is so wondrous. We may find it harder to take in another's glory than to take in the difficulties that arise in relationship. Yet to abide the seeing and to remain alive is our invitation and our call.

BLESSING

Today
now
this moment
may you see
the presence of God
in the face of another
and, in your seeing,
may you live.

# 9

## FAR REMOVED

Here's the thing, though. The lovers of the Song exist in a space that is largely idyllic. Within its poetic terrain, there are no dishes to do, no laundry to attend to, no piles of paperwork to sort. There are no jobs in this garden nor anxiety about the lack of employment. The lovers have no mortgage to pay, no teenaged children to worry over, no responsibilities to family or community. There is nothing mundane. The world of the Song seems far removed from the cares of daily life.

"Arise, my love, my fair one, and come away" (2:13). Well, who wouldn't want to?

Yet the Song offers a glimpse of a landscape that each intimate relationship needs: a space of seclusion; a pocket of time where care is, if not abandoned, at least laid aside for a while, and we can follow and delight in the voice of the one who calls to us. We may not be able to linger perpetually in the landscape of these lovers, yet they challenge us to cultivate spaces amid our days where we can tarry and savor and take our ease with our beloved.

### BLESSING

When your life has become
most frantic,
when fear and worry
have made their home in you
and anxiety attends your days,
may there come
from somewhere
the scent
of pomegranate and cedar,
apple and myrrh,
cinnamon, frankincense, fig.

# 10

## ALL DESIRES KNOWN

The Book of Common Prayer, which originated in England in the sixteenth century, contains a prayer that traditionally opens the liturgy of the Eucharist. In the 1662 version of the book, it begins, "Almighty God, unto whom all hearts be open, all desires known, and from whom no secrets are hid. . . . "[10]

*All desires known.* It is bold to call upon God in this way; it is courageous to bring ourselves before the One who already knows the longings of our hearts, especially when we don't always know, or want to acknowledge, these desires even to ourselves.

This prayer gave rise to the title of Janet Morley's book *All Desires Known*, a lush collection of litanies, prayers, and poems in which Morley searches fearlessly for language to bring before the living God. In the preface to her book, Morley writes of how the title became "a discipline and a comfort." She chose it, she writes, "because I understand the Christian life to be about the integration of desire: our personal desires, our political vision, and our longing for God. So far from being separate or in competition with one another, I believe that our deepest desires ultimately spring from the same source; and worship is the place where this can be acknowledged."[11]

How does desire find its way into your prayers? your reflection? your worship? What do your longings help you know about God?

### BLESSING

May you know
your desires
and may they draw you
toward the One
whose desire
is for you.

# 11

## THE HOUSE OF LONGING

"I think I'm addicted to longing," my friend Daniel once said to me. We talk about longing from time to time, how we are drawn to it, how it fuels us. It's a powerful thing, acknowledging what we want, what we yearn for, what we arc and ache toward.

Desire can offer clues to God's longing for our lives. Yet I've known the times when it has provided less of a map than a dwelling, a residence, a space where I have invited my longings in, entertained them lavishly, fed them well, and wound up being consumed in return. The House of Longing, I call it. The Place of Perpetual Ache.

How is it that we sometimes slip into a state where our longings leave us stuck? Where is the line we cross from desire into denial? Longing comes with its own enchantments: our yearning for what could be sometimes blinds us to what is and to what is truly possible and whole-making.

This is why it's crucial to learn to pray with our desires, to sit with what we think we want. Longing bids us to a kind of *lectio* in which we approach our desire as a sacred text, that we may discern where God is stirring within it and what God desires for us. Sometimes, in this kind of prayer, we find that it's time to leave the House of Longing, to step beyond its walls so that our vision can become restored. Or perhaps it's time to remodel the house or to reenvision it or to name it anew. Or maybe even to tear it down in order to see the stunning vista that it was blocking.

### BLESSING

That you will be wise
to the longings
that come to visit you.
That you will see their true faces
and know their true names.
That you will welcome the ones
that have gifts to bear.
That you will be graceful with yourself
for the ones

that took you a fool,
for they have their wisdom
that can be gained
no other way.


# 12

## SORTED OUT BY OUR DESIRES

We may find it hard to pray with our longings when such conflicting messages about desire and wanting abound. We find ourselves constantly bombarded with instructions about what we should want. Everywhere we turn, media confront us with advertisements designed to keep our "wanting" receptors in an overstimulated state while distracting us from what we really desire.

At the same time, much of the religious culture teaches us to be wary of what we want and to mistrust our instincts. Religion often works to inculcate us with the message, often with great subtlety, that God works against our desires and calls us to the places where we do not want to go. There is precedence for this, to be sure: think of Jonah going in the precise opposite direction from Nineveh, where God has sent him.

Although God often calls us to places beyond our imagining, it is also true that God lives within our longings and makes a habitation in the midst of our desires. Often it is in responding to our heart's deepest yearnings that we discover God's longing, God's call to us. The ultimate goal is that God's longing and our longing be one.

Janet Ruffing writes, "I understand that when we have the courage to sort out our desires and to be sorted out by them, our deepest and most authentic ones correspond to God's desires for us."[12]

How do you sort out your desires? How do you wander within the landscape of your longing? How do your yearnings serve to sort you? Where do you find God's desire within this?

May you have the courage
to sort through your desires

the humility
to be sorted by them

the vision
to look within your wanting

to find the God
who there makes a home.

# 13

## STILL YOUR WANTING

But there is this too: divesting ourselves, at least for a time, of our desires. *Still your wanting*, I sometimes find myself thinking. All this business of looking at our longings, of peering inside them and beneath them and behind them, sorting them and being sorted by them: this is good work, but it can be exhausting.

What might a sabbath from our desires look like? Not forever, but for a time—to fast, as it were, from what it is we want; to let go, to let be, and to see what comes our way. We may find yearnings we have clung to out of habit, desires we carry because it is our custom. What might we find in taking a break, taking a breath, taking a look around?

BLESSING

Amid your wanting
let there be stillness
and in your desiring
let there be silence.

Let there be release
and the simple grace

of breath,
of peace,
of rest.

# 14

## A SECRET LOVE

Some scholars have suggested that the love described in the Song is a secret love. The lovers, they say, have sought such landscapes as vineyard and garden because theirs is a love that needs enclosure, needs to be hidden from view, needs the protection of seclusion.

Every love has its labyrinth. We twist and spiral among the mysteries of attraction, desire, and loss, working to navigate and negotiate our path. Within this moving about, we have to discern continually how much to give of ourselves to each particular relationship—friendship, family, lover. Always there are spaces that only the two who share the labyrinth know. In some sense, every love is secret. And yet love cries out to come into the light of day.

There is a distinction between secret love and love that needs spaces of shared apartness, removal from the press of the world, in order to find renewal. Love that thrives in secret places—a vineyard, a garden—can be compelling. I have known these loves. Yet love that lives in hiding, love that is perpetually cloistered, cannot always survive the daylight. "Secret love is fragile," writes Alix Kates Shulman in *Drinking the Rain*, "but true love should be able to withstand exposure."[13]

Where does your love live? Have you had a love that you kept from view? What prompted the secrecy, and what was—or is—it like to live in this way? Where and how do we find the places where our love can thrive in fullness?

### BLESSING

In the labyrinth
of your loving,

may you see with clarity,
walk with integrity,
and abide the mysteries
that attend your way.


# 15

*The Secret Room*

## SAVANNAH

*for Gary*

We have spent three days
wandering the squares
of this Southern city:
Telfair, Chatham,
Washington and Franklin,
Lafayette and Liberty
and all their shaded kin.

Time and again
the trolley for the ghost tour
has rattled past us,
the guide pointing out
here a hotel where a Union soldier
wanders, carrying his severed arm,
and there a house
where spectral handprints
shimmer on the walls.

We two,
who began keeping company
on All Hallows' Eve,
know something of spirits.
We could give a tour
to make a body shiver

with delight and torment
by turns.

*On your left,*
*ladies and gentlemen,*
you could say,
*the house where I lived*
*with my former wife.*

*If you'll look to your right, folks,*
I could tell them,
*this is where the boy*
*I loved in childhood*
*would break my heart*
*a lifetime later.*
*And look, over there*
*is where a monk*
*told me of his desire.*

But here and now,
despite ghosts and shadows,
despite oaks dripping grey
with Spanish moss,
despite gardens
of good and evil,
I am feeling blissfully
less than gothic.

We are sitting in a café
on Chippewa Square,
you with coffee
and a book I have bought
for you,
I with jasmine tea
and a book you have bought
for me.

Two years from now
in this same city
you will ask me
to marry you.

We do not know this yet.
What we know is now,
the blessed enchantments
of the present:

tea, coffee,
books, quiet,
the companionable charms
of bodies
enfleshed and
familiar and
real.

Somewhere in the distance,
the ghost trolley
is spiriting its passengers
down the road

while here,
turning a page,
touching your solid,
beloved hand,
I am, for a moment,
utterly unhaunted
and content
down to my bones.


BLESSING

Amid the spirits
of loves past
and memories
that linger,

may you find
the blessed enchantments
of the present
and love
that welcomes you wholly
here and
now.

# 16

## THOSE SENTINELS OF THE WALLS

Just past its midpoint, the Song takes a dramatic turn. What has been a celebration of each other's presence becomes a lament of absence: "I opened to my beloved," sings the bride, "but my beloved had turned and was gone. . . . I sought him, but did not find him; I called him, but he gave no answer" (5:6). Absence then gives way to violence: "Making their rounds in the city," the bride continues, "the sentinels found me; they beat me, they wounded me, they took away my mantle, those sentinels of the walls" (5:7).

It is tempting to gloss over this seeming aberration within a generally rapturous poem. Yet the presence of loss and violence within this sacred text demands our attention and contemplation. Sometimes the most difficult passages benefit most from prayerful reflection: the practice of *lectio* invites us not to shrink from problematic or painful texts but to seek the presence of God who dwells even there.

I find myself thinking about a line from a John Gorka song in which he sings, "Love is our cross to bear." I used to cringe at this line. I have seen the torments and crucifixions of loving in abusive relationships where the recipients of abuse remain because they believe they are called to this form of sacrifice. There is something fatalistic—and sometimes fatal—about this kind of loving that compels someone to remain in a place so destructive and contrary to God's desire for wholeness.

At the same time, I have learned how the presence of love opens us to certain perils. We cannot control love; we cannot contain it; we cannot predict its effect upon us. When we give ourselves to love, we undertake a risk we can hardly fathom. It will take us down roads we cannot see at the outset. It will change us. It will demand the death of our false selves. It will open us to the eventual absence of the other. All the loss and all the piercing joy that come in the blessed binding of ourselves to our beloved: this cross is our fearsome and wondrous privilege to bear.

And so perhaps, reading the Song within the space of *lectio*, this is what the sentinels remind us of: that love will take us by surprise and strip us of the sureties we have clung to. Yet their presence reminds us too that God ever desires our wholeness. Within the vulnerability of love, we need to cultivate some part of ourselves that remains conscious, aware, and vigilant against the threat of real violence that diminishes, destroys, and is contrary to God's purpose for human loving.

## BLESSING

May you go
with the protection of God
who made you for wholeness,
the encompassing of Christ
who calls you beloved,
the grace of the Spirit
who bids us be as one.

# 17

## ANOTHER PIECE FROM THE NOVEL THAT MAY OR MAY NOT FIND ITS WAY

*Harlan*

Once was a man
who didn't even have to touch me
before I knew he would be
like a page from the book of Judges

like the part where the traveler
lets his concubine be raped

and left for dead
and then cuts her up
into twelve pieces

or where the daughter of Jephthah,
beloved of her father,
becomes his burnt offering.

Some men
you can smell danger upon.

But Harlan
one look and I knew
he would be all
Song of Solomon

deer and
vineyards and
spices and
dew.

BLESSING

May there be
discernment in your desire,
and may your loving ever be
a sanctuary
and a refuge.

# 18

## THE DAUGHTERS OF JERUSALEM

The daughters of Jerusalem, a near-constant presence throughout the Song, are the friends of the bride, her audience, her companions. Their relationship—as in so many friendships—is sometimes tense and strained, yet these are the ones to whom she tells her secrets and her delights. They are the ones she calls upon when her lover is absent. "I adjure you, O daughters of Jerusalem," says the bride, "if you find my beloved, tell him this: I am faint with love" (5:8).

Like good friends, they do not hesitate to respond to her and to question her frankly about the one whom she loves: "What is your beloved more than another beloved," they ask, "O fairest among women? What is your beloved more than another beloved, that you thus adjure us?" (5:9).

Who serves as your companions, your chorus on the path of love? Who accompanies you in the twisting labyrinth of longing and desire? Who offers their presence and wisdom along the way? Who asks you the questions you need to hear in your loving?

BLESSING

That there will be friends
to hold your secrets,
to share your delights,
to comfort and
to question,
and to bless you on
the way of love.

# 19

## WINE AND WHEAT

"Your navel," sings the groom in the Song, "is a rounded bowl that never lacks mixed wine. Your belly," he continues, "is a heap of wheat, encircled with lilies" (7:2).

Wine. Wheat. The elements of Eucharist.

At a table centuries later, Jesus will take bread, give thanks, share it with friends, call it his body. He will take wine, do the same, call it his blood. *Given for you*, he says as he shares these gifts of the earth, these ancient signs of hospitality and communion. As in the garden and the vineyard, the boundaries blur: wheat and wine are not distinct from Jesus, they *are* him. Body. Blood.

With his speech, his blessing, his invocation, Jesus both echoes the Song and reworks it. At this table, Jesus the bridegroom takes the qualities of the bride into himself. With this dramatic, poetic gesture, Jesus gives himself to the ones he loves.

This man who told parables of wedding banquets, who called himself a bridegroom, who reserved his first miracle for the marriage at Cana: was he thinking of the Song as he sat at that table, offering wine, offering bread, offering his very self with an extravagance that echoes the extravagance of the lovers in the Song?

BLESSING

May the Christ
who gives himself to us
with abandon
enfold you with
his extravagant love.

## 20

## BEAUTIFUL AND BELOVED

The Song compels us to recognize and consider the body for what it is: solid, real, incarnate. At the same time, the body is a thing of myth, of metaphor, of symbol and simile. The Bible presents the body as a garden, a vineyard, an ornate building, a sanctuary. It is a temple. A shelter. A place for liturgy and prayer. Perhaps such images gave rise to the evocative line from the wedding liturgy in the Book of Common Prayer: *With my body I thee worship.*[14]

The lovers in the Song speak of the body with great particularity. These are specific bodies, bodies they know, bodies upon which they lavish their depictions and descriptions. Their speech conveys the message that the body is not beloved because it is beautiful. It is beautiful because it is beloved.

The language of these lovers challenges us to speak with this kind of particularity about the body—our own and one another's. Oftentimes I have found the most eloquent descriptions of what it means to live as flesh and bone in this created world in the writings of those who struggle with their bodies. Among these writers is Nancy Mairs, whose writing includes forthright reflections on living with multiple sclerosis. Mairs writes,

> Illness and deformity, instead of being thought of as human variants, the consequence of cosmic bad luck, have invariably been portrayed as deviations from the fully human condition, brought on by personal failing or by divine judgment. The afflicted body is never simply that—a creature that suffers, as all creatures suffer from time to time. Rather, it is thought to be "broken," and thus to have lost its original usefulness; or "embattled," and thus in need of militaristic response, its own or someone else's, to whip it back into shape; or "spoiled," and thus a potential menace to the bodies around it. In any case, it is not the sort of thing your average citizen would like to wake up next to tomorrow morning.[15]

How do you experience your body? In its struggles and pleasures, do you experience it as a place of encounter with God and with others? What metaphors would you use to describe it?

BLESSING

May you see yourself
with the eyes of the One
who fashioned you:
beautiful and
beloved.

21

INVENTIVELY

The perceptions that Nancy Mairs describes have a vast impact in the realm of sexuality and intimate relationship. She writes of this, commenting on the widespread assumption that those with disabilities are, as she puts it, "out of the sexual running."[16] Mairs, who once wrote an essay that she titled "On Not Liking Sex," writes in her more recent book that "I really do like sex. A lot. Especially now that the issues of power and privacy that vexed me then have resolved themselves with time." She tells of how the changing bodies of her husband and herself have forced them to discover alternate means to intimacy.

> Oddly and ironically, my disability provides one of these. . . . After thirty-five years of acquaintance, and with two catastrophic illnesses, if we demanded enchantment, we'd be sorely let down. Our bodies hold few mysteries for each other. Once you've helped your wife change her wet pants, or watched the surgeon pop a colony of E. coli from the healing wound in your husband's belly, you have seen behind all the veils. I don't know what the sexual bond between us relies on, but it's not sorcery. The routine of caregiving doesn't seem to diminish our attraction; George's impotence, which has a physiological rather than a psychological basis, doesn't usually discourage either of us from lovemaking. And because we have grown so familiar with each other's physical realities, we love each other more unabashedly and inventively as time goes on.[17]

BLESSING

Within the borders
of your body
may you know
the beauty and grace
of the God
who takes flesh and form
in you.

# 22

## LATER

What would the Song of Songs read like thirty years later, forty years, fifty years, the lovers meeting and touching with bodies no longer in the spring-time of youth? What lyrics would they craft when the winter, which the groom once sang of as being over and past, begins to approach again? How to describe well-worn eyes, lips, faces, breasts, bellies? How to limn the scars and the creases that now line their bodies, a map of the living that has inscribed itself onto them? What vocabulary of praise shall the lovers—shall we—find then?

BLESSING

That the years
will take you deeper
in your loving.

That the changing
in your body
will open doorways
in your soul.

That you will
have the words
to tell of love
long past innocence
yet grown wise
with the seasons
and ripe with wonders
still to be found.

23

SOMETHING BORROWED

Early in my first pastoral appointment, a church member persuaded me to participate in the annual spring fashion show hosted by the United Methodist Women. That was the year they decided to feature wedding attire. The night of the show found me wriggling into a long-sleeved, wide-skirted, lace-and-satin dress while declining the proffered veil. Some weeks after the event I made a card for a couple of friends. On the front I had written, "When they told me the church was the bride of Christ . . . " Inside the card, " . . . I wasn't expecting this!" I had pasted in a photograph of myself in the borrowed bridal gown, walking down the aisle on the arm of a tuxedoed member of the United Methodist Men. In my note I commented that it was probably just as well that I'd had such an opportunity, since it likely was the fanciest wedding dress I'd ever wear. Perhaps the only one.

I was in my midtwenties at the time. Like many women at that age, I had accumulated a fair collection of bridesmaid's dresses, worn once and relegated to a corner of my closet. But somewhere along the way I had stopped assuming that I would have a wedding of my own. I valued companionship and still harbored hopes of making a home and sharing a life with someone. Eventually.

At the same time, I also possessed a strong sense of independence and a clear sense of vocation around which I was creating my life. In the midst of relationships that came and went, I was learning that my more pressing work lay in making a home and a life for myself. Over time I gained clarity about what I considered essential in a partner and with that clarity came the understanding that I would rather be alone than be in a relationship for which I had settled. I had learned that one of the most insidious forms of loneliness is the one that takes up residence in a relationship that doesn't fit.

When you were growing up, what ideas and expectations did you have about sharing your life with someone else? Where did these ideas come from? How has your experience matched your expectations? How have your ideas about sharing your life with someone changed? What dreams do you still have about a shared life?

### BLESSING

May it be
that you know your own soul.
May you be acquainted
with its mysteries and dreams,
take pleasure
in its solitude,
and be wedded
to the wonder
of a life
of your own.

# 24

## MAPLESS

Some years passed after shedding the fashion-show wedding dress. I moved from that congregation, became the artist-in-residence at San Pedro Center, and settled into a life whose contours I could hardly have imagined. It afforded tremendous freedom to be who I understood God calling me to be.

And then along came Gary and, with him, a sense of call that felt both foreign and somehow familiar. We discovered our common ground that included a commitment to a creative life, a kindred spirituality, and a voracious appetite for books. I realized this was someone I would love for a long, long time, someone with whom I could do the work of making a life together. Years later, I still delight in the sense of coming home that I felt at the outset. Even as I feel at home, being with Gary also stretches me into new and unfamiliar terrain in my soul. Gary's own landscape contains territory I had not sought or anticipated in a partner, including a teenaged son who, as a boy, had a level of extroversion and noise output that was in precisely inverse proportion to my introversion and need for quiet. I find the presence of this remarkable young man in my contemplative life a constant witness to God's sense of humor and to God's continual invitation to open ourselves to holy transformation.

In my relationship with Gary—as in so much of my journey—I often live with the sense of being without a map, of seeking to navigate, alone and together, a country with few signposts. I feel that I have found the Promised Land but still wonder where my house is. While being mapless sometimes leaves me feeling lost, it also invites me to be creative: to seek guidance where I might be tempted to forge ahead on my own, to practice being courageous when the way is dark, and to look at the terrain of my life from a different perspective. Doing these things keeps me from falling into expectations or stereotypes of what our relationship "should" look like and deepens my ability to engage the unexpected lay of the land and the treasures it holds.

BLESSING

And so let us give praise
for the places
that are mapless
chartless
without direction or sign.

Let us give thanks
for all they call forth:
for the questions
they require,
for the imagination
they summon,
for the path
they make
through the territory
of the heart.

# 25

## CONVERSION

As I came to know Gary, I began to realize I had underestimated the claim a
relationship could have on me. Earlier in my life, focusing on my vocation
had helped me create a life that I loved and that fit who I was. It had also,
for the most part, kept me operating with a keen sense of independence
in intimate relationships. In those relationships, sooner or later, a wall had
always emerged. Regardless of who first identified it or the level of pain it
caused, its presence meant I didn't have to go any farther down that road of
relationship. I didn't have to wrestle with questions of how much I revealed
of myself or whether I could give myself to a long-term relationship without
sacrificing the parts of my life that craved—and needed—solitude.

With Gary, the wall never appeared. This is not to say we have no
boundaries or that I have given over any sense of autonomy or responsibility
for continuing to live the life to which God has called me. What I do know

is that God has opened a path in which I—and we—have to grapple with what it means to know and be known so intimately. I have to work through questions about maintaining a contemplative life as I stretch myself into this community of two. In this stretching I continue to experience a radical shifting within myself, a transformation that I feel in my bones.

I have come to understand committed relationship as a process of conversion, in the sense that monastic folks use the term: entering the daily, ongoing work of allowing myself to be transformed by love in the crucible of relationship that brings me deeper into the heart of God. This ongoing conversion does not mean that I become any less than I am but, rather, that I become more who I am as I allow God to unhide me and to wear away whatever would insulate me from the holy. Conversion does not require a giving away of who I am at my core; rather, it offers abundant opportunities to peel back the layers of who I have known myself to be, that I may become more and more open to the God who seeks me both in solitude and in the knowing of another.

How do you come to know yourself in knowing another? Whatever their form, whether with a friend, a family member, or an intimate partner, what do your relationships reveal to you about your own soul? Do you experience your relationships as spaces that help you enter more fully into who you are? What do you long for in the journey of your loving?

BLESSING

May you give yourself
again and again and again
to that which will
wear away
all that is not God.

# 26

## REVELATION

When Gary and I met, I had recently begun research into illuminated prayer books from the Middle Ages called Books of Hours. These "jewels of devotion," as they have been called, fascinate me as an artist and writer who has focused particularly on creating artful books for reflection and prayer. My research led me to images from remarkable medieval manuscripts of the Book of Revelation, also known as the Apocalypse of John.

The images in these illuminated Apocalypses reawakened my curiosity about Revelation that had been stirred in a seminary class years earlier. I reimmersed myself in its text and in anything I could find on the illuminated versions of it. Although I pursued this activity with an eye toward a future art project, I eventually realized that a link probably lay between my fascination with the book and my relationship with Gary.

Although the Song and the Apocalypse may seem quite distinct on the surface, each book tells a story of a quest for the beloved, with its rhythms of seeking and losing, finding and being found, desire and desolation, and radical transformation. With their intensely visual, poetic, and mythic qualities, these books, by design, engage the imagination with great power. Medieval writers and artists alike recognized and responded to this. Not only did these two books draw the greatest number of scholarly commentaries in the Middle Ages (sometimes accompanied by rich illuminations to further engage the reader); the resonance between the books was made explicit by the fact that they were sometimes bound together.[18]

Although the word *apocalypse* has popularly come to refer to a destructive ending of impressive magnitude, at its root it simply means "revelation." And revelation—that act of knowing and being known—lies at the heart of the Song as well as the Apocalypse. But the work of revelation brings its own occasions of destruction: of familiar ways of being, of the illusions we have tried to protect ourselves with, of worlds we have known. It is no mistake that the library places its books on weddings beside its books on death.

BLESSING

That God will make
of your heart
a book.
Pages luminous
with your longing.
Prayers inscribed

by fire.
Stories written
in flame.
Open and
unbound.
On every page
your true name.

# 27

## THE PRACTICE OF LOVING

I have come to appreciate being in relationship as a spiritual path. Rather than paralleling my personal journey of faith, loving is a spiritual practice that encompasses all that I am, and it intertwines with all the other practices that draw me deeper into God.

Loving is an ascetic practice in its own right. As we learned from the desert mothers, our word *ascetic* comes from the Greek *askein*, which means "to exercise" or "to work." Forms of asceticism are infinite, and for many the word evokes images of the more extreme practices that we often associate with earlier Christians: severe fasting, self-flagellation, hair shirts. Fundamentally, however, asceticism involves habits that take us outside our familiar terrain in order to draw us more deeply into who God has created us to be: not for ourselves alone, but for the life of the world.

Ascetic practices enable us to examine familiar habits, to question our accustomed ways of being and responding, to divest ourselves of all that hinders us from meeting God within one another and ourselves. We stretch: we exercise, develop muscles that enable us to move as the Spirit wills. These practices help prepare us for the changes that come, rather than letting the changes catch us unawares. They train our eyes to find the wellsprings in the landscape, to spot the manna that waits for us when the way is most difficult. They open us to the pleasures that come as we practice.

BLESSING

May you find pleasure
in the practices
that draw you deeper
into the heart of God.


# 28

## IN GOOD COMPANY

As I have moved more deeply into my life with Gary and the spiritual path to which our relationship calls me, I have found some of my best companions among the monastics, those women and men who offer wisdom from their own call to a life encompassing both solitude and relationship. The desert mothers and fathers, those ammas and abbas in the early centuries of Christianity who left the city to encounter God in the wilderness, teach me about vigilance, humility, fierce honesty with oneself, devotion to love, radical dependence on God, and, in the words of Abba Poemen, the necessity to "teach your mouth to say that which you have in your heart."[19] These folks encountered at least as many obstacles to God in the desert as they did in the city. So the desert mothers and fathers remind me that if we flee toward something—a place, a relationship—expecting to escape our demons, we will find them waiting for us there.

Medieval mystics, including Julian of Norwich and Teresa of Ávila, have given me windows into seeking divine love with a sense of abandon that does not diminish self but refines it. John of the Cross gives words to the reality of the dark night of the soul, bearing witness to the ways that entering into the mystery of loving sometimes leads us down paths thick with shadows. Beguines such as Mechthild teach me the delights that come in devotion. Being part of Saint Brigid of Kildare Monastery helps me attend to the monastic layer of my own soul, to the ways I am called to live out the Benedictine values of *ora et labora*—prayer and work—in the rhythm of relationship and elsewhere in my life. My connections with a Franciscan community have deepened my understanding of the ways that a vowed life ultimately leads not to deprivation but to a freedom to welcome others with deep wellsprings of hospitality and love.

The monastics—these companions and teachers on the ascetic path—have taught me of the grace that emerges when we move into our true vocation, when we take the vows to which God has called us. Abba Macarius once told the story of encountering two monks who astonished him with their way of life, one he could hardly imagine being able to endure. They told him, "It is God who has made this way of life for us."[20]

What teachers or companions have helped you engage your relationships as a spiritual practice? What ammas or abbas from across the ages have helped you find the way of life that God has made for you? What have they offered on your path? Where have you encountered surprising wisdom?

BLESSING

May you know
the way of life
that God has made for you.

May you find
the sustenance that comes
in traveling its paths.

May you have
good company
to inspire and to guide you
and the graces
that come in going
where only you can go.

# 29

## SOMEDAY

From very early in our relationship, Gary and I felt called to make a life together. Those who know us recognized it too. And so for years we have been fielding the question, "So when are you two getting married?" For a long time, it was difficult to know how to respond. For all our clarity, we had much yet to do before I could plan to put on a wedding dress again— for real this time. Most days I have lived with a sense of peace that the answer was "someday" and that, like the monks whom Macarius encountered, this was the way of life that God has made for us. On other days it has felt like desert waiting, walking through the uncharted wilderness. Yet there has been manna along the way. And even in the desert, there are deep joys as well as thresholds to be crossed.

Once, during a visit from Canada a few years ago, my sister suggested we go look at wedding dresses. With the knowledge that it could be a long time before I needed one, I took her up on the invitation and entered the foreign world of bridal shopping. I still did not imagine myself wearing a poofy, traditional gown like the one I wore for that long-ago fashion show. But I pulled something slim and elegant off the rack. Standing in the changing room, shimmying into the beaded satin, I felt a shift. Dressing in that ceremonial garb did set me to wondering in earnest about what it means to prepare to become a bride, to make ready for that rite of passage, to cross the threshold into the vowed community of two.

### BLESSING

May you abide
the places in between:
the thresholds, the passages,
the spaces of waiting
and patience and preparing.

May you give yourself
to the mysteries
that move us from what was
toward what is yet to be.

May you know
the company of the angels
who come only
to those betwixt

and who love
the liminal places
and the treasures
that they hold.

# 30
## CROSSING THE THRESHOLD

So now we have a date and a place and the beginning of plans. By the time you read this, God willing, Gary and I will be married. Here's how we imagine the long-awaited celebration: a fine spring day, an abundance of family and friends surrounding us, a joyous gathering on a farm that has been in the Richardson family for generations. It is a place that holds my heart, the place of my beginnings, a place that will remind me who I am as Gary and I set out on this journey.

Eager as I am for that day and to finally make a home and a life with my beloved, I am aware too that across that vowed threshold lies a life that I can hardly perceive or imagine from where I stand now. I anticipate many occasions when I echo the words I wrote in that long-ago, post-fashion show card: ". . . I wasn't expecting this!" All my thoughts about relationship as a spiritual practice, all my ponderings of the rhythms of conversion, revelation, and asceticism that I find here, are set in the reality of continuing to have my own space. For now, I can always return to the quiet and solitude of the studio apartment where I live and work. Within this small space is a sense of spaciousness and freedom that has to do with more than the skylights and large windows. I know that when I walk out this door for the final time, it will likely be with some wistfulness for the life I have lived within these walls. But it will also be with the knowledge that making a home and a life for myself—enough in itself—also provided the best possible preparation for becoming a true bride and for recognizing the one who is my beloved.

BLESSING

That you will make a life
that you will fall in love with.

That you will become
your own beloved.

That you may so know
God's delight in you
that it spills out,
spills over,
spills forth
to become a drenching,
welcoming blessing
for one who thirsts
for you.

# 31

## POSTSCRIPT: IN WHICH WE CLOSE WITH A WEDDING AND A BLESSING

On a bright day at the far edge of spring, I slip into my wedding dress. A perfect combination of simplicity and elegance, the dress showed up just weeks before the wedding on a shopping foray with my friend Francesca. We found it at a store that my sister and I had visited all those years before, when this wedding day was an imagining and a dream.

My sister zips me into the dress, places my mother's strand of pearls around my neck, buckles my shoes. When it is time, we climb into my uncle's convertible. Clad in a red beret, my cowboy uncle drives us to the farm, down the lane, toward the barn where I can begin to make out the crowd that has come to celebrate with us.

Walking down the aisle on my father's arm, moving toward my beloved, I take in the faces that surround me. From across more than four decades, friends and family have gathered. Here, in one place. I am startled by the tears that spring to my eyes.

We take our places, faces turned toward the pastureland that stretches away from the barn and the lake that lies beyond the land. Gary's son, Emile, now a young man of sixteen, stands, steps toward the front, and, in a voice clear and strong, begins.

"My beloved speaks and says to me," Emile reads, "'Arise, my love, my fair one, and come away; for now the winter is past, the rain is over and gone. The flowers appear on the earth; the time of singing has come'" (Song 2:10-12).

On this day, in this landscape, among this community, the words we have chosen from the Song remind us how love is elemental, rooted in the earth and grounded in the generations; how its ancient longing spirals through seasons and twists through our marrow (*bone of my bones and flesh of my flesh*). How it draws us deeper into our own terrain even as it unearths us, unmakes us, lays us bare, and creates us again.

How it is our first sanctuary and our final home.

As my beloved and I dreamed our way toward this day, the word *blessing* kept visiting us. *And so let this be a day of blessing*, we decided: a time to gather up those who have blessed us, a time to give thanks, a time to offer a blessing in turn. Blessings weave through our wedding day, offered by family and friends who speak powerful words for Gary and me and for the community that has journeyed with us to this place.

Wanting to offer a blessing of my own, I placed this one in our wedding program. I give it to you in gratitude. May it grace the path ahead of you.

## HERE: A BLESSING

Some other day, perhaps,
I could draw you a map of this place:
could show you the stand of trees
that has always seemed to me
haunted by those
whose arrowheads still surface
now and again by the lake;
could show you the spot
where eagles keep their nest;
the silo
where my grandfather and his siblings
carved their names
into the new concrete;
the place where I stood
the night the old depot burned.

But I think today is a day
for remembering
how all our history
comes down to our hands,
how we carry the lines
that our ancestors
pressed into our palms:
a geography of the generations
inscribed upon us like a map.

And so let it be
that before we leave
this place
this day
we lay our hands—
the topography
ever etched into our skin—
upon this ancient terrain
in gratitude and praise

and then, rising,
turn them skyward:
a blessing
a benediction
a prayer
that the wind will carry
far and far
from here.

## FURTHER READING

*Aphrodite: A Memoir of the Senses* by Isabel Allende, trans. Margaret Sayers Peden. New York: HarperCollins Publishers, 1999.

*The Conscious Bride: Women Unveil Their True Feelings about Getting Hitched* by Sheryl Nissinen. Oakland, CA: New Harbinger Publications, 2000.

*Desert Quartet: An Erotic Landscape* by Terry Tempest Williams with artwork by Mary Frank. New York: Pantheon/Knopf Doubleday Publishing, 1995.

*The Erotic Word: Sexuality, Spirituality, and the Bible* by David M. Carr. New York: Oxford University Press, 2005.

*The Ink Dark Moon: Love Poems by Ono no Komachi and Izumi Shikibu, Women of the Ancient Court of Japan* trans. Jane Hirshfield with Mariko Aratani. New York: Vintage/Knopf Doubleday Publishing, 1990.

*The Song of Songs: A New Translation* by Ariel Bloch and Chana Bloch. Berkeley, CA: University of California Press, 1998.

*The Song of Songs: A New Translation and Interpretation* by Marcia Falk. San Francisco: HarperSanFrancisco, 1990.

*The Soul of Sex: Cultivating Life as an Act of Love* by Thomas Moore. New York: HarperCollins Publishers, 1998.

## NOTES

1. Marcia Falk, *The Song of Songs: A New Translation and Interpretation* (San Francisco: HarperSanFrancisco, 1990), 105.

2. Renita J. Weems, "Song of Songs," in Carol A. Newsom and Sharon H. Ringe, eds., *The Women's Bible Commentary* (Louisville, KY: Westminster/John Knox Press, 1992), 156.

3. Ariel Bloch and Chana Bloch, *The Song of Songs: A New Translation* (Berkeley, CA: University of California Press, 1998), 15.

4. Ibid., 29.

5. Ibid., 35.

6. Weems, "Song of Songs," 156.

7. Ariel and Chana Bloch, *The Song of Songs*, 32.

8. Molly Peacock, *How to Read a Poem . . . and Start a Poetry Circle* (New York: Riverhead Books/Penguin Putnam, 1999), 17.

9. Falk, *The Song of Songs*, 168.

10. The Book of Common Prayer (New York: Henry Holt, 1992), 242.

11. Janet Morley, *All Desires Known* (Harrisburg, PA: Morehouse Publishing, 1992), xi.

12. Janet Ruffing, "Spiritual Direction with Women: Reclaiming and Reinterpreting Key Themes from the Spiritual Tradition," in *Presence: An International Journal of Spiritual Direction* 12, no. 3 (September 2006): 45.

13. Alix Kates Shulman, *Drinking the Rain* (New York: Penguin Books, 1996), 239.

14. Book of Common Prayer, 310.

15. Nancy Mairs, *Waist-High in the World: A Life among the Nondisabled* (Boston: Beacon Press, 1996), 47–48.

16. Ibid., 51.

17. Ibid., 52–53.

18. See, for instance, Suzanne Lewis, *Reading Images: Narrative Discourse and Reception in the Thirteenth-Century Illuminated Apocalypse* (New York: Cambridge University Press, 1995) and Frances Carey, ed., *The Apocalypse and the Shape of Things to Come* (Toronto: University of Toronto Press, 1999).

19. Benedicta Ward, trans., *The Sayings of the Desert Fathers: The Alphabetical Collection*, rev. ed. (Kalamazoo, MI: Cistercian Publications, 1984), 175.

20. Ibid., 126.

*This page constitutes an extension of the copyright page. The publisher gratefully acknowledges the use of the following:*

*Hadewijch: The Complete Works*, Translation and Introduction by Mother Columba Hart, O.S.B. Copyright © 1980 by The Missionary Society of St. Paul the Apostle in the State of New York. Paulist Press, Inc., Mahwah, NJ. Reprinted by permission of Paulist Press, Inc. www.paulistpress.com.

"Shepherd Me, O God" by Marty Haugen. Copyright © 1986 by GIA Publications, Inc.; 7404 S. Mason Ave., Chicago, IL 60638. www.giamusic.com. 800.442.1358. All rights reserved. Used by permission.

Excerpts from *Hildegard of Bingen: Scivias*, translated by Mother Columba Hart and Jane Bishop. Copyright © 1990 by the Abbey of Regina Laudis: Benedictine Congregation Regina Laudis of the Strict Observance, Inc. Paulist Press, Inc., New York/Mahwah, NJ. Reprinted by permission of Paulist Press, Inc. www.paulistpress.com.

"Where I'm From" from *Where I'm From: Where Poems Come From* by George Ella Lyon © 1999 by George Ella Lyon. www.georgeellalyon.com. Used by permission of the author.

Excerpts from *The Sayings of the Desert Fathers: The Alphabetical Collection*, revised edition, translated by Benedicta Ward, SLG, copyright © 1984 by Cistercian Publications. Published by Liturgical Press, Collegeville, MN. Reprinted with permission.

Several readings in chapter 6 appeared in an earlier form in the article "Becoming the Bride: Belonging to a Community of Two," in *Weavings: A Journal of the Christian Spiritual Life*, Vol. XX, No. 3, May/June 2005: 6–13.

Several readings have been adapted from reflections on Jan's blogs The Painted Prayerbook (paintedprayerbook.com) and The Advent Door (theadventdoor.com).

*About the*

# AUTHOR

Jan L. Richardson is an artist, writer, and ordained minister in the United Methodist Church. She serves as director of The Wellspring Studio, LLC, and travels as a retreat leader and conference speaker. Widely known for such books as *Sacred Journeys* and *In Wisdom's Path*, Richardson lives in Florida with her husband, the singer/songwriter Garrison Doles.

You can find Richardson's distinctive artwork, writing, and more at her blogs and Web sites:

*The Painted Prayerbook*
paintedprayerbook.com

*The Advent Door*
theadventdoor.com

*Jan Richardson Images*
janrichardsonimages.com

and her main Web site

JANRICHARDSON.COM

Please visit the companion site for
*In the Sanctuary of Women*
sanctuaryofwomen.com